The Gothic and death

Manchester University Press

The INTERNATIONAL GOTHIC Series

The Series' Board of General Editors

Elisabeth Bronfen, University of Zurich, Switzerland
Steven Bruhm, University of Western Ontario, Canada
Ken Gelder, University of Melbourne, Australia
Jerrold Hogle, University of Arizona, USA (Chair)
Avril Horner, Kingston University, UK
William Hughes, Bath Spa University, UK

The Editorial Advisory Board

Glennis Byron, University of Stirling, Scotland
Robert Miles, University of Victoria, Canada
David Punter, University of Bristol, England
Andrew Smith, University of Glamorgan, Wales
Anne Williams, University of Georgia, USA

Previously published

Monstrous media/spectral subjects: imaging gothic from the nineteenth century to the present Edited by Fred Botting and Catherine Spooner
Globalgothic Edited by Glennis Byron
EcoGothic Edited by Andrew Smith and William Hughes

The Gothic and death

Edited by Carol Margaret Davison

Manchester University Press

Copyright © Manchester University Press 2017

While copyright in the volume as a whole is vested in Manchester University Press, copyright in individual chapters belongs to their respective authors, and no chapter may be reproduced wholly or in part without the express permission in writing of both author and publisher.

Published by Manchester University Press
Altrincham Street, Manchester M1 7JA, UK
www.manchesteruniversitypress.co.uk

British Library Cataloguing-in-Publication Data is available

ISBN 978 1 7849 9269 9 hardback
ISBN 978 1 5261 3947 4 paperback

First published by Manchester University Press in hardback 2017

This edition first published 2019

The publisher has no responsibility for the persistence or accuracy of URLs for any external or third-party internet websites referred to in this book, and does not guarantee that any content on such websites is, or will remain, accurate or appropriate.

Typeset in Arno Pro by
Servis Filmsetting Ltd, Stockport, Cheshire

Contents

Part II: Gothic revolutions and undead histories

Part III: Gothic apocalypses: dead selves/dead civilizations

Part IV: Global Gothic dead

Part V: Twenty-first-century Gothic and death

List of figures

List of contributors

Katherine Bowers is Assistant Professor of Slavic Studies at the University of British Columbia. She is working on a monograph on the influence of eighteenth-century Western Gothic fiction on Russian realism. In 2015 her co-edited volume *Russian Writers and the* Fin de Siècle: *The Twilight of Realism* appeared; the collection's chapters focus on why nineteenth-century Russian literature tends towards the gloomy. Her work has appeared in American, British, and Russian publications.

Conrad Brunström is Lecturer in English at National University of Ireland, Maynooth. He has published two monographs on William Cowper (2004) and Thomas Sheridan (2011) as well as essays on Samuel Johnson, Frances Burney, Charles Churchill, and a variety of other eighteenth-century authors and topics including religious poetry, oratory, nationalism, and queer studies.

Carol Margaret Davison is Professor and Head of the Department of English Language, Literature, and Creative Writing at the University of Windsor. Her published books include *History of the Gothic: Gothic Literature 1764–1824* (2009) and *Anti-Semitism and British Gothic Literature* (2004). She has published on a wide variety of Gothic-related authors and topics, and has just completed a co-edited collection of critical essays devoted to the Scottish Gothic for Edinburgh University Press with Dr Monica Germanà. She is currently at work on a casebook of criticism of the British Gothic, 1764–1824.

Sibylle Erle, FRSA, is Senior Lecturer in English at Bishop Grosseteste University Lincoln, author of *Blake, Lavater and Physiognomy* (2010), co-editor of *Science, Technology and the Senses* (special issue for RaVoN, 2008), and volume editor of *Panoramas, 1787–1900: Texts and Contexts* (2012). With Morton D. Paley she is now co-editing *The Reception of William Blake in Europe* (forthcoming). She has co-curated the display 'Blake and Physiognomy' (2010–11) at Tate Britain and devised an online exhibition of Tennyson's copy of Blake's *Job* for the Tennyson Research Centre (2013). Apart from reception, she is working on 'character' in the Romantic period.

Emma Galbally is a doctoral student at National University of Ireland, Maynooth. Her research focuses on the employment of Gothicism during the eighteenth century, and the thesis employs an interdisciplinary approach to the manipulation of Gothic simulacra during the eighteenth century. It is an amalgamation of new historicism, structuralism, and psychoanalytical criticism, employed for the purpose of extrapolating examples of Gothicism from the architecture, poetry, literature, and theatre of the period, arguing that Gothic staging, as a whole, provided a framework for the playing out of potential outcomes of politically sanctioned violence and repression, and their impact on society, within a fictive mini-narrative.

John Cameron Hartley is conducting doctoral research at the Open University on incidences of the 'romantic macabre' in the fiction of Hugh Walpole (1884–1941), and that writer's relationship with literary modernism. His Master's thesis applied Freud's model for the development of self to Mary Shelley's three-volume 1818 edition of *Frankenstein*. In July of 2013 he presented a paper on Walpole at the 'Maverick Voices and Modernity 1890–1939' International Conference, at St John's College, Durham University. He is also a published poet, runs a small-press imprint, and contributes articles on film, science fiction, comics, and cult TV to various online publishers.

Neal Kirk received his BA in English Literature and Mass Communications (*cum laude*) from University of Denver, and his MSc from University of Edinburgh. He is currently a PhD candidate at Lancaster University. His work is included in the collections, *Twenty-first Century British Fiction – Critical Essays* (Leggett and Venezia,

2015) and *Digital Horror: Haunted Technologies, Network Panic and the Found Footage Phenomenon* (Aldana-Reyes and Blake, 2016). He teaches Sociology, Media and Cultural studies, and English literature courses, which allow him to explore his interests in digital media and culture, and contemporary Gothic scholarship.

Yael Maurer teaches at the Department of English and American studies at Tel Aviv University. Her PhD centres on Salman Rushdie's rewriting of Indian history as a science fictional site. Her monograph *The Science Fiction Dimensions of Salman Rushdie* was published in 2014.

Vijay Mishra is Professor of English Literature at Murdoch University, Australia. He is also a Fellow of the Australian Humanities Academy. He has written widely on the Gothic, Australian, and postcolonial literatures, Medieval Indian devotional poetics, Bollywood cinema, and multiculturalism. He has completed a manuscript entitled 'The Genesis of Secrecy: Annotating Salman Rushdie'.

Matthew Pangborn is Associate Professor of Modern Languages at Briar Cliff University in Sioux City, Iowa. In addition to publishing articles on eighteenth- and nineteenth-century American literature in *Poe Studies* and *Arizona Quarterly*, he has contributed to edited collections on Hitchcock and the ABC television show *Lost*. His book project, titled *Founding Others: Oriental Tales of the Early American Republic*, examines early American challenges to the oriental other constructed by period authors to ease the nation's entry into an imperialist Franco-British world system. His teaching interests include eighteenth- and nineteenth-century American and British literature, literary criticism, the Gothic, and film.

Christina Petraglia received her PhD in Italian literature from the University of Wisconsin-Madison in 2012. Her dissertation focused on the figure of the *Doppelgänger* in selected works by Igino Ugo Tarchetti, Luigi Capuana, and Emilio De Marchi. She is currently an Assistant Professor of Italian Studies at Gettysburg College where she teaches courses on gothic and fantastic literature, post-war film, and Italian language and culture. Her research interests include representations of the uncanny and the supernatural, depictions of monstrosity and psychopathology, and portrayals of science, doctors, and technology in late nineteenth- and early twentieth-century Italian fiction.

Jennifer Schell received her PhD from the University of Pittsburgh in the English Department's Critical and Cultural Studies Program. Her specialties include eighteenth- and nineteenth-century American literature, print culture, transnational studies, and environmental humanities. She is the author of 'A Bold and Hardy Race of Men': The Lives and Literature of American Whalemen (2013) and has published articles on J. Hector St. John de Crèvecoeur's Letters from an American Farmer, William Wells Brown's Clotel, and Herman Melville's Moby-Dick. She is currently at work on a series of articles about the ecogothic and a book manuscript on ecocatastrophes.

Michelle J. Smith is an Alfred Deakin Postdoctoral Research Fellow in Literature at Deakin University, Australia. She completed her doctorate at the University of Melbourne in 2007. Her monograph Empire in British Girls' Literature and Culture: Imperial Girls, 1880–1915 (2011) won the European Society for the Study of English's award for best first book in 2012. With Kristine Moruzi, she is the co-editor of the anthology Girls' School Stories, 1749–1929 (2013) and Colonial Girlhood in Literature, Culture and History, 1840–1950 (2014). Her research focuses on gender in Victorian literature and culture, as well as children's literature. She recently published a chapter on True Blood in Open Graves, Open Minds: Vampires and the Undead from the Enlightenment to the Present (2013).

Dr Serena Trowbridge is Lecturer in English Literature at Birmingham City University, where she completed her PhD in 2010. Her monograph Christina Rossetti's Gothic was published by Bloomsbury in 2013. Her research interests include Victorian Gothic, pre-Raphaelitism and eco-criticism. Recent publications include a chapter on Christina Rossetti and the environment in Victorians and the Environment (ed. Lawrence Mazzeno) (Ashgate, 2017), Insanity and the Lunatic Asylum (edited with Thomas Knowles) (Pickering & Chatto, 2014) and Pre-Raphaelite Masculinities (edited with Amelia Yeates) (Ashgate, 2014).

Adam White is an editor in the Faculty of Arts and Social Sciences at The Open University. He taught for a number of years in English and American Studies at the University of Manchester and Manchester Metropolitan University and is a Fellow of the Higher Education Academy. He has published a number of comparative essays on Romantic-period writing, including 'John Clare, William Wordsworth, and the Poetry of Childhood' in *English* (2015), 'The Love Songs and Love Lyrics of Robert Burns and John Clare' in *Scottish Literary Review* (2013), and 'Identity in Place: Lord Byron, John Clare and Lyric Poetry' in *The Byron Journal* (2012). For *The Literary Encyclopedia* he has written a wide variety of articles, including those on Byron's *Hours of Idleness, The Two Foscari,* and *Sardanapalus.* He is a regular book reviewer for the British Association of Romantic Studies and is currently working on a monograph on John Clare.

Bruce Wyse is Instructor in the English and Film Department at Wilfrid Laurier University and Lecturer in the English Department at the University of Waterloo. His PhD dissertation was on Romantic drama, and his current research interests include the representation of mesmerism in nineteenth-century literature, psychoanalytic approaches to Gothic, the 1890s, neo-Victorianism, and adaptation.

Series editor's preface

Each volume in this Series contains new essays on the many forms assumed by – as well as the most important themes and topics in – the ever-expanding range of international 'Gothic' fictions from the eighteenth to the twenty-first century. Launched by leading members of the International Gothic Association (IGA) and some editors and advisory board members of its journal, *Gothic Studies*, this Series thus offers cutting-edge analyses of the great many variations in the Gothic mode over time and all over the world, whether these have occurred in literature, film, theatre, art, several forms of cybernetic media, or other manifestations ranging from 'Goth' group identities to avant garde displays of aesthetic and even political critique.

The 'Gothic Story' began in earnest in 1760s England, both in fiction and drama, with Horace Walpole's efforts to combine the 'ancient' or supernatural and the 'modern' or realistic romance. This blend of anomalous tendencies has proved itself remarkably flexible in playing out the cultural conflicts of the late Enlightenment and of more recent periods. Antiquated settings with haunting ghosts or monsters and deep, dark secrets that are the mysteries behind them, albeit in many different incarnations, continue to intimate what audiences most fear in both the personal subconscious and the most pervasive tensions underlying Western culture. But this always unsettling interplay of conflicting tendencies has expanded out of its original potentials as well, especially in the hands of its greatest innovators, to appear in an astounding variety of expressive, aesthetic, and public manifestations over time. The results have transported this inherently boundary-breaking mode across geographical and cultural borders into 'Gothics' that now appear throughout the world: in the settler communities of Canada, New Zealand, and Australia; in such post-colonial areas as India and Africa; in the Americas and the Caribbean; and in East Asia and several of the islands within the entire Pacific Rim.

These volumes consequently reveal and explain the 'globalisation' of the Gothic as it has proliferated across two-and-a-half centuries. The General Editors of this series and the editors of every volume, of course, bring special expertise to this expanding development, as well as the underlying dynamics, of the Gothic. Each resulting collection, plus the occasional monograph, therefore draws together important new studies about particular examples of the international Gothic – past, present, or emerging – and these contributions can come from both established scholars in the field and the newest 'rising stars' of Gothic studies. These scholars, moreover, are and must be just as international in their locations and orientations as this Series is. Interested experts from throughout the globe, in fact, are invited to propose collections and topics for this series to the Manchester University Press. These will be evaluated, as appropriate, by the General Editors, members of the Editorial Advisory Board, and/or other scholars with the requisite expertise so that every published volume is professionally put together and properly refereed within the highest academic standards. Only in this way can the International Gothic series be what its creators intend: a premiere world-wide venue for examining and understanding the shape-shifting 'strangeness' of a Gothic mode that is now as multicultural and multi-faceted as it has ever been in its long, continuing, and profoundly haunted history.

Acknowledgements

I would like to thank the Board of General Editors and the Editorial Advisory Board of this International Gothic Series, particularly Andy Smith (University of Sheffield), Bill Hughes (Bath Spa University), and Jerry Hogle (University of Arizona), for their enthusiastic support of this collection, which, I hope, will pave the way for further scholarship in this domain of Gothic Studies. I also owe special thanks to Matthew Frost at Manchester University Press for his patience and advice during the production process. Tremendous thanks also goes to the University of Windsor for research support in the form of a Humanities and Social Sciences Research Grant (2015) that allowed me to procure the invaluable services of Ashley Girty, a former student and editorial/research assistant, now a stellar doctoral candidate at McGill University. Ashley's efficient, assiduous, and incisive editorial assistance, in combination with her friendship during the production process made for lighter, vastly improved work. Last but not least, I would like to thank the collection's contributors for their tremendous patience and commitment to this project, and their insightful chapters that are certain to lay valuable groundwork for generations of future scholars.

This volume is dedicated to Andy Smith for his tremendous friendship and scholarly advice and support over the years, particularly after the very dark and traumatic year of 2010 when I felt the light in me had been extinguished.

Carol Margaret Davison
Windsor, Ontario, Canada

Carol Margaret Davison

Introduction - the corpse in the closet: the Gothic, death, and modernity

'The earth is a tomb, the gaudy sky a vault, we but walking corpses.'
Mary Shelley, 'On Ghosts', 1824.[1]

Gothicists readily identify death as one of the foremost terrors at the heart of their cultural field of study. Certainly, the engine of terror that Horace Walpole identifies in the Preface to the first edition of *The Castle of Otranto* (1764) as fuelling that work (1982: 4) exemplifies Edmund Burke's concept of sublime terror with its '*apprehension of pain or death*' (emphasis added) ([1757] 1767: 96). The threat of death, in different manifestations, has since served as a key feature in Gothic works across various media. Curiously, an overview of the existing critical literature reveals a dearth of scholarship that explicitly engages with the subject of death in the Gothic. Death has been, to date, only tangentially referenced, 'discussed' by implication, and minimally theorised in association with the Gothic, a few noteworthy exceptions being the stellar, pioneering work of Elisabeth Bronfen and Barbara Creed on the abject female body/corpse, and insightful studies by Angela Wright and Dale Townshend devoted to the role of mourning and melancholia in the works of Ann Radcliffe. As the fifteen chapters in *The Gothic and Death* illustrate, bringing the Death Question into relief in the Gothic helps us make greater sense of this protean mode/aesthetic that, 'with its invitation to melancholia and its obsession with the undead', as Peter Walmsley aptly characterises it, partook of 'a tradition of nationalist discourse about death' that became pronounced in the late eighteenth century (2009: 53). Recognition of the prevalence of what I have elsewhere called the Gothic's *necropoetics*

– comprised of death-focused symbols and tropes such as spectrality and the concept of *memento mori* – in combination with its necropolitics, which featured intergenerational power dynamics between the (un)dead and the living, further substantiates Walmsley's claim while rendering more understandable the historical emergence of the Gothic (Davison, 2015). As Sarah Webster Goodwin and Elisabeth Bronfen have rightly noted, 'Representations of death necessarily engage questions about power: its locus, its authenticity, its sources, and how it is passed on' (1993: 4–5). Drawing on the exciting body of scholarship in the burgeoning field of Thanatology Studies, the chapters in this collection aim to unearth a sense of the cultural work carried out by the Gothic in relation to death, dying, mourning, and memorialisation and, in the process, to expose and explore the role these experiences played in shaping the generic register of the Gothic. This volume also hopes to contribute both to the growing body of scholarship devoted to the intellectual history of death and loss, and to the joint domains of cultural theory and literary historiography by shedding new light on why the Gothic has served, across cultures and eras, as the aesthetic of choice through which to engage such issues. Notably, several of the chapters in this volume offer up an explanation, when we step back into history, as to why the changing face of the Death Question in the Gothic has been only tangentially examined.

According to sociologist Zygmunt Bauman in his groundbreaking book *Mortality, Immortality & Other Life Strategies* (1992), death is the 'most persistent and indifferent' adversity faced by humanity. Using notably Gothic rhetoric to describe it, Bauman deems death unmasterable by the Age of Reason. It is the 'guilty secret [and] ... skeleton in the cupboard left in the neat, orderly, functional and pleasing home modernity promised to build' (134). This description places Gothicists in recognisable territory as *memento mori*, the complex warning/reminder that we will all die, which is significantly 'fissured between future and past' (Royle, 2002: 196), litters the Gothic landscape. Death serves as the quintessential emblem of the Freudian uncanny in the Gothic; while being 'of the home' and familiar, it also remains secret, concealed, and unfamiliar, a reality that has become, like mourning, 'obscene and awkward', according to Jean Baudrillard (2007: 182), in the face of which we have – at least in our everyday lives – fallen silent. The advent of secular modernity, the putative triumph of Reason, and the unsettling of religious certainties during the Enlightenment about the existence of God, the soul, and the afterlife, constituted a type of cultural trauma that alienated us from an earlier familiarity with death while giving rise to greater anxieties and uncertainties about mortality, loss, and remembrance. Elisabeth Bronfen astutely describes the result of this defamiliarisation as 'a retreat from death in a double gesture of denial and mystification' (1992: 86) accompanied by a deeply entrenched cultural schizophrenia where we denied and deferred the death of the self while recognising and even celebrating the death of the Other. This defamiliarisation is perhaps best captured in the line from Edward Young's renowned Christian consolation poem *Night Thoughts* (1742–45): 'All men think all men mortal but themselves.' As Thanatology historian Philippe Ariès has argued, in stark contrast to and in defiance of the grotesque realities of the putrefying corpse, which generated our deep-seated anxiety and fear of our own death and the loss of our individuality, we created a new, beautiful, more spectralised Other who remained incorruptible and individually identifiable in his/her post-mortem state. This mixed response to death remains in evidence in our death-denying Western culture where discussion of our personal experiences with death is treated as taboo and shameful while we feed on a steady diet of graphically rendered, usually visually projected, carnage. How may we account for these phenomena and how has the Gothic served to mediate this paradoxical response?

While no chapter in this collection deals with Mary Shelley's death-saturated and fixated Gothic masterpiece, *Frankenstein; or The Modern Prometheus* (1818), that work sheds light on this transitional era (late eighteenth to early nineteenth century) in Western attitudes towards death. Shelley's monomaniacal, overreaching scientist also holds lessons for our death-denying culture. On the heels of his mother's sudden death from disease, a traumatised Victor, then a young student of natural philosophy, turns his attention to eradicating death and disease from the world. To this end, ironically, he produces a macabre, fleshly Creature fabricated from a multitude of different putrefying corpses collected from the charnel house, the dissecting room, and the slaughter-house (Shelley, 1997: 83). Gazing upon his newly made, inanimate Creature that signals for Victor the advent of a new era of undeath, he rapturously praises its beauty. As the Creature's shocking and terrifying moment of birth and immediate paternal rejection further signal, however, in combination with his nightmarish crusade of carnage, Victor's delusional dreams of attaining immortality can never be realised. The unpalatable fact persists: the reality of death may be repressed but remains utterly ineradicable. Indeed and arguably, no more powerful embodiment of *memento mori* exists in Gothic literature than Victor's eight-foot tall, abjected, 'hideous progeny', a type of uncanny neo-mort, to borrow a term from the work of Giorgio Agamben, positioned between life and corpse. In an act of tremendously tragic irony, Victor achieves, as Elisabeth Bronfen aptly phrases it, the opposite of what he intended: thinking he has created a new being that is 'beyond mortality, … he produces a death-machine, bent on the total destruction of his maker's social world' ([1998] 2009: 115). Indeed, the devastation is far more intense and personal as Victor's own description of the destruction makes clear. In his words, the Creature becomes 'my own vampire, my own spirit let loose from the grave, and forced to destroy all that was dear to me' (57). In a strategically manipulated Monster-Maker dynamic that brilliantly exemplifies the Freudian death drive, Victor learns that while one may run from Death, one cannot hide. Several years later and subsequent to the sudden death of her husband, in her powerful yet unsettling essay 'On Ghosts' (1824), the source of this chapter's epigraph, Mary Shelley, makes eminently clear that we all, as Victor's literal walking corpse of a Creature reminds us, carry our future corpse within us: all who live must, inevitably, die. 'One is mortal', Todd May powerfully observes, echoing Shelley, 'not only at the end of one's life, but all throughout it' (2009: 7).

As several chapters in this volume attest and as *Frankenstein* suggests, much inheres, from the Enlightenment onwards, in the multivalent corpse. Positioned at the threshold of the (possible) next world where it signals the paradoxically dreaded-yet-desired annihilation of our subjectivity and signposts a (possible) secular cul-de-sac, the corpse has become the 'supreme signifier for anything from human destiny and its redemption to life's meaninglessness' (Webster Goodwin and Bronfen, 1993: 17). Bound up with the exercise and abuse of political power, corpses also tap the deep Romantic well of affect to different ends. They are crucial to the expression and exploration of subjectivity while also serving as contested sites, and figurative battlefields, for various ideas and debates, particularly those that involve religious ideologies and philosophies and their moral authority. As is repeatedly illustrated in the Gothic, this uncanny subject/object that often refuses to stay dead, has been 'imbued with otherworldly powers' (Quigley, 1996: 18), invested with our pre-Enlightenment superstitious beliefs and ideas, and figuratively buried. This process notably occurred in tandem with our invention of funerary receptacles such as coffins with screwed-down lids and sealed, concrete burial vaults (Ragon, 1983:

16), to hide the offending 'thing' from our collective view. Our mixed post-Enlightenment sentiments of denial, dread, and desire in relation to death have been projected onto this socio-cultural body/corpse that serves,[2] as Alan Bewell has rightly noted, 'as the nexus of all spiritual imagery … [as] all narratives about life after death can be reduced to and derive their formal organisation from a primary confrontation, which every culture and every individual repeats, with the bodies of the dead' (1989: 190). Such repressed anxieties and desires have been especially projected onto the abjected *female* corpse (Bronfen, 1992: 86) that serves as a grotesque Bakhtinian reminder of one's origins (birth) and telos (death), a projection registered in the proliferation of the supernatural, uncanny undead in the Gothic.

That corpses occupy such a prominent place in the Gothic and the collective consciousness at the advent of a secularising modernity makes sense given the shifting meaning of *memento mori* in combination with the pre-eminence of corpses during the French Revolution, a cataclysmic series of historical events that figure prominently in Part II of this collection. *Frankenstein* references this transition in the execution of the innocent Justine that resonates powerfully with the state-sanctioned massacre of tens of thousands of purported 'enemies of the revolution' by guillotine during the bloody Reign of Terror (September 1793 to July 1794). Against this backdrop, corpses not only registered power dynamics between the living, but between the living and the dead, the latter emblematising previous generations and the past more generally. Indeed, a new cultural epistemology was in the process of being negotiated that involved the creation of a religiously and nationally inflected social contract between the living and the dead. This negotiation featured prominently in socio-political and theological debates. The necrocracy (dominion of the dead) famously identified by Edmund Burke in his *Reflections on the Revolution in France* as characterising the British constitution – 'an entailed inheritance (1790: 47) that grips the state and its citizens in a type of "mortmain for ever"' (1790: 48) – was condemned as classist, archaic, and a type of 'necrophiliac abomination' (Duggett, 2010: 50) by such thinkers as Thomas Paine and William Wordsworth. Their writings suggest that they favoured Thomas Jefferson's philosophy as articulated in a letter to James Madison in 1789: 'the dead have neither powers nor rights over the earth' which 'belongs in usufruct to the living' (Jefferson, 1945: 130).

Gothic novels published during its early, classical era (1764–1824) grant expression to this new cultural epistemology positioned between what is represented as a perverse, superstitious Roman Catholic necrocracy characterised by a dominion of the dead, and the careless abuse and annihilation of the dead as promoted in Anglo-American radical philosophy. Indeed, the latter abuses, exemplified by the spectacular excesses and violations perpetrated during the September Massacres,[3] led to a revitalised brand of Gothic that radically transformed its established tropes, as Ronald Paulson has shown (1983: 221), and positioned its necropoetics and necropolitics more centre stage as illustrated in Matthew Lewis's *The Monk* (1796) and the works of Ann Radcliffe. Death was notably and frequently represented in the early, classic Gothic as a destabilising, disruptive force involving intergenerational, historical crimes/sins requiring exposure, recognition, and appeasement by way of mourning rituals and memorialisation processes. Across literary forms, Anglo-American Gothic meditations on mortality and Life's Big existential and ontological Questions also subsequently altered, in radical and powerful ways, the face of literary history, reaching their efflorescence in what Robert D. Hume has categorised as a type of metaphysical Gothic in the early to mid-nineteenth century (1969: 290).

In the face of Enlightenment-generated anxieties about the afterlife and the loss of subjectivity, ideas, sites, and practices around mourning and memorialisation were radically altered. Mourning became a more fraught process that could lend itself, as readers readily recognise in the cases of both Heathcliff and Victor Frankenstein, to melancholic excess, an emotional extreme that characterises most Gothic hero-villains. Notably, mourning was extended in this industrialising era of rapid change, to the past more generally – to former, lost belief systems and certainties rendered obsolete due to historical shifts. As Jolene Zigarovich has accurately noted, underlying the 'embrace of death was an uneasiness about the rapidity of change. Anxieties regarding the moral, physical, and spiritual decay of people and culture were inevitably personified and figured in narrative' (2012: 5). Given its elaborate mourning rituals and what has been called its 'pornography' of death (see Gorer, 1965), Victorian England has been provocatively and aptly described, for example, as a necroculture in 'mourning for lost fixtures, in the world and of the spirit, which the acceleration of a coveted yet feared modernity had swept away' (Tucker, 1999: 122). That the Gothic continued to flourish in newly transmuted forms throughout that period was largely the result of that nation's monomania about death. Britons also encountered multifarious cultural rituals and attitudes towards death in the course of their imperialist ventures that were channelled into Gothic literature.

The memorialisation of the dead likewise assumed greater importance in the face of anxieties induced by modernity. A failure or refusal to memorialise contributed, among other things, to the concept of persecutory, haunting ghosts associated with the Gothic hero-villain who is often also a persecutor. As Terry Castle has argued in *The Female Thermometer* (1995), the new model of haunted consciousness that arose during the Enlightenment evidences a new spectrality that, while featuring ghosts of a different, non-Catholic, non-Purgatorial order, nevertheless signify the presence of guilt arising from past transgressions or, as Avery Gordon persuasively argues about the driving forces behind the ghost story, 'a repressed or unresolved social violence' (2008: xvi).

In allowing a cultural space for the imaginative, post-Enlightenment treatment of the Death Question by way of ghosts and corpses and a host of other undead, the Gothic rendered death fascinating and offered the unique invitation to experience what Elisabeth Bronfen describes as 'death by proxy' (2009: 114), an attractive and even desirable experience because 'apparently unreal' (113). It also allowed readers to engage with death-related subject matter considered too macabre, controversial, or sensitive within certain cultures and societies. In its pages, readers may indulge dark death-related fantasies and fears, the Gothic becoming, as Dale Townshend has claimed drawing on the work of Coral Ann Howells, 'a socially symbolic site of mourning' that permitted and promoted the expression of the 'more macabre realities of corporeal decomposition and religious insecurity' and what Townshend calls a 'negated grief' that ranged beyond what tame neo-Classical proprieties dictated and allowed (2008: 89).

Attentive to our changing, often ambivalent experiences with death and bereavement, and the changing status of corpses – whether portrayed as dead or undead – as social bodies that must be critically analysed and 'read' in the light of their shifting cultural and historic contexts, *The Gothic and Death* is organised around five pre-eminent death-related themes/preoccupations spanning the eighteenth to the twenty-first centuries. The chapters in Part I, 'Gothic graveyards and afterlives', coalesce around anxieties about, and representations of, the grave and post-mortem spiritual existence and experience as expressed in eighteenth- and nineteenth-century Gothic literature and its hugely influential precursor, Graveyard Poetry. Both forms lent expression to anxieties and desires about the grave while contributing to 'a tradition of nationalist discourse about death' (Walmsley, 2009: 53) and engaging in a type of immortalising process. According to Deidre Shauna Lynch, both notably enabled 'the British public to probate [their] … literary inheritance' in the form of medieval romance, and foregrounded a 'ghost-seeing' that 'sought to keep open lines of communication with the literary dead' (2008: 51). This proliferation of historically fixated cultural forms 'quest[ed] for intimacy with the dead' more generally (Westover, 2012: 8), engendering what Paul Westover has nicely called 'Necromanticism', 'a complex of antiquarian revival, book-love, ghost-hunting, and monument-building that emerged in the age of revolutions and mass print' (3).

In 'Past, present, and future in the Gothic graveyard' (Chapter 1), Serena Trowbridge examines the development of an aesthetic of mortality in Graveyard Poetry that influenced later Gothic novels. She notes their shared atmospherics and preoccupations with the past as a means of envisaging the future, as well as their common reliance on a Christian belief system that heralds and celebrates life after death while engendering reflections on the inevitability of mortality. Focusing on denominational beliefs and changing metaphysical attitudes towards death in the seventeenth century that were predicated on a body/soul division, Trowbridge's chapter is also attentive to death's transformation in the wake of Graveyard Poetry from signalling a reminder of death with an eye to a future world to inducing anxiety in the Gothic given the prospect of a post-mortem loss of individuality. Sibylle Erle's chapter, '"On the very Verge of legitimate Invention": Charles Bonnet and William Blake's illustrations to Robert Blair's *The Grave* (1808)' (Chapter 2), extends Trowbridge's investigation in its analysis of William Blake's illustrations for Graveyard Poet Robert Blair's *The Grave* (1808) and the reception of that edition. According to Erle, these illustrations interceded in European debates about the immortality of the soul and evidenced Blake's awareness of the physiognomical theory of Johann Caspar Lavater, for whom he had created earlier engravings (1789–98). The chapter examines Blake's relationship to the Gothic's obsession with death and dying and argues that his images superseded the Gothic and visual quality of the language of Blair's text by asserting the immediacy and reality of afterlife existence and experiences.

Moving into the Victorian era where, as Francis O'Gorman has incisively articulated, what made 'the cultural history of the Victorians and

the dead distinctive and important, was not, in fact, death [but] …
life: eternal life' (2010: 255), Bruce Wyse (Chapter 3) considers the
Gothic's changing relationship to Christianity and its worldview on
death as reflected in Horace Smith's little known novel, *Mesmerism: A
Mystery* (1845). In this unusual hybrid of Gothic fiction and its contrary,
the novel of religious faith, mesmerism takes centre stage, a phenomenon that, its proponents claimed, demonstrated the latent paranormal
powers of the mind as a vehicle for fantasising about death's universal
mystery. Wyse demonstrates in 'Entranced by death: Horace Smith's
Mesmerism', how the central tenets of Christianity recede in Smith's
novel while Death itself assumes the place of the principal redeemer of
humankind. Indeed, death becomes a metonym for heaven in a work
that remains, given Smith's introduction of a provocative, psychological analysis of its protagonist, marked by irresolution and a tension
between the Gothic and the novel of faith.

Part II, 'Gothic revolutions and undead histories', considers the
Death Question in association with the concept of gothicised history and inheritance, ideas inextricably bound up with the French
Revolution during the 'Classic Gothic' era (1764–1824). As several of
the chapters in this volume suggest, history was not only a condition of
modernity, it was itself gothicised at the advent of modernity when it
was popularly represented as a form of Gothic emplotment marked by
a haunting dialectic between the barbaric, obscurantist past (the dead)
and the progressive, civilised present (the living). Thus did mourning
and melancholia become inextricably bound up with modernity, an
association central to what David L. Eng and David Kazanjian call
'an intellectual history of loss' (2003: 6) that was expressed across a
variety of history-inflected literary genres including, and especially, the
Gothic. Notably, and in keeping with Walter Benjamin's characterisation of the historical materialist's ongoing and open 'dialogue' with
the past, such cultural productions were underpinned by a healthy
melancholia – rather than a pathological form of mourning as Freud
defines it in his early writings on the subject – that brought modernity's
'ghosts and specters, its flaring and fleeting images, into the present'
(Eng and Kazanjian, 2003: 4).

Recognising these historical complexities and dynamics, in '"This
dreadful machine": the spectacle of death and the aesthetics of crowd
control' (Chapter 4), Emma Galbally and Conrad Brunström consider
the French Revolution as both a Gothic and an anti-Gothic moment
that redeployed the barbaric horrors of mass execution in the name of

'Enlightenment'. They investigate the guillotine as a symbol of this tension, offering, as it did, the mechanisation of terror while, in the highly popular form of theatrical presentations of mock execution, allowing for mass entertainment and social commentary. To this end, they consider James Boaden's *Aurelio and Miranda* (1798), an adaptation of Matthew Lewis's *The Monk* (1796), and George Reynolds' *Bantry Bay* (1797), as stage entertainments that accommodated and sanitised this spectacle as part of the Revolutionary Gothic.

In 'Undying histories: Washington Irving's Gothic afterlives' (Chapter 5), Yael Maurer then turns to an examination of the aftermath of the French Revolution and the guillotine – its spectacular instrument of mechanised terror – in the context of the American Gothic. She analyses Washington Irving's deployment of a 'gothic engine' in 'The Adventure of the German Student' (1824), and discusses 'Rip Van Winkle' (1819) and 'The Legend of Sleepy Hollow' (1820), as exemplifying Irving's reimagining of history as a Gothic site, where what Robert Hughes has called 'the nightmare of history' manifests itself in the form of ghosts and revenants. In Chapter 6, 'Deadly interrogations: cycles of death and transcendence in Byron's Gothic', Adam White then offers a psychoanalytic reading of Byron's *The Two Foscari* (1821), *The Prisoner of Chillon* (1816), as well as *Manfred* (1817) and *Sardanapalus* (1821), in relation to Sigmund Freud's death-drive principle. White examines the compulsion to repeat scenes and images of death in these works, as well as – in a move away from the Gothic – their depictions of transcending death. He especially attends to the Walpolean Gothic trope of 'the sins of the fathers being visited upon the sons', asking how the dead, ancestral past interacts with the living present.

Part III of this collection, 'Gothic apocalypses: dead selves/dead civilisations', considers death as a Gothic vector for exploring the spectres of cultural and global degeneration and annihilation in texts ranging from the ecoGothic and 'Lost World' fictions to the zombie cinema. The scholars in this section examine how depictions of mass death in the Gothic have, since the late eighteenth century, registered social concerns about expansion, scarcity, and resource management. Adopting an ecocritical approach to the Gothic, Jennifer Schell (Chapter 7) investigates how the writings of Mary Shelley and Nathaniel Hawthorne extrapolate upon the fears that arose out of Georges Cuvier's work on extinction in the late eighteenth century. Schell's chapter, 'The annihilation of self and species: the ecoGothic sensibilities of Mary Shelley and

Nathaniel Hawthorne', identifies and discusses emergent scientific and environmental anxieties, as well as contemporary concerns about how British and American expansion would have an impact on ecological stability and, ultimately, whether this would lead to *human* extinction. In 'Death cults in Gothic "Lost World" fiction', John Cameron Hartley (Chapter 8) then turns to a popular Anglo-American nineteenth-century novelistic sub-genre penned by such authors as Edgar Allan Poe, James De Mille, and H. Rider Haggard. Focusing on Haggard's lucrative imperial adventure novels at the *fin de siècle*, an era that saw a tremendous public enthusiasm for Egyptology and other archaeological discoveries, Hartley considers how, by way primarily of the characters of Allan Quatermain and Horace Holly, contact with various cults of death served as meditations upon notions of personal, national, and imperial evolution and degeneration.

Finally, in 'Dead again: zombies and the spectre of cultural decline' (Chapter 9), Matthew Pangborn traverses between evocations of the 'zombie' in British debates on the French Revolution through to twentieth-century film. His chapter examines that uncannily undead figure as a metaphor for a disturbing dynamic – namely, that if a culture 'naturally' matures, it must also be impelled – as if from the 'other side' – into decrepitude and dissolution. As Pangborn cogently discusses and illustrates, this dynamic is especially in evidence in the contemporary resuscitation of the zombie figure that is frequently employed to engage with the energy crisis and the 'Green Revolution'.

Part IV, 'Global Gothic dead', provides evidence of the Death Question as a transcultural and transhistorical phenomenon and preoccupation from Bollywood to the Caucasus that has attracted, significantly and with a variety of objectives, a Gothic treatment. As these authors show in a spectrum of cinematic and literary productions set against various national backgrounds marked by distinct socio-cultural and theological attitudes to death – Italian, Russian, and East Indian – *memento mori* remains a powerful yet variously meaningful concept. Each dialogues with the Anglo-American Gothic, to different ends and with unique agendas, while forging its own aesthetically innovative and culturally unique expressions. Beginning in Italy (Chapter 10), a popular Southern European backdrop for much British Gothic fiction exploring what is traditionally represented as abusive Roman Catholic authority, we move on to Russia (Chapter 11), where some readers may be surprised to see, in various nineteenth-century naturalist works, the traces of Anglo-American Gothic influence. Part IV concludes in

India (Chapter 12) where, in a nation decidedly marked by British imperialism yet utterly distinct in its cultural, theological, and philosophical contexts, a cinematic flirtation with the Gothic is not only discernible but strategically manipulated.

In 'A double dose of death in Iginio Ugo Tarchetti's "I fatali"' (Chapter 10), Christina Petraglia considers the literary moment of the *Scapigliatura* that, in its shared stylistic affinities with the European Gothic, constitutes an Italian style Gothic. More specifically, Petraglia investigates the marriage of death and the double in the oeuvre of the Italian progenitor of fantastic literature, Iginio Ugo Tarchetti, a marriage made before this connection was established in psychoanalytic literature. Taking Tarchetti's short story 'I fatali' as her primary case study, Petraglia outlines how the author embodies death in father-and-son pair Count Sangrezwitch and Baron Saternez. Moving into the domain of Russian naturalism in 'Through the opaque veil: the Gothic and death in Russian Realism' (Chapter 11), Katherine Bowers demonstrates how a movement that called for 'realistic' depictions of dying curiously engaged Gothic elements imported from Western models. Her chapter evaluates how authors such as Ivan Turgenev and Anton Chekhov employed these Gothic elements not merely to embellish the experience of dying, but to serve as a literary modus operandi that allowed for the interrogation of deeper existential questions about the fear of death. The section concludes with Vijay Mishra's fascinating chapter, 'Afterdeath and the Bollywood Gothic noir' (Chapter 12), an examination of a sub-genre of the capricious Indian cinematic melodrama that asks how culturally distinct figurations of death and an afterlife influence cinematic engagements with timeless 'Gothic' questions. Mishra examines a number of classic Bollywood Gothic film noirs, paying specific attention to the ways in which the idea of eternal recurrence enters into the Indian demotic of ghosts and spirits to interrupt the logic of reincarnation.

This collection's concluding section, Part V, 'Twenty-first-century Gothic and death', explores how the advent of contemporary advancements in technology in such areas as media and healthcare influenced Gothic-related cultural productions dealing with the Death Question. On the heels of a century that has seen horrifying global wars and mass exterminations where we may be said to suffer from an overexposure to death, as Benjamin Noys maintains in *The Culture of Death* (2005), twenty-first-century Gothic treatments of the Death Question register what Philippe Ariès calls the 'invisible death' (1981: 557), which is divested of ritual, and where the dying/the dead are ignored and unmourned. Part V's contributors ask how twenty-first-century technological advancements have complicated our ideas of mourning, haunting, and the 'afterlife' of the self. In 'Dead and ghostly children in contemporary literature for young people' (Chapter 13), Michelle J. Smith opens this section by surveying a burgeoning genre of young adult and children's literature from the past decade that draws on the Gothic while featuring dead and ghostly children. She advances the idea that vastly improved child mortality rates, among other cultural shifts, have dramatically altered the meaning of child-death in literature. Whereas Victorian and Edwardian fictions were inclined to present child-death in a comforting light due to a commonly short lifespan, contemporary fictions frequently use this theme as a vehicle for social critique as expressed and exposed in the past wrongs of adults that require redressing. Her chapter further examines a unique strain of contemporary Gothic literature involving child revenants whose symbolic weight has shifted in the face of twenty-first-century violence.

In 'Modernity's fatal addictions: technological necromancy and E. Elias Merhige's *Shadow of the Vampire*' (Chapter 14), Carol Margaret Davison addresses the motion picture's obsession with death, particularly as represented in the form of the sexually fetishised, murdered female corpse. Building from Leo Tolstoy's observation that cinematic technology has the peculiar quality of rendering the film star an 'undead', regnant figure, she turns to E. Elias Merhige's *Shadow of the Vampire* (2000) as a critical commentary on the 'vampirism' of cinematic technologies. Her chapter theorises about the stakes involved in our contemporary media addiction to, and cultural fascination with, the dead woman on screen. Finally, moving into the domain of contemporary technology's aim to immortalise the human subject, Neal Kirk (Chapter 14) explores the 'Be Right Back' episode of Charlie Brooker's Gothic small-screen series, *Black Mirror*, that engages the issue of how users of new, addictive, spectralised media technologies encounter death, loss, and memorialisation. In '"I'm not in that thing you know ... I'm remote. I'm in the cloud": networked spectrality in Charlie Brooker's "Be Right Back"', Kirk reads the episode through the lens of what he calls 'networked spectrality'. He considers the relevant developmental, technical, social, and political dynamics of digital networks and dependent technologies, and asks the complex, provocative question as to how and with what implications the concept of 'haunting' is adapted to convey a digital undead presence that persists after death.

As evidenced by its necropoetics and necropolitics, its melancholic characters in mourning, and its narrative preoccupation with mortality, the ineffable, and undeath/the undead, the Gothic has, since its inception, fetishised death and been deeply invested in death-related and religiously/spiritually inflected post-mortality issues. Indeed, this quintessential product of its Romantic, revolutionary historic moment, registered, like various other cultural forms of the Enlightenment era, the 'obsession with death' that Marilyn Butler identifies as prevalent in British literature between 1760 and 1790 (1981: 27). True to form and in keeping with Western thanatological attitudes post-Enlightenment, death served ambivalently in the Gothic, then as now, as both a centripetal and centrifugal narrative force.

This volume endeavours to unearth and theorise the nature of the death obsession cited by Butler as it was manifested across dozens of Gothic productions, which feature different national, historical, and socio-cultural contexts. In each instance, the mode provides an index of various death-related anxieties, terrors, and desires. In this objective, this pioneering scholarly volume aims to be suggestive rather than comprehensive or exhaustive, hoping to lay some necessary and valuable groundwork for future scholarship. While death is always, as Webster Goodwin and Bronfen rightly underscore, misrepresented, as it is ultimately unknowable (1993: 19), cultural engagements with this complex and multifaceted subject that possesses aspects simultaneously physical and metaphysical, literal and symbolic, are eminently fascinating to intellectual and cultural historians.

As Vijay Mishra's chapter in this volume cogently argues, attitudes towards death, such as the concepts of haunting, *memento mori*, and the afterlife, vary significantly across cultures and historic periods. While some of death's terrors, like those generated by the prospect of subjectivity's annihilation and the silencing of voice, have remained constant, significant transmutations have occurred in their narrative treatment. What Thomas Laqueur has characterised as a changing 'culture of death' (2001: 23) has been in evidence in Gothic literature since its inception. In the works of Ann Radcliffe, for example, a more middle-class, Protestant 'culture of death' was featured, one that positioned itself in opposition to a Roman Catholic 'culture of death' by promoting death's compartmentalisation from life alongside its domestication, sanitisation, and sentimentalisation. More contemporary Anglo-American Gothic texts push the boundaries on the graphically grotesque very self-reflexively, almost daring their viewers, who are violence- and death-saturated as a result of sensational news and other media, to watch bloody, gruesome horrors unfold as the protagonist hovers on the brink of death.

It has been said that '[m]any of the cultural systems concerned with death are in fact constructed to give a voice to the silenced dead' (Webster Goodwin and Bronfen, 1993: 6). The same is true of certain cultural forms. Graveyard Poetry and other eighteenth-century British literature worked to tame death-related terrors and appease mourners with visions of a peaceful afterlife of family reunion. As such, these works served as a new type of Protestant consolation literature that, albeit indirectly, assisted those in mourning, an experience that is ultimately universal. While the Gothic functioned in this capacity, it also granted expression to both the irrepressible terrors generated by the prospect of the grave and of encounters with the spectral and corporeal undead who, often unmourned and unmemorialised, lay beyond it. In thus reflecting on our relationship to personal, socio-political, and cultural history, the Gothic tapped questions about our inheritances from, and debts to, our dead forefathers and foremothers. Such Gothic meditations continue to this day, interrogating and challenging Hamlet's poetic description of death as 'the undiscovered country, from whose bourn / No traveller returns'. Despite concerted contemporary scientific efforts to prolong life indefinitely, the terror of death that annihilates subjectivities and silences voices remains, spectres abound, and the Gothic persists, popular and relevant. Gothic engagements with death may immortalise their authors and, for a time, reader-survivors may engage in the process of cultural reception, thinking with relief, '*Lugeo ergo sum*: I mourn, therefore, I am'. Identified and characterised by Terry Castle, this new mantra of devotionalism in Radcliffe's era that signposted a 'new immortalizing habit of thought' (1995: 135), reaffirmed interests on both sides of the grave: the memorialisation of the lost loved one and the ongoing existence of the surviving mourner. True to form, however, the Gothic continues to reassert, in a compelling multitude of ways, its other most powerful and unsettling warning – *memento mori* – in the face of which some of us, striving for immortality of another order, will continue to create cultural productions.

Notes

1 See Shelley, 1990, p. 336
2 One of the most curious post-Enlightenment superstitious practices relating to corpses involved the belief that the touch of a freshly hanged man's hand could cure physical ailments and ward off dangers and bad health. See Davies and Matteoni, 2015.
3 It is noteworthy that, from the establishment of the Directory in France in November of 1795 onwards, as part of an attempt to return a greater sense of socio-political stability and normalcy to the Republic, 'the corpse once again ... [became] taboo in the public sphere' (de Baecque, 2001: 11).

References

Ariès, P. (1981) *The Hour of Our Death*, trans. Helen Weaver (New York and Oxford: Oxford University Press).
Baudrillard, J. (2007) *Symbolic Exchange and Death* [1976] (London: Sage Publications).
Bewell, A. (1989) *Wordsworth and the Enlightenment* (New Haven, CT: Yale University Press).
Bronfen, E. (2009) 'Death' [1998], in M. Mulvey Roberts (ed.), *The Handbook of Gothic Literature* (Basingstoke: Palgrave Macmillan), pp. 113–16.
Bronfen, E. (1992) *Over Her Dead Body: Death, Femininity, and the Aesthetic* (Manchester: Manchester University Press).
Burke, E. (1790) *Reflections on the Revolution in France* (London: J. Dodsley).
Burke, E. (1767) *A Philosophical Enquiry Into the Origin of Our Ideas of the Sublime and the Beautiful* (London: J. Dodsley).
Butler, M. (1981) *Romantics, Rebels and Revolutionaries: English Literature and Its Background, 1760–1830* (Oxford and New York: Oxford University Press).
Castle, T. (1995) *The Female Thermometer: Eighteenth-Century Culture and the Invention of the Uncanny* (Oxford and New York: Oxford University Press).
Creed, B. (1993) *The Monstrous-Feminine: Film, Feminism, Psychoanalysis* (London: Routledge).
Davies, O. and F. Matteoni (2015) '"A virtue beyond all medicine": The hanged man's hand, gallows tradition and healing in eighteenth- and nineteenth-century England', *Social History of Medicine*, 29.4: 1–20.
De Baecque, A. (2001) *Glory and Terror: Seven Deaths Under the French Revolution* (New York and Oxford: Oxford University Press).
Duggett, T. (2010) *Gothic Romanticism: Architecture, Politics, and Literary Form* (Basingstoke: Palgrave Macmillan).
Eng, D. L. and D. Kazanjian (eds) (2003) 'Introduction: Mourning Remains', in *Loss: The Politics of Mourning* (Berkeley: University of California Press), pp. 1–25.
Gordon, A. (2008) *Ghostly Matters: Haunting and the Sociological Imagination* (Minneapolis, MN: University of Minnesota Press).

Gorer, G. (1965) 'The Pornography of Death', in *Death, Grief, and Mourning in Contemporary Britain* (London: The Cresset Press), pp. 169–75.

Hume, R. D. (1969) 'Gothic Versus Romantic: A Re-evaluation of the Gothic Novel', *PMLA*, 84.2: 282–90.

Pogue Harrison, R. (2004) *The Dominion of the Dead* (Chicago and London: The University of Chicago Press).

Jefferson, T. (1945) *Jefferson's Letters*, ed. Willson Whitman (Eau Claire, WI: E. M. Hale and Company).

Joseph, G. and H. F. Tucker (1999), 'Passing On: Death', in H. F. Tucker (ed.), *A Companion to Victorian Literature & Culture* (Oxford: Blackwell), pp. 110–24.

Laqueur, T. (2001) 'In and Out of the Panthéon', *London Review of Books*, 23.18: 3–8. Available at: http://www.lrb.co.uk/v23/n18/thomas-laqueur/in-and-out-of-the-pantheon. Accessed 5 December 2014.

Lynch, D. S. (2008) 'Gothic Fiction', in R. Maxwell and K. Trumpener (eds), *The Cambridge Companion to Fiction in the Romantic Period* (Cambridge: Cambridge University Press), pp. 47–63.

May, T. (2009) *Death* (Stocksfield: Acumen).

Noys, B. (2005) *The Culture of Death* (London and New York: Berg).

O'Gorman, F. (2010) 'The Dead', in F. O'Gorman (ed.), *The Cambridge Companion to Victorian Culture* (Cambridge: Cambridge University Press).

Paulson, R. (1983) *Representations of Revolution (1789–1820)* (New Haven, CT, and London: Yale University Press).

Quigley, C. (1996) *The Corpse: A History* (Jefferson, NC: McFarland and Company).

Royle, N. (2002) 'Memento Mori', in M. McQuillan (ed.), *Theorizing Muriel Spark: Gender, Race, Deconstruction* (Basingstoke: Palgrave Macmillan), pp. 189–203.

Shelley, M. (1990) 'On Ghosts' [1824], in B. T. Bennett and C. E. Robinson (eds), *The Mary Shelley Reader* (Oxford: Oxford University Press), pp. 334–40.

Shelley, M. (1997) *Frankenstein; or, The Modern Prometheus* [1818], ed. D. L. Macdonald and K. Scherf (Peterborough, ON: Broadview Press).

Townshend, D. (2008) 'Gothic and the Ghost of Hamlet', in D. Townshend and J. Drakakis (eds), *Gothic Shakespeares* (Abingdon: Routledge), pp. 60–97.

Walmsley, P. (2009) 'The Melancholy Briton: Enlightenment Sources of the Gothic', in M. L. Wallace (ed.), *Enlightening Romanticism, Romancing the Enlightenment: British Novels from 1750 to 1832* (Aldershot: Ashgate), pp. 39–54.

Walpole, H. (1982) *The Castle of Otranto* [1764] (Oxford: Oxford University Press).

Webster Goodwin, S. and E. Bronfen (eds) (1993) *Death and Representation* (Baltimore, MD, and London: Johns Hopkins University Press).

Westover, P. (2012) *Necromanticism: Travelling to Meet the Dead, 1750–1860* (Basingstoke: Palgrave Macmillan).

Wright, A. (2004) '"To live the life of hopeless recollection": Mourning and Melancholia in Female Gothic, 1780–1800', *Gothic Studies*, 6.1: 19–29.

Zigarovich, J. (2012) *Writing Death and Absence in the Victorian Novel: Engraved Narratives* (Basingstoke: Palgrave Macmillan).

Part I

Gothic graveyards and afterlives

1

Serena Trowbridge

Past, present, and future in the Gothic graveyard

Ways of memorialising the dead have changed over the centuries; yet reflection on death has been a consistent preoccupation. Often, this takes place at a graveside where the memorial stone and the proximity of the corpse, juxtaposed with the unchanging and tranquil setting, elevate the mind to consider the eternal and sublime. Such a scene is offered by the most famous 'graveyard' poem, Thomas Gray's 'Elegy Written in a Country Churchyard' (*c.*1745–50), which illustrates this combination, causing the poem to serve as a memorial to the poet as well as a *memento mori* for the reader. In Gray's poem, corpses receive little mention, although they are implicitly at its heart. Earlier poems such as Edward Young's *The Complaint: or Night-Thoughts on Life, Death, & Immortality* (1742–45) and Robert Blair's 'The Grave' (1743) are more explicit in their concern for the fate of the body, contrasting it with the onward journey of the soul. This last work, in particular, relates to the beginning of a shift in the cultural significance of the corpse as Philippe Ariès (1981) indicates, and which is evident in Gothic fiction.

The concept that Gothic literature was influenced by Graveyard Poetry is entertained briefly by David Punter and Glennis Byron: 'It is also important to notice that as early as the 1740s we can trace the development of a form of poetry which was radically different from anything Pope advocated, and which came to be called "Graveyard Poetry". Graveyard Poetry is significant here because it prefigures the Gothic novel in several ways and its emergence was sudden and dramatic' (Punter and Byron, 2004: 10). Similarly, Andrew Smith mentions this poetic form, suggesting that the graveyard poets 'made a significant contribution to developing a Gothic ambience (by dwelling on feelings of loss), and provided an investigation into life and death that constituted a peculiarly Gothic metaphysic' (2004: 52). Such discussions of Graveyard Poetry in relation to Gothic literature tend, however, to be cursory. Fred Botting explores the iconography of the graveyard, directing readers to reflect on mortality, as a counter-cultural undercurrent that challenged Enlightenment thought; the aesthetics of the graveyard were increasingly used 'to evoke intense feelings' (1996: 35) as Gothic evolved, yet bear the traces of their Protestant origins in Graveyard Poetry. This chapter offers a brief exploration of the aesthetics and metaphysics that both Graveyard Poetry and the Gothic modes share, and examines ways in which death is refigured in the wake of Graveyard Poetry from a warning to the living into a horror-fiction that bears the traces of its Graveyard precedent. Graveyard Poetry indicates a concern for the body as a site for remembrance; Gothic, building on this and transforming the notions of death as the Graveyard presents it, manifests a deeper concern for loss of individuality post-mortem, and a deep anxiety about the very existence of an afterlife. The cultural position of the corpse in these related but contrasting schema – Graveyard and Gothic – is also relative to denominational beliefs, and this, along with the metaphysical shift in thought about the corpse, evident in eighteenth-century changing representations of the body after death, is explored here.

The graveyard serves as a site for both corpses and spectres. In the context of the Gothic, a form supremely concerned with religion and religious differences between Catholicism and Protestantism, ghostly presences are usually associated with Catholicism, relegating it to superstition. Belief in Purgatory, largely absent in Britain post-Reformation, permitted the existence of ghosts awaiting the Resurrection, while Protestant belief, on a more 'rational' basis, saw the soul as taken directly to Heaven with no possibility of remaining on earth. Consequently, Terry Castle has argued that, in the post-Enlightenment, spectres were likely to be understood as a product of the mind rather than as separate entities (1995: 161). Castle proposes that, 'In the very act of denying the spirit world of our ancestors, we have been forced to relocate it in our theory of the imagination' (143). Moreover, she argues that literature about ghost-seeing began, in the early eighteenth century, to focus on the ghost as the product of mental disturbance rather than a physical reality. Thus did 'thought itself …

[become] a spectral process' (164). Castle's discussion suggests that whereas before the Enlightenment it was considered possible to see a spectre, a gradual transition began which forced the spectre into the realms of the mind, considering it a projection of the ghost-seer's unconscious rather than of the spirit world.

The focus on the corpse, always present in some form in Graveyard Poetry and frequently in Gothic literature, indicates the fluctuating concern with the physical corpse and the treatment of the dead according to Philippe Ariès. Here, the 'schism' (1981: 297) that occurs is not between Catholic and Protestant, but with regard to individuals' approach to death. The reverence with which death and dying were treated shifted in the seventeenth century, Ariès states, where death became 'something metaphysical that ... [was] expressed by a metaphor, the separation of the soul and the body' (300). As faith waned, the focus on the body increased, especially with the advent of medicine promising an extended life. As objects of scientific investigation, the corpse was useful to the living; otherwise, it was 'nothing but a handful of dust, which was returned to nature' (394). Into the eighteenth century, however, the respect for the body after death increased. Rituals surrounding burial and mourning indicated anxieties about the onward journey of the soul, creating a 'cult of the dead' (508). These socio-historical shifts are registered in the treatment of corpses and spectres in Gothic literature.

'Graveyard Poetry' is a problematic label; while books on eighteenth-century poetry tend to list a few poets (including Gray, Blair, Young, and Thomas Parnell), and describe the features of Graveyard Poetry, it was not part of a 'movement'. Although these writers may be grouped together as a 'school', even this suggests more coherence than the poets and poetry deserve. Nevertheless, as Mary Snodgrass points out, the 'graveyard poets' certainly produced a 'recognisable canon' (2005: 161). More fruitfully, Eric Parisot offers a detailed taxonomy of the graveyard mode, suggesting that it is 'most productive to view eighteenth-century Graveyard Poetry as the culmination of a number of literary precedents' (2013: 2), from *Hamlet* to Milton's 'Il Penseroso', taking in funeral sermons and devotional literature along the way. Significantly, Parisot also offers a definition of Graveyard Poetry, in which 'Night, solitude and self-examination are all key tropes of the Graveyard Poetry, but it is the accretion of these tropes into a specific consideration of death and mortality that is the essential characteristic of this poetic mode' (15). This characterisation of the mode is particularly significant given the dearth of criticism on the graveyard 'school'.

Derrida (1996) writes of the 'gift' of death in Western philosophy, arguing that the traditional theology of Christianity presents death as a gift to the living, in two senses: the sacrifice of Christ so often commemorated on tombstones by way of the statement, 'I am the resurrection, and the life' (John 11:25), and in the way that this sense of an ending offers meaning to life by emphasising the individual's inescapable fate. Underscoring the mysticism inherent in the human understanding of death, Derrida binds together the threads of the past (our historical understanding of death, which he problematises), a present in which we must face our own death and take responsibility for it, and the unknowable future, the 'new experience of death' (1996: 6). One of Derrida's concerns here is the self and its unique identity:

> The sameness of the self, what remains irreplaceable in dying, only becomes what it is, in the sense of an identity as a relation of the self to itself, by means of this idea of mortality as irreplaceability. (1996: 45)

Derrida's arguments centre on the construction of the self, and what death as an event can mean to the living. His focus on selfhood in relation to death suggests that poets like those of the graveyard school can be read as finding meaning in life, and a way of depicting their mortality, while ensuring their immortality as writers. Parisot posits that such self-awareness combines with the 'poetic methodology' of Graveyard Poetry to offer 'a particular aesthetic manoeuvre as a symptom of religious/poetic crisis', 'seek[ing] death and the dead as a source of poetic revelation' (2013: 81).

The locus of death provides a focal point where the poetic and the constructed self meet, uniting the rational and the sublime in contemplating the terrible and unknowable, and replacing the pre-Reformation prayers for the dead with a Protestant contemplation of the hereafter. Familiar *memento mori*, including grave markers, depict the passing of time as life's enemy, but time is also crucial to the poet's conception of death. Taking Gray's 'Elegy' as an example, the poet, situated in the graveyard, looks outward to the world around him, and opens with an indication of the present time: 'The curfew tolls the knell of parting day' (line 1), indicating in the lexicon time, death, and a sense of loss. With a subtle shift, the poem moves backwards in time to remember those who have died and are buried around the speaker, recalling small domestic details such as the 'blazing hearth' (line 21) and the children welcoming home their returning father. This backward gaze is not merely sentimental; it is absorbed in the aesthetics of the poem, in the 'ivy-mantled tower' and the 'yew-tree's shade' (lines 9, 13). The poet's focus on the appearance of the graveyard is mingled with the construction of historical pasts, both real and imagined, such as the 'village-Hampden' and 'mute inglorious Milton' (lines 57, 59). The past, for Gray and others, is a way of re-imagining the future – of considering our own eventual fate, and the purpose of life, by considering those who have been forgotten. Only among the graves of the dead can we learn what our own future will be. The future is not uncertain, then, but clear: 'The paths of glory lead but to the grave' (line 36). The closing stanzas of the poem consolidate this moral, by shifting from the unnamed, unknown dead, to 'thee', who will one day join them. This is the future to which the poem looks, though unlike many others of its time it does not anticipate the joys of Heaven until the very last line when the dead are envisioned as resting in 'The bosom of his Father and his God' (line 128).

The preoccupation with the past as a way of enlightening and envisaging the future is one which is familiar from the Gothic novel. It is a truism of the genre that history, particularly in the form of a romanticised medieval past, provides a staple backdrop to which Gothic persistently returns. Yet in, for example, Matthew Lewis's *The Monk* (1796), the distance in time and place allows Lewis to be extremely critical of rigid religious practices. Ann Radcliffe's novels, although set contemporaneously, are steeped in the past and in antiquated beliefs and behaviours, yet permit her heroines a certain subversive freedom of behaviour given the gender norms context of the period. The past, then, is a way of reading the present, and one that links Gothic to the graveyard school. Moreover, as Clive Bloom points out, 'Its [Gothic] obsession is with death' (2010: 64). Exploring the past unavoidably confronts the dead, the processes of dying, and the future that awaits us after death.

The physical disintegration of the body and the trepidation relating to what awaits the soul is a preoccupation that is represented metaphorically in Horace Walpole's *The Castle of Otranto* (1764). Here, a gigantic helmet appears, killing the heir to Otranto. While the events of the story unfold concerning the future of the lineage of the ruling family, other parts of a giant knight are seen, including a foot and a sabre. While these supernatural manifestations are ludicrous, they have a logical conclusion; they represent Alfonso the Good whose heir is

the true lord of Otranto. Alfonso is seen in his entirety in a portrait in
the gallery and an effigy in the chapel; his body parts are thus reunited
only in family history and in a place of worship. The metaphorical disintegration of the body of Alfonso, representative of the literal decay
of his body, reminds the living of his claim. The wholeness of the body
in the church and gallery indicates the memorial that is lasting and
more precious – that of lineage, and faith – and reminds the living that
immoral behaviour will ultimately fail them.

The first proponent of the graveyard school, Thomas Parnell's 'A
Night-Piece on Death', was published by Alexander Pope after its
author's death in 1722. This poem is often credited with inspiring later
Gothic novelists, a connection rarely explored in detail, though Patrick
Bridgwater suggests that 'the Gothic state of mind goes back, via the
cult of Spenser and Milton, to the second quarter of the eighteenth
century (Parnell, Young, Blair and Gray)' (2013: 506), alluding to the
relationship between Radcliffe's work and the 'Night-Piece'. Oliver
Goldsmith commented that '"The Night Piece on Death" deserves
every praise, and I should suppose, with very little amendment, might
be made to surpass all those night pieces and church-yard scenes that
have since appeared' (1854: vol. 4, 143–4). Reading the poem provides
a curiously intertextual effect; Parnell is looking back to earlier poetic
precedents, perhaps seeing himself as an inheritor of the traditions of
Milton and Spenser, whose inventiveness and style he praises in his
Preface to 'An Essay on the Different Stiles of Poetry' (1713) (iii). In
looking backwards to his poetic predecessors, Parnell is conforming
to Gothic's desire for the past, its styles, ideas, and aesthetics. Parnell's
poem is, however, also looking forward: to death, and Heaven. As
David Fairer and Christine Gerrard point out:

> the Night-Piece checks and even undercuts its own Gothic frisson. It is Death who
> reprimands foolish man for frightening himself with macabre phantasms. Death,
> for the enlightened Christian, is but a passage to Heaven. The poem thus moves
> steadily from images of darkness and entrapment to those of flight, transcend-
> ence and sublimity. (2004: 61)

The poem begins with a 'wakeful night', lit by a flickering flame. With
a brief diversion to the glories of nature, the poem moves on to its real
subject: the wisdom that we may learn in the graveyard rather than
from scholars. The reader is advised to:

> … think, as softly-sad you tread
> Above the venerable Dead,

Time was, like thee they Life possest,
And Time shall be, that thou shalt Rest. (lines 25–8)

The warning is not uncommon; *memento mori* paintings, containing skulls or hourglasses, for example, were still common in Europe during Parnell's lifetime, and earlier literary precedents include Thomas Browne's *Hydriotaphia, Urne-Burial, Or A Discourse of the Sepulchrall Urnes lately found in Norfolk* (1658). The poetic form of Parnell's work focuses the reader's mind on the elegiac appropriation of death, accompanied by the aesthetic trappings of the graveyard. The 'objects' that will be imported into the Gothic make an appearance; from graves and headstones, tombs and 'Arms, Angels, Epitaphs and Bones' (line 42), we move to more fanciful items such as the Shades, 'wrap'd with Shrouds', the Yew, the Charnel House, Ravens, Clocks, Sable Stoles, Cypress and Palls, among others. But these aesthetics point to a deeper meaning. The horror of the 'peal of hollow groans' (line 59) and the 'visionary crouds' (line 50) of the dead are not there simply to provide a pleasurable frisson of terror but to point to an eternal truth – namely, that 'Death's but a Path that must be trod, / If Man wou'd ever pass to God' (lines 67–8). Such phantoms and imaginings are of our own making, and can be dismissed by true faith.

Gothic literature thus occupies a precise poetic relation to the poetry of mortality. A reflective atmosphere of melancholy prevails, for example, in the novels of Ann Radcliffe, particularly relating to bereaved heroines such as Emily St Aubert in *The Mysteries of Udolpho* (1794). Radcliffe employs poetry both as epigraphs and within the text to evoke a mood of sublime contemplation inspired by the surrounding landscape. The melancholy poetry that Radcliffe uses in her novels as epigraphs to set her melancholy scenes offers one way back to the graveyard from within Gothic novels. A chapter of *The Italian* (1797), in which the heroine Ellena's murder is discussed, opens with a fine example of this:

Along the roofs sounds the low peal of Death,
And Conscience trembles to the boding note;
She views his dim form floating o'er the aisles
She hears mysterious murmurs in the air … (Radcliffe, 1998: 171)

Here, the sound and sight of Death approaching pricks the conscience; the parallels with the thematic structure of Parnell's poem are clear. Although the 'sound' and 'dim form' of death may be imaginary, its effect is nonetheless potent, causing the conscience to tremble. This sign of fear is, of course, the fear of God, of retribution for lifetime sins that must be addressed before death. What is lacking in the majority of poetic fragments in Radcliffe's novels is the optimism of life after death that Parnell and Gray, among others, use to conclude their graveyard meditations. Both for the graveyard poets with their ultimate focus on the sublime and hope of Heaven, however, and for Radcliffe with her spectres that are explained away, the atmosphere of death and decay is not dispelled. It is so strongly evocative, so emotionally charged, and in many ways so pleasurably unpleasant, as well as necessary to remind the reader that their focus should be not on the decay of the body, but the heavenly future awaiting them. The Gothic, like the graveyard, is ultimately about the terrors and bondages of the world; Parnell dismisses these fears, reminding us, in the closing lines of his poem, that the future holds freedom and hope:

> …when their Chains are cast aside
> See the glad Scene unfolding wide
> Clap the glad wing and tow'r away
> And mingle with the Blaze of Day. (lines 87–90)

Such instances are perhaps shadowed by the more graphic *memento mori* that infamously features as *Udolpho*'s cliffhanger, in which Emily glimpses a corpse behind a black veil deep in the castle, a reminder of death that magnifies Emily's fears for her own life. Yet, as Timothy Baker discusses, *Udolpho* 'repeatedly gives the reader the image of death but not the thing itself' (2014: 18); what Emily believes to be death is merely a graphic reminder of the graveyard, modelled in wax. This is because the novel is predicated on mourning, Baker argues, as the only way in which we might 'know' death, and provides an instructive lesson to the reader not only as a 'model of mourning' but 'in differentiating between death and its image' (18). Consequently, Emily is not exposed to death itself, but to what her fearful mind interprets as death, though Townshend's essay (2014) counters this by indicating that mourning is itself an encounter with death, and some detailed passages in the novel also outline her contact with her father's corpse. Radcliffe's novels have been criticised for 'explaining away' the supernatural, and here she might be accused of undercutting the experience of death by providing a proxy corpse. Yet she offers a distinct position in relation to the death and the supernatural. Like Parnell, her ghosts are of human creation, and offer both characters and readers a way to understand life and death, maintaining the instructive strain of the graveyard poets. Castle (1995) posits that the division of the world into homely and uncanny (in itself a troublesome proposition), and the division of a Gothic novel into Gothic/domestic, which is common in Gothic criticism, echoes the too-comfortable binaries of living and dead. This distinction, she argues, is not present in Radcliffe's work due to her unifying use of spectral language; it is in the domestic scenes where memories of the dead overwhelm Radcliffe's characters. The result of this is that 'the supernatural is not so much explained in *Udolpho* as it is displaced' into the 'everyday' (1995: 124). This highlights a striking disjunction between the poetry of the graveyard and the spectres of the Gothic; in poems such as Parnell's, the horrors of the decaying bodies and the spectres of death are confined to their appropriate place – the graveyard. In the novels of Radcliffe and other Gothic writers, these spectres and corpses, reminders of death, exit the graveyard and enter the home, threatening the domestic centre. The description of Emily's discovery of the waxen corpse in *Udolpho* is intended to frighten:

> Beyond, appeared a corpse, stretched on a kind of low couch, which was crimsoned with human blood, as was the floor beneath. The features, deformed by death, were ghastly and horrible, and more than one livid wound appeared in the face. (Radcliffe, 1980: 348)

It is no wonder that Emily faints. When the mystery of the corpse is explained, the horror is intentionally undiminished; in some ways it is magnified with mention of 'the habiliments of the grave' and 'the face ... partly decayed and disfigured by worms' (Radcliffe, 1980: 662). The explanation, that it was created as a penance for an ancestor, seems to undermine its significance both as a Christian reminder of death and as an object of fear in the novel, but it remains a reminder of the graveyard, and it is noteworthy that this memento mori is a more fearful concept in the novel than the supernatural phenomena, again indicating the primacy of the physical over the metaphysical. As Dale Townshend points out as he explores the construct of Emily as a woman in mourning for her father, 'ghosts are invoked ... in order to be eventually exorcised as the unbearable objects of horror and terror' (2014: 233). The first glimpse of death in *Udolpho* overshadows much of the novel, but finally reveals the truth behind the 'counterfeit renditions of death' (233). Emily's experiences of death indicate her education by fear, and thus her growing maturity, which involves 'appropriate mourning' (233).

Two further corpses, slightly resembling each other, are notable in early Gothic fiction. Both are described in their putrefying state and, as such, serve as *memento mori*, but despite their similarities they occupy distinctive spaces in the text. The first is the child of Agnes in *The Monk*. Agnes's heart-rending story is that she has fallen pregnant out of wedlock, whilst residing in a nunnery against her will. When the eponymous Monk, Ambrosio, discovers her secret, he informs the Prioress who orders that Agnes be locked away in a room beneath the nunnery and left to die. When Agnes begs for mercy for her unborn child, the Monk remains unbending:

> Dare you plead for the product of your shame? … Expect no mercy from me either for yourself, or Brat! Rather pray, that Death may seize you before you produce it; Or if it must see the light, that its eyes may immediately be closed again for ever! (Lewis, 1998: 410)

This and other speeches by the Prioress indicate an emphasis on suffering and bodily death as a means of purification of the soul, offering salvation. Agnes's crimes can only be expiated by mortification, a Roman Catholic concept, for which Lewis demonstrates deep mistrust. Agnes's punishment resembles a living death, immured in a crypt and left without food or light to die; she is placed upon a 'wicker Couch' which would ultimately 'convey [her] … to [her] … grave', and she rests her hand upon 'something soft': 'What was my disgust, my consternation! In spite of its putridity, and the worms which preyed upon it, I perceived a corrupted human head' (1998: 402–3). Such *memento mori* traumatise Agnes, though she survives her incarceration. The most macabre element of her experience, however, is the fate of her child who dies a few hours after birth. Agnes describes her refusal to give up the corpse, an indication of her mourning:

> It soon became a mass of putridity, and to every eye was a loathsome and disgusting Object; to every eye, but a Mother's. In vain did human feelings bid me recoil from this emblem of mortality with repugnance: … I endeavoured to retrace its features through the livid corruption. (1998: 413)

This moment in the novel manifests the charnel-house atmosphere of Graveyard Poetry. In 'The Grave', Blair notes those who are mourned in the graveyard, including

> … the child
> Of a span long, that never saw the sun,
> Nor press'd the nipple, strangled in life's porch. (lines 517–20)

The child, the poet notes, dies just as all others do. Yet the death of a child is significant, causing a particularly poignant reflection on the brevity of life and the necessity of salvation. The focus on the infant's corrupted body in *The Monk* provides a graveyard reflection on the transformation from living, beloved being to object of disgust. Moreover, the transformation of the once-beautiful Agnes herself into a near-corpse underlines – or perhaps undermines – Mario Praz's argument (1970: 31) that 'to such an extent were Beauty and Death looked upon as sisters by the Romantics that they became fused into a sort of two-faced herm, filled with corruption and melancholy'. As Agnes's beauty is transformed to the point of death, so her soul is also transformed.

A similar scene appears in Maturin's novel *Melmoth the Wanderer* (1820). Here, the graveyard trope of the proximity of the mouldering body, again of an infant, prompts a reflection on future deaths. Isidora, Melmoth's wife, is imprisoned by the Inquisition along with their child. When officers arrive to remove the child, she gives them instead the corpse of her daughter, which she had been nursing: 'Around the throat of the miserable infant, born amid agony, and nursed in a dungeon, there was a black mark ... deemed ... the fearful effect of maternal despair' (Maturin, 2000: 593). This death is quickly followed by Isidora's who asks, in her dying breath, 'Paradise! *Will he be there?*' (596). Her preoccupation is not her own death, but the ultimate destination of her husband's soul. Comfort for the bereaved often implied a reunion in Heaven with the dead, yet contrary to this belief are the words of Mark 12:25: 'For when they shall rise from the dead, they neither marry, nor are given in marriage'. This passage 'abrogates not only the essential human faculty of sexual love and relationship and the need for procreation but even the very survival of human ties' (Simon, 1958: 217). The implication is that there will be no recognition of individuality in heaven; the earthly body will be discarded, yet the hope of reunion remains, particularly in this Roman Catholic context.

These examples of disintegrating bodies and departing souls may seem removed from the context of Graveyard Poetry, but the melodramatic depictions of death and emphasis on the brevity of life indicate their status as *memento mori*. While in the case of *The Monk* and *Melmoth the Wanderer* the gruesome depiction can in part be attributed to the 'horror Gothic' that Ann Radcliffe deplored, the beliefs towards which they gesture are also significant. Gothic fiction absorbed much of the atmosphere of Graveyard Poetry, which is manifest in its aesthetics as well as its appropriation of corpses and revenants, but as Eve Kosofsky Sedgwick discusses in *The Coherence of Gothic Conventions*

(1986: 140–67), the aesthetics on which the genre depends for its atmosphere are also indicative of what lies beneath. We ignore the aesthetics at a cost, because they are all a writer can offer; the 'meaning' depends on a complex web of allusions, history, and social and religious contexts, which constitutes a shared ideology of mortality. This is especially true of the relationship between the widely read Graveyard Poetry and the later, more widespread, Gothic. Both, in their different forms, remind the living that 'the paths of glory lead but to the grave'.

References

Ariès, P. (1981) *The Hour of Our Death*, trans. Helen Weaver (London: Penguin).

Baker, T. (2014) *Contemporary Scottish Gothic: Mourning, Authenticity, and Tradition* (Basingstoke: Palgrave Macmillan).

Barbauld, A. L. (2000) 'On Romances' [1773] and 'On the Pleasure Derived from Works of Terror' [1773], in R. Norton (ed.), *Gothic Readings: The First Wave 1764–1840* (London: Continuum), pp. 279–80.

Blair, R. (2010) *The Grave, to which is added Gray's Elegy in a Country Church-Yard. A new edition, with notes, moral, critical and explanatory* [1814] (London: British Library).

Bloom, C. (2010) *Gothic Histories: The Taste for Terror, 1764 to the Present* (London: Continuum).

Botting, F. (1996) *Gothic* (London: Routledge).

Bridgwater, P. (2013) *The German Gothic Novel in Anglo-German Perspective* (New York: Rodopi).

Castle, T. (1995) *The Female Thermometer: Eighteenth-Century Culture and the Invention of the Uncanny* (Oxford: Oxford University Press).

Derrida, J. (1996) *The Gift of Death* [1992], trans. D. Wills (Chicago and London: University of Chicago Press).

Fairer, D. and C. Gerrard (2004) *Eighteenth-Century Poetry: An Annotated Anthology* (Chichester: Blackwell Publishing).

Freud, S. (1953) 'The Uncanny' [1919], in J. Strachey (ed. and trans), *The Standard Edition of the Complete Psychological Works of Sigmund Freud* (London: Hogarth), pp. 219–52.

Goldsmith, O. (1854) *Works*, ed. P. Cunningham (London: John Murray).

Gray, T. (1966) *The Complete Poems of Thomas Gray*, ed. H. W. Starr and J. R. Hendrickson (Oxford: Clarendon Press).

Lewis, M. (1998) *The Monk* [1796], ed. E. McEvoy (Oxford: Oxford University Press).

Maturin, C. R. (2000) *Melmoth the Wanderer* [1820], ed. V. Sage (London: Penguin).

Parisot, E. (2013) *Graveyard Poetry: Religion, Aesthetics and the Mid-Eighteenth-Century Poetic Condition* (Farnham: Ashgate).

Parnell, T. (1989) *Collected Poems of Thomas Parnell*, ed. C. Rawson and F. P. Lock (London: Associated University Presses).

Parnell, T. (1713) *An Essay on the Different Stiles of Poetry* (London: B. Tooke).

Praz, M. (1970) *The Romantic Agony* [1933], trans. A. Davidson (Oxford: Oxford University Press).

Punter, D. and G. Byron (2004) *The Gothic* (Oxford: Blackwell).

Radcliffe, A. (1980) *The Mysteries of Udolpho* [1794], ed. B. Dobrée (Oxford: Oxford University Press).

Radcliffe, A. (1998) *The Italian* [1797], ed. F. Garber (Oxford: Oxford University Press).

Sedgwick, E. K. (1986) *The Coherence of Gothic Conventions* (London: Methuen).

Simon, U. (1958) *Heaven in the Christian Tradition* (London: Rockliff).

Smith, A. (2004) *Gothic Literature* (Edinburgh: Edinburgh University Press).

Snodgrass, M. E. (2005) *Encyclopaedia of Gothic Literature* (New York: Facts on File).

Townshend, D. (2014) 'Shakespeare, Ossian, and the problem of "Scottish Gothic"', in E. Bronfen and B. Neumeier (eds), *Gothic Renaissance: A Reassessment* (Manchester: Manchester University Press), pp. 218–43.

Walpole, H. (1982) *The Castle of Otranto: A Gothic Story* [1764], ed. W. S. Lewis and J. W. Reed (Oxford: Oxford University Press).

Young, E. (2005) *The Complaint: or Night Thoughts on Life, Death, and Immortality* [1742–5] (London: Folio Society).

2

Sibylle Erle

'On the very Verge of legitimate Invention': Charles Bonnet and William Blake's illustrations to Robert Blair's *The Grave* (1808)

Blake was extremely fond of drawing souls. It is, however, often impossible to tell the living soul from the dead body. This is especially true of the illustrations to the new edition of Robert Blair's *The Grave* published by R. H. Cromek in 1808,[1] which was so successful that much of Blake's posthumous reputation rested on it. Blake's illustrations allegorise death by communicating the experience of dying through dramatic scenes depicting body and soul, male and female figures, parting from one another. The sublation of death culminates in their reunion on the Day of Judgment followed by domestic bliss in Heaven. How did Blake represent the incorporeal essence of a person? The answer has a traumatic dimension and a parallel in Swedenborgian thinking because Blake, after nursing his brother Robert through his final illness, said that he saw his 'spirit ascend heavenward through the matter-of-fact ceiling, "clapping its hands for joy"' (Gilchrist, 1998: 60). Blake kept his brother alive in his imagination. This kind of effacement between reality and fantasy was attacked by reviewers of *The Grave* who realised that Blake's visual language systematically undermined Blair's as it blurred the boundary between the literal and the figural and even distorted the boundaries of gender. The illustrations are uncanny because, rather than supporting the scenarios described by Blair, they create an alternative reality and tease viewers into confronting death (Freud, 1985: 370–2). It is Blake's Gothic aesthetic that this chapter investigates.

The Grave is a religious poem of Calvinist orientation and consists of 767 lines in blank verse. Blair's speaker, walking in a graveyard, asks for the support of the 'Eternal King' (line 8), God, to be able

'To paint the gloomy horrors of the tomb' (line 5) but quickly turns his attention in another direction: 'O Grave, dread thing!' (line 9). Blair's language luxuriates in death imagery but it never loses sight of its didactic purpose (Parisot, 2013: 60–3). Cromek, in other words, asked Blake to illustrate a text that permitted the exploration of the supernatural as well as emotional alienation but comforted readers with the existence of God. The speaker, looking at the tombstones in the graveyard, talks about death as equaliser and becomes increasingly preoccupied with physical decay. He moves non-chronologically from loss and burial to dying. Natural progression from material to spiritual life was a popular conceit in elegiac poetry classified as Graveyard Poetry. Blake engages with its iconographic focus, the graveyard, but collapses the corporeal into the spiritual in the death and resurrection scenes where the boundaries between bodies, corpses and souls are blurred.

Cromek's plan had been to include a facsimile from the manuscript of Blair's poem but changed his mind when he saw Thomas Phillips's portrait (Bentley, 2001: 290). Blake was well-known for his 'visionary communications' when he sat for Phillips in 1807 (Bentley, 2001: 265). He had visions all his life, said that they were external to him and had no problems recording them even in his late sixties. To get him into the desired pose, Phillips provoked him by saying that Raphael was a superb painter of angels. Blake took the bait and started gushing about how the archangel Gabriel had told him that he preferred Michelangelo (Bentley, 2001: 166). The *Anti-Jacobin Review* commented that it 'represents a man about the middle period of life, with an open, expressive countenance, but accompanied by a wildness in the eye' (Bentley, 2004: 274). Phillips's portrait is a semiotic as well as artistic statement about Blake; it conflates two kinds of likeness by juxtaposing physical likeness with behaviour. The resulting contiguity of image and anecdote turns Blake's face into an index of his character but also a site for narrative via the story about Gabriel. Cromek made the most of Blake's reputation. To say, however, that Blake's illustrations are sensationalist would ignore their European context. This chapter contextualises Blake's manipulation of Blair's text by explaining, via its historical context, how Blake's illustrations supersede the visual quality of Blair's language. Blake added to the poem. The scenes are not spontaneous sketches depicting the supernatural in the Gothic tradition founded by Walpole, but evidence of an awareness of the Zwinglian minister Johann Caspar Lavater (1741–1801) and the debate about immortality, kindled by Lavater's contemporary, the Swiss philosopher Charles Bonnet (1720–93) (Luginbühl-Weber, 1994: 114–48).

Blake knew of Lavater because he engraved four plates for *Essays on Physiognomy* (1789–98) and read and annotated *Aphorisms on Man* (1788), which had been translated by Lavater's classmate, Henry Fuseli. Identity, in physiognomical theory, is associated with appearance, which in turn is linked to the notion of the physical manifestation of character in the face. Lavater's revival of physiognomy pulled together different strands of popular belief and typical Enlightenment principles, such as improvement and education. In *Essays on Physiognomy* he discussed the moral qualities and intellectual abilities of real people and moved away from categorising human beings into types, which had dominated the thinking of the previous centuries, to analysing individuals. Lavater was a prolific writer who, at the outset, concentrated on small tractates for his parishioners in Zurich. He had already written on the continued bodily existence of the soul in *Aussichten in die Ewigkeit* (1768–78) when he joined the immortality debate with his translation of Charles Bonnet's *Palingéné philosophique* (1769). Encouraged by Bonnet's explanations about body-soul relationships, Lavater set out to find empirical evidence for the soul; this search determined all of his publications on physiognomy, starting with *Von der Physiognomik* (1772) and culminating in the English translation of *Physiognomische Fragmente* (1775–78) in the 1790s.

Bonnet's works were known in England. In *Contemplation de la Nature* (1764), translated in 1766, Bonnet made a direct comparison between what he identified as the behaviour of the immaterial soul and organisms that self-generated (Bonnet, 1766: I. xxiv). He explained self-generation in theological terms but talked of embodiment in terms of epigenesis, the biological model used to explain the regeneration observed in worms and polyps. In this work, Bonnet undertook to reconcile epigenesis with preformationism, and the Christian doctrine of the unity of the soul in particular, to argue that individual development strictly adhered to an original plan. Preformation, he postulated, was the result of an unfolding seed-like core or soul inside the body. In *Palingéné Philosophique*, he argued that the resurrected soul was a perfected version of its mortal equivalent. In the afterlife, consequently, human identity became fully exposed due to the self-generating soul. The best example for this progression was the metamorphosis of Jesus into Christ (Pestalozzi, 1975: 285). Bonnet was pleased with Lavater's translation but worried that he had taken his metaphors too literally (Luginbühl-Weber, 1997: I. 191). Bonnet published parts of *Palingéné Philosophique* in 1770 and it was this abridged edition that was translated as *Philosophical and Critical Inquiries Concerning Christianity* in 1787. John Lewis Boissier (1742–1821), Dragoon Guard and son of a Swiss expatriate from Geneva, Bonnet's hometown, had heard the Bishop of Chester preach about Bonnet in Bath and decided to translate the work because he liked Bonnet's philosophical approach (Bonnet, 1787: v). The sentiment that nothing Bonnet had written should be taken for a universal truth is expressed in the work's preface where Bonnet writes, 'I have not spoken of *demonstration*, but of *probability* only' (author's emphasis) (Bonnet, 1787: vii).

With Blake's portrait as frontispiece the emphasis is on the authenticity of the visions. While the text offers many of the themes, it was their rendering as images that caused a moral outrage. Robert Hunt, writing for the *Examiner*, targeted the illustrations that showed what was beyond human experience. Singling out 'The Reunion of the Soul & the Body' and 'The Meeting of a Family in Heaven', he rejected the figures' 'most indecent attitudes' and the 'appearance of libidinousness' to then ask 'how are we to find out that the figure in the shape of a body is a soul?' (Bentley, 1975: 120–1). Blake took his inspiration from the text, because Blair designated the soul as female, though not consistently, and he consciously broke with familiar artistic conventions insofar as he represented the soul as female as well as active.[2] Hunt responded to the viewing process, the readers' movements between text and images, as well as movements between ideas triggered by either the text or the images.

Death grounds human existence. All representations of death are culturally coded. Blair, Scottish poet and minister, moves between designating the soul as 'she' or 'it' and as part of the self as well as Other. For example, 'The Soul hovering over the Body reluctantly parting with Life' illustrates the lines 'How wishfully she looks / On all she's leaving, no longer is her's!' (lines 357–8). The body has been dead for a while; it is already in a shroud but the soul cannot leave. Her grief-stricken face confirms, on a metaphorical level as well as in Bonnet's sense, that body and soul are intertwined. Blake's decision to illustrate these lines puts the soul's memory of her enjoyment of life on display. Blair's point, however, is a lot more abstract. It is regret combined with forgiveness: 'O might she stay to wash away her stains, / And fit her for the passage! mournful sight!' (lines 360–1). Blair describes how, in the face of death, the relationship between body and soul disintegrates (Lacan, 1989: 1–8), when his speaker addresses his soul: 'Sure 'tis a serious thing to die! My soul, / What a strange moment must it be, when near / Thy Journey's end, though hast the gulf in view!' (lines 369–71). The soul survives death but Blair's speaker has already othered his soul as female and sinful. The split is complete when he admits that he cannot offer any final revelations about the afterlife: 'Ask not how this can be' (line 437) (Parisot, 2013: 110–11). Blake, by comparison, offers a window into the afterlife by means of his illustrations.

For Hunt, Blake's resurrected couples signified renewed sexual activity and it is hard to disagree with him because Blake's illustrations walk a tightrope between the literal and the figural. Blair speaks of male bodies and female souls metaphorically, 'For part they must – body and soul must part! / Fond couple! link'd more close than wedded pair' (lines 376–7), but not towards the end, when the trope translates into the literal: 'Nor shall the conscious soul / Mistake its partner; but amidst the crowd / Singling its other half, into its arms / Shall rush with all th' impatience of a man / That's new come home' (lines 754–8). When Blake visualised the reunion of body and soul, which is gender-less at this point in Blair, he opted for kissing and embracing couples. While Blair's readers are reminded that death and dying are solitary experiences in the poem, 'We make the grave our bed, and then are gone!' (line 763), 'The Meeting of a Family in Heaven' has three couples and is, therefore, a direct translation of Blair's 'Thrice happy meeting!' (line 760). Hunt, when criticising Blake's loose morals, was not simply rejecting his visions: he identified the paradox of representing death. He attacked this design because Blake made the inexpressible familiar as well as sexual. Taking a second look, this illustration can be interpreted as reaching beyond the text and resisting a psycho-sexual reading because the young boy, running towards the central couple and entirely Blake's invention, suggests that we are witnessing a literal reunion of a family torn apart by death. The boy has no female double or soul to meet. Blake highlights in this illustration that literalness amounts to an adjustment to natural limitations and, here specifically, to artistic conventions. Very little has been imagined. Ignoring the male-female body-soul dichotomy, Blake projects Heaven as a place of passion.[3]

While Hunt protested that Blake left nothing to the imagination, Henry Fuseli, who on Cromek's request wrote a new preface, claimed the opposite. Regarding the contiguity between text and illustration and considering Blake's approach to Gothic horror ('the varied Imagery of Death leading his Patients to the Grave'), Fuseli argued that Blake's was a 'less ambiguous, and less ludicrous Imagery, than what Mythology, Gothic Superstition, or Symbols as far-fetched as inadequate could supply' (Bentley, 2004: 211). He was full of praise for Blair: 'His Invention has been chiefly employed to spread a familiar and domestic Atmosphere round the most Important of all Subjects, to connect the visible and the invisible World, without provoking Probability, and to lead the Eye from the milder Light of Time to the Radiations of Eternity' (Bentley, 2004: 211). The expression 'without provoking probability' implies, in Bonnet's sense, that Blair represented what is intellectually plausible, and applied to Blake this means that he represented the inexpressible as part of a 'familiar and domestic' setting. The word 'familiar' circumscribes the relationship between sign and meaning. Using Charles Sanders Peirce's categories of signs, it becomes clear that Fuseli perceived the relationship between text and image as indexical, because he explained that the illustrations connect two diametrically opposite states of being and 'lead the eye'. In Peirce's words, the action set in motion during the viewing process is 'in dynamical ... connection both with the individual object ... and with the senses or memory of the person for whom it serves as sign' (Peirce, 1940: 107). Contiguity of association also explains the response of the journalist Henry Crabb Robinson: 'the soul appears hovering over the body, which it leaves unwillingly; in others we have the reunion of both at the Resurrection and so forth. These are about the most offensive of his inventions (Bentley, 2004: 597). The abruptness of the last sentence suggests that this viewer is distressed not by the resemblance between body and soul but by the fact that both are resurrected. What may have troubled Robinson is the unsettling and unexplained duplicity of the female Other created by Blair and represented by Blake, because in the illustrations the female figures simultaneously signify soul and companion (Lacan, 1985: 48–50).

How an artist visualises what is feared because it cannot be known is a matter of style. In its response to 'The Death of the Good Old Man' (Figure 2.1) the *Anti-Jacobin* declaimed that if Blake had wanted to make a believable connection between the visible and the invisible, which Fuseli said he had, he should have done so 'with threats of silk and not with bars of iron' (Bentley, 2004: 270). By the same token, the *Examiner* ridiculed the idea that Blake's illustrations enhanced the moral quality of the text by embodying the soul: 'How "*the visible and*

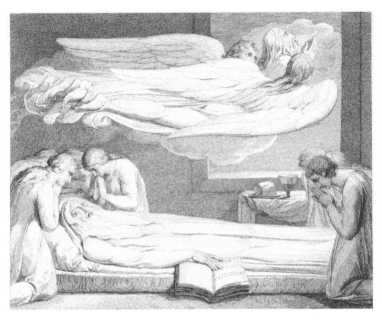

2.1 *The Death of the Good Old Man.*

the invisible world" can be *connected* by the aid of the pencil without
"provoking probability," nay even without outraging it, none but such
a visionary as Mr. Blake, or such a frantic as Mr. Fuseli, could possibly
fancy' (author's emphasis) (Bentley, 2004: 259). That Blake and Fuseli
are thrown together by their unappreciating critics is little surprising.
If Fuseli had not told Blake about Bonnet, Blake might have read John
Wesley's cheap translation of Bonnet's *Conjectures Concerning the
Nature of Future Happiness* (1785). He read and annotated works by
Lavater and Swedenborg, probably on Fuseli's suggestion, and could
have read Bonnet alongside Swedenborg because Bonnet's *Conjectures*,
reprinted in London in 1790, formulates ideas about human nature
similar to those found in Swedenborg. But while Swedenborg, building on his theory of correspondence, extrapolates his dream-journeys
and conversations with the dead, Bonnet wrote about the power of the
imagination that enabled individuals to anticipate their future (Bonnet,
1790: 5). In the same vein he wrote about the afterlife: 'If, however, a
thick cloud conceals this *future* happiness which our hearts pant after,
from our most eager search, we may nevertheless perceive, though
faintly, some of the principal sources from whence it will proceed'

(author's emphasis) (Bonnet, 1790: 6–7). His visual language, typical of the language of the sublime, helps to explain why Blake conceived dying as evolving. Bonnet stressed that the connection between body and soul is never interrupted, not even by death: 'Death is not a *break* in the *chain*: it is the link which connects the two lives' (author's emphasis) (Bonnet, 1790: 23). Blake insisted his dead brother Robert was always with him (Gilchrist, 1998: 71). Though not mentioned in the text, he included him as his uncanny double into *Milton* (1804–10). The full-picture plate 'Robert' is the mirror image of 'William', which is supposedly a self-portrait because Blake is a character in his epic poem's journey of self-discovery.

The death scenes in *The Grave* required that Blake represented corpses as well as souls. Fuseli remarked, drawing on the language of the sublime and thus firmly rooting Blake's illustrations in the Gothic tradition, that the designs generally evoked 'Wonder' and 'Fears' in the viewer, because Blake 'play[ed] on the very Verge of legitimate Invention' (Bentley, 1975: 112). This expression describes the designs' Gothic qualities, which, again, arise from Blake's style. Fuseli, well aware of the challenges to conventional modes of representation, had defined the difference between horror and terror, when pondering 'the *limits* of expression', in his lectures on painting: 'sympathy and disgust are the irreconcileable parallels that must for ever separate legitimate terror and pity from horror and aversion. We cannot sympathise with what we detest or despise, nor fully pity what we shudder at … we loathe to inspect the actual process of the crime; mangling is contagious, and spreads aversion from the slaughterman to the victim' (author's emphasis) (Knowles, 1831: II. 262–3). This is precisely what propelled Blair's writing and what Blake magnified in 'Death of the Strong and Wicked Man' (Figure 2.2).

Death in Blake's illustrations is private, but it is also a public event because it takes place in a family setting. Only the poor die alone. In his study on the iconography of death scenes, Philippe Ariès differentiated between secular and Christian images and analysed the changing arrangements of those in attendance. 'The Death of the Good Old Man' is a typically Christian scene because the soul is led away by angels while the children are praying. Here the dialogue between the deceased and his family continues beyond the moment of death (Ariès, 1984: 100–12). 'Death of the Strong Wicked Man' counterpoints the serene death represented in 'The Death of the Good Old Man' and it also recalls *Ars moriendi* (art of dying), medieval manuals that assisted

2.2 *Death of the Strong Wicked Man.*

the dying to prepare for a good death, which was conceptualised as
the result of having lived a good and morally upright life. Whereas
medieval images used death as a moment of crisis to raise awareness
and remind the viewer that they too had moral choices, Blake, just like
Blair, emphasises the paraphernalia of a death scene in order to reflect
back on a life well-lived. 'The Death of the Good Old Man' illustrates
the lines, 'Heard you that groan! / It was his last' (lines 277–8). Death
at the end of a good life is painless (Ariès, 1984: 155–64). The goblet
on the table near the window symbolises that life continues because its
contents have been preserved, while the other broken goblet near the
hand of the strong man signifies that life has been wasted even at the
very end. Blake increased the physical horror of 'Death of the Strong
Wicked Man' by doubling the pain of the dead with that of his escaping soul. The connection between body and soul is enhanced through
the pillow bursting into flames, carrying the soul out of the window.
It was this resemblance, the raw physicality of the soul-figure echoing
that of the doomed man, which caused concern at the *Anti-Jacobin*:
'when to all this is superadded a perfectly *corporeal* representation of
"the masculine soul" of the dying man ... the mind is shocked at the

outrage done to nature and probability' (author's emphasis) (Bentley, 2004: 270). Here Blake was not interested in the dialogue between the dying and his family but in the physical and spiritual realms of existence. He added 'wicked' in the caption which suggests that he wanted the face of the strong man to be read as a *memento mori*; its distorted physiognomy is a trope for a sinful life and the face of the soul serves as its mirrors: 'Just like a figure drowning! Hideous sight! / O how his eyes stand out, and stare full ghastly!' (lines 273–4). Blair reveals to the reader the futility of physical strength (Parisot, 2013: 68), but Blake's death scene draws attention to pain continuing beyond the moment of death. In addition, the pain, evoked through contorted faces, also affects the two women. If this man was wicked, why is he being mourned? At the deathbed a drama is unfolding: the older female flings herself at the corpse. Her face expresses utter distress. The younger is standing in the right-hand corner with her face buried in her hands. Both the head of the dead man and the feet of his soul touch the body of this daughter-figure which seems an afterthought as it is crammed into the available space. Through it Blake's design links the body and soul of the strong man. The figure accentuates the horror of the scene and the viewer is left to imagine the pain of this woman. Fuseli had used the words 'familiar and domestic' to describe Blair's poetry and ever since Ellen Moers's *Literary Women* (1976) we can defer to the term Female Gothic, but did Fuseli think that 'Death of the Strong Wicked Man' captured loss and mourning as well as fears of entrapment caused by a socioeconomic change? If the answer is yes, then by his definition, the women – not the dying – are the victims.

'Christ Descending into the Grave' (Figure 2.3) features another death scene that integrates the viewer into Blake's conception of the afterlife. This illustration faces the first page of the poem and its caption, 'Eternal King! whose potent Arm sustains / The Keys of Hell and Death' (lines 8–9), is part of the speaker's invocation. The juxtaposition between 'Eternal King' and Christ causes hesitation because apart from the doubling of a divine figure, the reader-viewer seems to encounter Christ a lot earlier than Blair's speaker; but Blair not only delays meeting Christ, he has his speaker imagine it: 'Methinks I see him / Climb the aerial heights, and glide along / … but the faint eye, / Flung backwards in the chase, soon drops its hold / Disabled quite, and jaded with pursuing' (lines 678–82). Through this doubling Blake pre-empts and makes concrete what Blair wanted to remain obscure. Blair's speaker

2.3 *Christ Descending into the Grave.*

never actually meets Christ (Parisot, 2013: 65). Whereas Blair associates death with sleep, to be interrupted on Judgment Day, in 'Christ
Descending into the Grave' Blake has Christ step down towards the
reader-viewer. This positioning is typical for Blake who wanted his
viewers to transform through his art; on account of a feeling of dislocation they have to actively engage and reorient themselves. In *A
Vision of the Last Judgment* (1810), the description of the lost eponymous painting, he explains this technique: 'If the Spectator could
Enter into these Images in their Imagination … then he would arise
from his Grave, then would he meet the Lord in the Air & then he
would be happy' (Blake, 1988: 560). Meeting Christ is possible but
conditional.

    In 'Christ into the Grave' viewers are, if they look closely, inside a
ring of flames. Ariès explains such iconographic allusions to Purgatory,
unusual in Protestant thinking, with changing attitudes towards
death. From the eighteenth century onwards, death was perceived as
a personal experience rather than a fate shared by all; Purgatory, associated with a time and place of punishment, came to stand for the

relationship between the living and the dead and signified waiting. Popular belief was that all would meet again, sooner or later, in Heaven (Ariès, 1984: 147ff., 171–83). A more immediate vision or meeting with Christ, in fact, is introduced in the poem dedicating Cromek's edition of *The Grave* to Queen Charlotte because text and design, Blake's inventions, blur the boundaries between life and death in interesting ways. The drawing shows a young female who, keys in hand, floats towards a door:

> The Door of Death is made of Gold,
> That Mortal Eyes cannot behold;
> But, when the Mortal Eyes are clos'd,
> And cold and pale the Limbs repos'd,
> The Soul awakes; and, wond'ring, sees
> …
> The Grave is Heaven's golden Gate,
> And rich and poor around it wait;
> O Shepherdess of England's Fold,
> Behold this Gate of Pearl and Gold! (lines 1–10)

Possibly modelled on Blair's speaker's experience, Blake evokes a somatic state when he compares dying to the body falling asleep. The final lines of the dedicatory poem, however, suggest that the door of death is the gate of Heaven which can be seen by the living as well as the dead. Life and death collapse because Blake eradicates waiting.

'Christ Descending into the Grave' is a full-length portrait of Christ that, in Bonnet's sense, combines bodily and spiritual aspects of human identity into one androgynous whole. This Christ, as noted by reviewers, is far too human looking and his gender is ambiguous.[4] Blake is asking Blair's readers to transcend their own sense of identity: if individual, bodily identity, as suggested by Bonnet, survived death, embracing one's feminine qualities was an important step towards spiritual liberation. For the viewing process this means that all readers, male and female, should see parts of themselves in the face of Christ, whose body, according to the Christian faith, symbolises mankind.[5] If the fear of death, furthermore, is suppressed and therefore latent, it is bound to surface during the viewing of 'The Descent of Christ into the Grave', because this illustration aligns the viewer's point of view with that of the dead inside the grave. According to the Christian faith, Christ meets the resurrected on Judgment Day. Figuratively speaking, this belief puts the viewer into a position that becomes intelligible through Lacan's *aphanisis*, the appearance and disappearance of the subject, because while examining Christ's portrait viewers have to alternate between feeling alive and imagining themselves resurrected. Blake, consequently, creates a viewing experience that oscillates between conscious and unconscious mental acts; it hovers between acknowledging and denying death (Lacan, 1977: 204–7). This illustration is the result of a number of strategic choices. We can imagine dying, but to imagine being-dead-for-ever is impossible, which is why we fear death. This impossibility, however, is also a comfort to the survivor who, in this case, is the reader of *The Grave*.

Notes

1 Blake made forty drawings but Cromek chose fifteen (first prospectus), then twelve (second prospectus) and asked Luigi Schiavonetti (not Blake) to etch them (Bentley, 2004: 213, 216–17). To promote and finance the book Cromek travelled across Britain and gathered 589 subscribers (Read, 2011: 19–43).
2 Angels lead souls, normally naked and genderless, to paradise (Ariès, 1984: 147).
3 For the limitations of the literal, see George (1980): 77.
4 Christ's demeanour is more masculine looking in the preparatory sketch (Essick and Paley, 1982: fig. 4 [n.p.]).
5 Blake expressed similar ideas about gender and Christ in *Milton* (George, 1980: 158, 168–70).

References

Ariès, P. (1984) *Bilder zur Geschichte des Todes* (*Images de'l Home Devant la* Morte) (Munich and Vienna: Carl Hanser Verlag).
Bentley Jr., G. E. (2004) *Blake Records*, 2nd edn (New Haven, CT, and London: Yale University Press).
Bentley Jr., G. E. (2001) *The Stranger from Paradise: A Biography of William Blake* (New Haven, CT, and London: Yale University Press).
Bentley Jr., G. E. (ed.) (1975) *William Blake: The Critical Heritage* (London and Boston: Routledge and Kegan Paul).
Blake, W. (1988) *The Complete Poetry and Prose of William Blake*, rev. edn, ed. D. V. Erdman (New York: Day Anchor Books).
Bonnet, C. (1790) *Conjectures Concerning the Nature of Future Happiness*, trans. J. Wesley (London: Printed and sold at the New-Chapel, City-Road).
Bonnet, C. (1787) *Philosophical and Critical Inquiries concerning Christianity*, trans. J. L. Boissier (London: John Stockdale; Charles Dilly; William Creech).
Bonnet, C. (1766) *The Contemplation of Nature*, trans. from the French, 2 vols (London: T. Longman; T. Becket; P.A. de Hondt).
Essick, R. N. and M. D. Paley (eds) (1982) *Robert Blair's The Grave, Illustrated by William Blake: A Study with Facsimile* (London: Scholar Press).

Freud, S. (1985) 'The Uncanny' [1919], in J. Strachey and A. Dickson (eds), *Art and Literature* (Harmondsworth: London), pp. 339–76.

George, D. H. (1980) *Blake and Freud* (Ithaca, NY, and London: Cornell University Press).

Gilchrist, A. (1998) *The Life of William Blake* [1863], ed. W. G. Robertson (Mineola, NY: Dover Publications).

Knowles, J. (1831) *The Life and Writings of Henry Fuseli, Esq. M. A. R. A.* (London: Henry Colburn; Richard Bentley).

Lacan, J. (1989) *Écrits. A Selection* [1977], trans. Alan Sheridan (London and New York: Routledge).

Lacan, J. (1985) *Feminine Sexuality (Jacques Lacan and the École Freudienne)* [1975], eds J. Mitchell and J. Rose, trans. J. Rose (New York: W. W. Norton).

Lacan, J. (1977) *The Four Fundamental Concepts of Psycho-Analysis* [1973], ed. J. A. Miller, trans. A. Sheridan (Harmondsworth: Penguin).

Luginbühl-Weber, G. (1997) *Johann Caspar Lavater – Charles Bonnet – Jacob Benelle: Briefe 1768–1790: Ein Forschungsbeitrag zur Aufklärung in der Schweiz*, 2 vols (Bern: Peter Lang).

Luginbühl-Weber, G. (1994) '"Zu thun, … was Sokrates gethan hätte": Lavater, Mendelsohn und Bonnet über die Unsterblichkeit,' in K. Pestalozzi and H. Weigelt (eds), *Das Antlitz Gottes im Antlitz des Menschen: Zugänge zu Johann Kaspar Lavater* (Göttingen: Vandenhoeck and Ruprecht), pp. 114–48.

Parisot, E. (2013) *Graveyard Poetry: Religion, Aesthetics and the Mid-Eighteenth-Century Poetic Condition* (Farnham: Ashgate).

Peirce, C. S. (1940) *The Philosophy of Peirce: Selected Writings*, ed. J. Buchler (New York: Harcourt, Brace and Company).

Pestalozzi, K. (1975) 'Lavaters Utopie', in H. Arntzen, et al. (eds), *Literaturwissenschaft und Geschichtsphilosophie: Festschrift für Wilhelm Emrich* (Berlin and New York: de Gruyter), pp. 283–301.

Read, D. M. (2011) *R. H. Cromek, Engraver, Editor, and Entrepreneur* (Farnham: Ashgate).

3

Bruce Wyse

Entranced by death: Horace Smith's *Mesmerism*

While there may be 'nothing more terrible, nothing more true' than death, as Philip Larkin avers in his bleak poem 'Aubade' (2013: line 20), many Gothic works aggravate the terrors of death and supplement its facticity with profoundly disturbing fantasies that perversely amplify dread and revulsion. This is most patently and crudely manifested in palpably macabre Gothic paraphernalia (corpses, skeletons, charnel houses, and so on) that both condense and displace the fear of death. At about the midpoint of Horace Smith's *Mesmerism: A Mystery* (1845), the author interrupts his narrative to announce, 'The main purport of our tale is to remove that mistaken terror of death which is often … pushed to such a morbid excess as even to sadden and embitter life' (1846: 141). This strange but sanguine novel makes the case for a radical transvaluation of death and it draws on Gothic elements to effect this. As Smith acknowledges, 'we contemplate the descent into the grave with aversion, if not with horror' (1846: 141), a horror often distended and warped in Gothic scenarios, and it is this that Smith is determined to refute and counteract through his narrative. In certain respects an anti-Gothic Gothic text, *Mesmerism: A Mystery* obsessively addresses the subject of death to alleviate, if not eliminate altogether, the fear of death.

As Fred Botting observes, since 'Enlightenment rationalism displaced religion as the authoritative mode of explaining the universe', 'Gothic works [can be approached as] attempts to explain what the Enlightenment left unexplained, [as] efforts to reconstruct the divine mysteries that reason had begun to dismantle' (1996: 22). To some extent this makes the religious and Gothic novels homologous, although they approach these mysteries quite differently. Unlike other perhaps dubious mysteries, death is an irreducible mystery, one not definitively voided by Enlightenment thinking. The generic subtitle of Smith's novel signals a double affiliation to the Gothic and the Romantic twist on the medieval mystery play in works such as Byron's *Cain: A Mystery* (1821) and *Heaven and Earth: A Mystery* (1823). The title itself declares the novel's engagement with the controversial phenomenon of mesmerism and Smith explains that his 'imagination had been strongly excited by the Mesmeric wonders which have latterly bewildered so many minds' (1846: 'Preface'). At the time, mesmerism or alternatively animal magnetism, the forerunner of hypnotism, was not just a highly contentious, physically non-invasive, alternative treatment for a variety of disorders, particularly of the 'nervous' variety. It was also more dubiously touted by partisan investigators as demonstrating ordinarily latent paranormal powers of mind. Particularly sensitive mesmeric subjects in the somnambulistic state exhibited uncanny abilities such as thought transference, clairvoyance, and prescience, and some singular somnambulists, already etherealised by bodily infirmity and spiritual yearning, gave evidence of mediumistic communication with both the spirits of the dead and the spirits of a different metaphysical order. Smith's narrative addresses, if only in passing, two charges levelled against the practice: charlatanism and diabolical agency. The heroine Jane's clergyman father voices his misgiving that mesmerism is 'little better than a perilous phantasy; or ... if it really [has] any foundation in fact, may possibly originate in some satanic agency', but Jane counters 'that mesmerism and its prodigies, however startling they may appear, are of divine origin'. When her father expresses his Enlightenment hostility towards 'all mystery, because [he] cannot help suspecting it', Jane offers a defence by analogy, saying, 'we are surrounded by mysteries of all sorts. What enigmas can be more inscrutable than life and death?' (Smith, 1846: 123)

Universal yet unknowable, death is itself uncanny. In their itemisation of 'forms that the uncanny can take', Andrew Bennett and Nicholas Royle (2009: 36) suggest that death is 'something at once familiar – "all that lives must die", as Gertrude puts it ... and absolutely unfamiliar, unthinkable, unimaginable. As the Anglican *Book of Common Prayer* declares, "In life we are in the midst of death"' (39). Many Gothic works foreground this ineluctable co-presence of death and life and complicate this through disturbing, supernatural scenarios involving the interpenetration of the living and the dead, the mortal and the immortal. These imaginative, extra-doctrinal destabilisations of the boundary between life and death, although nightmarish, also evince a certain ambivalence about death. Elisabeth Bronfen writes, 'Gothic representations of death are so resonant because they occur in a realm clearly delineated as other than ordinary, the supernatural realm of ghosts and spirits.' Consequently, death may even become 'attractive, because it is apparently unreal' (2009: 113). For Bronfen, 'Gothic representations of exquisite corpses, revenants, spirits or monsters articulate both an anxiety about and a desire for death, … [they paradoxically] enraptur[e] with depictions that also disgust or terrify' (115–16).

As Todd May observes, 'One is mortal, not only at the end of one's life, but all throughout it' (2009: 7). The melancholy burden of this pervasive sense of immanent mortality and ever-imminent death is expressed by Mary Shelley in 'On Ghosts': 'the earth is a tomb, the gaudy sky a vault, we but walking corpses' ([1824] 1990: 336). The basic insight need not of course assume a gothic cast; there is nothing necessarily morbid, fancifully macabre, or even visionary in the sobering reminder that 'In life we are in the midst of death', a devotional axiom that, rightly considered, is productive of serious spiritual introspection. *Mesmerism: A Mystery*, however, while wholeheartedly embracing the conviction that the 'glorious hope of heaven [is] more than a compensation for the certainty of a grave' (Smith, 1846: 165), tends to deform this aspect of faith through its very extremism. Its disproportionate emphasis on death per se, its polemical drive to reconceive 'the universal destroyer' (1846: 166) as 'THE UNIVERSAL FRIEND' (1846: 167), coupled with the recurrent and mildly uncanny manifestation of a personified Death as a beautiful, serene, and enthralling male phantom to whom the heroine Jane is unmistakably attracted, tip the text towards the Gothic in spite of the heroine's many professions of spiritual confidence and joy.

Smith's *Mesmerism: A Mystery* appropriates the mysterious agency of mesmerism as a vehicle for fantasising about the more fundamental and universal mystery of death, one that particularly preoccupied the Victorians. Francis O'Gorman writes:

> Death and the Victorians are indeed particularly tangled. But … what renders
> the cultural history of the Victorians and the dead distinctive and important, was
> not, in fact, death. It was life: eternal life. It was the period's restless probing of
> theological conceptions of the durability of the soul and the Christian notion of
> the resurrection of the dead. (2010: 255)

Social historians have argued that the discourses of death undergo a shift in the nineteenth century. Philippe Ariès argues that the nineteenth century could be characterised as the age of the 'beautiful death':

> Since death is not the end of the loved one, however bitter the grief of the survivor, death is neither ugly nor fearful. On the contrary, death is beautiful… Presence at the deathbed in the nineteenth century is … an opportunity to witness a spectacle that is both comforting and exalting. (1981: 473)

Pat Jalland proposes an alternate paradigm: 'if death in nineteenth-century Britain is to be characterised in terms of a single model or an ideal, then it should be the Evangelical "good death" and not Ariès's "beautiful death"' (1997: 8). Gerhard Joseph and Herbert F. Tucker, however, suggest, 'In death as in philosophy, of course, the romantically beautiful and the evangelically good might prove compatible' (1999: 114). Smith's *Mesmerism* certainly assumes and instantiates this compatibility. However, in its increasingly obsessive emphasis on death, not just as a release and a 'momentous transformation,' but as a 'precious birthright' and the 'all-sufficing recompense for life' (1846: 167), coupled with a notable indifference to many of the central tenets or concerns of Christianity (certainly Evangelicalism) like sin, judgment, and atonement, Smith's novel seems to develop a rather eccentric creed.[1] In fact, while heaven frequently figures in the thoughts and words of Jane and her clergyman father, and the idiosyncratically devout Jane certainly worships the 'Creator, who is all love' (1846: 135), Christ seems altogether absent from the novel; it is almost as if Death instead assumes the place of the principal redeemer of humankind.

Written before the advent of spiritualism proper, Smith's *Mesmerism* charts a course from mesmeric experience to spontaneous, unmediated visions of both the spirits of deceased family members and an initially enigmatic phantom who ultimately proves to be the (now beneficent) angel of death, eventually graced with the sobriquet 'THE UNIVERSAL FRIEND' (1846: 151, 167, 168). The novel provides an uneasy synthesis of elements of Gothic fiction – including an attenuated Gothic ambivalence about the reality and the nature of the supernatural – and elements of a religious novel, albeit a curiously lopsided and reconfigured one. *Mesmerism* is certainly an odd generic amalgam. Opening as a novel of clerical life concerning the disappointments of the Anglican clergyman, Jaspar Harvey, it is also a novel of manners. In the central story of Harvey's independently minded daughter Jane, the novel stages a clash between social expectations and individual principle.

Jane is 'a delicate, pale, and highly excitable girl, whose unnaturally pre-cocious intellect assumed [a] morbid … character', a 'tremulously sen-sitive' girl who, 'Without any specific and tangible illness, … had grown up a confirmed invalid' (1846: 118). She is also 'subject to epileptic fits' (118) and prone to somnambulism. Given unusual intellectual latitude in her upbringing, she becomes accustomed to thinking for herself on all questions, which puts her at odds with social opinion, particularly in her opposition to restrictive Sabbath observance.

Her propensity for unconventional sentiments becomes a deter-mined strain of eccentricity after her one life-altering experience of mesmerism. In spite of her father's reservations, she eagerly agrees to undergo mesmeric treatment in London for her chronic conditions and, while in the somnambulistic state, she receives a form of divine assurance, not that she is saved, but that her epilepsy is cured, which proves to be reliable. Her therapeutic mesmeric session, however, has other, more profound ramifications. Like 'the pythonesses and priest-esses' (124) of antiquity, she proves to be an exemplary mesmeric subject, rapidly entering into a 'death-like trance' (127). Once Dr Peterson, a mesmerist of the utmost probity, stimulates her very pro-nounced phrenological 'organ of veneration', she undergoes a 'spiritual ecstasy' (128), 'soar[ing] far above all sublunary thoughts and feelings, … no longer a creature of flesh and blood, but a spirit' (129). In this 'temporary apotheosis', she encounters a mysterious phantom 'figure attired in black', but with a 'countenance … perfectly radiant with benignity', who 'beckon[s her] upwards … towards the throne of grace' (129). Then as her 'very heart and soul' seem to her to be 'deif[ied]', 'he gradually … [becomes] invisible, and … [appears] to be extinct' (129). Asked afterwards for an interpretation of Jane's clairvoyant rapture and 'the meaning of the figure in black', Dr Peterson predicts that at some 'future period' the radiant phantom will 'again reveal itself, and explain the meaning of its apparition' (130).

Peterson theorises that mesmerism can provide a foretaste of the liberation of the spirit that comes when, 'freed by death from this earth-binding clog, the disembodied spirit … may find … that almost unlimited knowledge which was its first inheritance' (134). Positioned 'between the natural and the supernatural', the mesmerised clairvoy-ant is 'partly corporealised' but has the power to 'see … and foresee … without the intervention of the senses' (134). Jane, then, has entered into a liminal state between life and death, spirit and matter, and by the end of the novel she recognises that the 'barrier between the visible and

invisible worlds is only the width of a grave' (165). Her premature spiritualisation, precipitated by her mesmeric, mystical experience, renders
this boundary permeable. In a series of spontaneous bouts of clairvoyance, her spiritualised sense reveals to her the invisible dimension of
death itself, or rather Death himself.

The traditional iconography of Death and the Maiden typically
consists of a ghastly, skeletal, predatory, and perhaps amorous Death
claiming a forlorn and appalled or resigned virgin, sometimes in an
unexpected embrace. The juxtaposition instantiates the theme of the
vanity of the flesh but also erotically conflates unrealised female sexuality with premature death. In the novel's affirmative reconception of
this motif, the beautiful, benign, angelic, and smiling male phantom
of her mesmeric vision reappears to Jane repeatedly, reassuringly and
even enticingly. Unlike the spirit communications and manifestations
in later Spiritualist narratives, the central supernatural phenomenon of
Smith's novel has a curiously archaic, even 'Gothic' quality, recreating
while updating the medieval allegorical manifestation of Death. The
emblematical nature of the personification of death is slightly obscured
by the formal traces of the Gothic in the construction of the figure's
mystery and also by the very different valence given the iconic figure.
Although the intermittent manifestations of Death are unearthly and
his identity and purpose are ostensibly unknown, he is unfailingly cast
as benign and his appearances reassuring. His representation then
straddles the Gothic and the religious novel, a double orientation captured in the narrative's alternative descriptors: he is a 'phantom' but
also an 'angel' (165).

From the start, Jane seems constitutionally suited for this singular
revelation of death. She believes that 'her days [are] numbered [and]
she [has] but a small portion of life to lose' (119). Certainly this sense
of her impending demise, cheerfully borne, is the source of both her
intellectual independence and her independence from marital expectations. The connection between her anticipated death and her disinclination to marry is foregrounded when her self-serving cousin Steven
Maule later proposes to her with a mind to appropriating her eventual
inheritance. In a markedly Gothic pronouncement, she tells him, 'the
only bridal array I shall ever wear is the shroud, and ... my bridegroom
is to be sought in another world. You might as well unite yourself to a
corpse as dream of marrying me' (160). As already, proleptically dead,
she is compatible with the dead or perhaps more appositely with Death
himself.

In a telling but tentative Gothic gesture, the text makes the association between her visionary encounters with the phantom and possible amorous feelings. When Jane first describes the 'beautiful figure'
of her mesmeric vision, her father suggests that she has 'conjure[d]
up the impersonification of some individual whom [she] had seen in
London, and by whose prepossessing appearance [her] imagination
had become deeply affected' (139–40), but Jane protests that, given
her tenuous grasp on life, she has 'never had an eye' or 'still less a heart,
that took note of men's forms and faces' (140). She does, however,
admire the surpassing, preternatural beauty of the entrancing figure
in black, and while he emphasises his universal role as friend and not
destroyer, he appears to Jane alone. This unique relationship may not
be emphatically eroticised, but when, at the close of the action, the
phantom faithfully makes his final visit to her, she is ecstatic, thinking
as he approaches, '"My heart seems to leap out of my bosom for joy … I
see him, I see him! 'tis he! 'tis he!"' and at his icy touch '"murmur[s], in
a languid voice, "but what a thrill of ineffable rapture has it sent to my
heart, to my very soul"' (167).

In the wake of her initial mesmeric vision, Jane encounters the
mysterious phantom a number of times, prompting a dramatic reassessment of death. She returns home believing that 'she ha[s] been
placed in spiritual communion with heaven' (134), a conviction that
is corroborated by a sequence of three visions about which she retro-
spectively confides to her father. In the first vision she sees a 'mysterious effulgence' that develops into 'a manifest representation of [her]
self' (138). On the following evening, this appearance of a 'fac-simile
of [her]self' reoccurs, from which she infers that it is 'the perceptible
form' of her 'own separated and yet impersonated mind' (139). The
more elaborate third vision evinces 'a most distressing object' as she
sees her younger sister Mary 'absorbed by … the pale but beautiful
figure' of the stranger seen originally in her 'mesmeric trance' (139).
This is repeated when Mary's twin, Fanny, similarly 'evaporate[s]' in
the returning image of the 'stranger' (140). The vision closes with
the sight of Jane's mother's tomb and the sound of a tolling bell. Jane
concludes that it portends 'some danger impending over the twins,
danger even unto death' (140). Her broadly symbolic prevision proves
accurate: 'the sinister conclusions that she had so quickly drawn from
it were unhappily destined to receive as quick a confirmation' (141).

It is at this point in the text that Smith announces his narrative purpose in a dialogic and didactic interpolation, dramatically reframing

what is to come. He directly addresses the reader's irritation with a narrative that introduces characters – twin sisters – only to immediately consign them to death, but Smith insists, 'The main purport of our tale is to remove that mistaken terror of death which is often … pushed to such a morbid excess' (141). Shifting from coyness to stirring conviction, he adds, 'Possibly the progress of our tale may familiarise the reader with [the] triumphs of the "fell destroyer," as men most absurdly term him; possibly he may be presented in some new and unexpected form[, as] … on the contrary, the friend, comforter, and benefactor of mankind' (141).

The depiction of the deaths of the twins in Smith's novel does more than exemplify the glorification of death characterised by Ariès as the beautiful death. The voluble treatment borders on inadvertent caricature. We are told, 'What an interesting, what a beautiful, what a heart-soothing and soul-elevating scene was the deathbed of the twins! What a triumph of the spirit over the flesh' (141–2). Jane feels that they are particularly blessed to '"be summoned to the skies in all their innocence and beauty"' (142) and they both die with joyful affirmation, as 'the phantom … smile[s] itself away into thin air' (143).

The fulfilment of her vision, the narrator admits, has a 'disadvantageous effect upon the character of Jane' (143) in the eyes of the world. Feeling herself to be 'a kind of votaress of heaven' (144), she virtually becomes Death's evangelist. She openly flouts social conventions, refusing to wear mourning clothes and purposing to henceforth 'celebrat[e] the day of [each sister's] death with the same joyous observances' typically 'devoted to … birthdays' (144). This 'abominable affectation' (1846: 144), which is decried as 'a sort of monomania' (145), renders her worthy of 'social excommunication' (144). Her notoriety is only exacerbated when she again exhibits this socially unaccountable behaviour following the death of her respected father while, ironically, mourning the supposed death of her brother Alfred who, as an unrepentant sinner, presumably does not undergo 'the great change' (151) with the same 'unwonted delight' as her father (152).

Although the mysterious phantom punctually presides over the deaths of Jane's family members, he makes a few other appearances that have a more direct relation to Jane herself. In one episode, Jane, almost falls into a ravine, but is arrested by the palpable apparition of her sister Fanny's hand that 'transfix[es] her to the spot.' Like a 'guardian angel, … commissioned by heaven to hover around' Jane (146), Fanny has saved her life. Given that death increasingly appears to be exceedingly desirable, this intercession can only mean that this is not her time and yet, when she looks over the precipice, she 'start[s] back' because there 'at the bottom of the abyss' is 'the mysterious figure in black' smiling as always and 'holding out his arms as if to catch her in the event of her falling' (147). This ambiguous manifestation suggests that he also serves as an appointed guardian to preserve her life, but the reader detects a darker purpose. Since 'on this occasion he wore the semblance of an embodied being', she calls down to him, asking him to explain his presence, but his answers, which may 'clear … up all the mysteries by which she had been recently haunted' (147),[2] are inaudible. 'Resolved to know her fate', she hastens to the bottom of the ravine, but he has disappeared without leaving 'a single footmark' behind in the soft ground, and she is 'utterly aghast with bewilderment' (147). This is one of the more uncanny moments in a text that generally subsumes the uncanny in the rhetoric of wonder. It also suggests that benign supernatural agencies may work at cross purposes or that Death personified is not an independent agent determining the time and place of each individual's death.

While the primary plot purposefully attenuates the unsettling dimension of the Gothic trope of the mysterious phantom, insistently associating it with benignity, the novel's secondary concerns and plotlines exhibit a complementary strategy. The sections of the narrative that concern the men in Jane's life – her father Jaspar Harvey, her brother Alfred, and her disingenuous suitor Steven Maule – function to siphon off much of the Gothic potential of the central plot's supernatural element. For example, Jaspar Harvey comes to suffer from a profound religious pessimism which is given a markedly Gothic cast.

Harvey's conventional attitude towards death acts as a foil to his daughter's unconventional one. In the opening chapter Harvey's 'domestic felicity' is 'blighted' (118) by the loss of his wife which engenders his anxiety for his young children. In a traditional iteration of *memento mori* imagery, Harvey, who knows that 'the insidious and fatal malady [is] often hereditary', cannot 'help sometimes imagining that, beneath the curling ringlets … of the little one that climbed his knee or kissed his lips, he could discover a death's head!' (118) The mix of dread and revulsion in Harvey's sense of the presence of death in life is the antithesis of the text's sanguine belief in death as the Universal Friend. In time, however, Jane's exposition of her visions of her sisters' and father's deaths help her father share her fervent belief in death as a welcome and glorious transition. Although he finds it difficult to resign himself to the loss of the twins, he eventually renounces any 'wish for prolonging [their] earthly existence' (142). Later, in the vision of his imminent demise, Jane's mother points towards 'the dark phantom' with 'the same angelic countenance' and formally identifies him as 'THE UNIVERSAL FRIEND! who will soon restore us to each other' (151). Prepared 'for the great change that is so shortly to occur' (151), he feels 'exhilarated and filled with unwonted delight' (152) when death approaches.

The depiction of Harvey's death contributes to the novel's transvaluation of death, but this ultimately affirmative scene is jeopardised in his final days by 'anxious misgiving' against which Jane must contend (148). Having fallen prey to the 'gloom of Calvinism', he becomes 'haunted' by 'spiritual horrors'. When he considers his own death, he 'recoil[s] with terror and great agony of soul from the eternal torments which [he] feel[s] that [he has] merited' (149). The narrator dismisses this 'as superstition' and Jane musters arguments against the debilitating impiety of transferring 'features of human depravity ... to the Supreme Being' (150). She recalls her father to a trust in 'a God of infinite mercy' and 'chase[s] away the hideous phantasmagoria by which he had been haunted' (150). Horror and terror are expunged from death, seen to be the unfortunate consequences of factitious and pernicious beliefs.

In the concluding pages of the novel, Jane finally gets the opportunity she has been yearning for to speak with the phantom. The lead-up to this penultimate encounter exemplifies the narrative's strategic incorporation of Gothic potentialities. Braving a 'perilous' ledge, Jane is momentarily 'appalled' when she sees 'the mysterious figure in the dark vestments' but, characteristically, 'her confidence in the protection of heaven' soon restores her 'self-possession'. She is driven by 'curiosity' to ascertain 'the nature and object of this ambiguous visitant' and when he approaches and stands before her, 'so far from exciting terror', his presence 'sooth[es] her spirit with a glad serenity' (165). The affect apposite to a Gothic scenario is clearly evoked, only to be superseded.

The phantom now proves to be surprisingly communicative, if enigmatic, disputatious, and self-vindicating. Asked to confirm that this unusually sustained reappearance (his penultimate one) signals that she is soon to 'quit the narrow company of the living, to join the mighty multitude of the dead', he informs her with riddling generality, 'I am perpetually hovering around you, and around all your fellow-creatures, though you do not always see me' (166), substantiating *The Book of*

Common Prayer's teaching that 'in the midst of life we are in death'. He adds that he is intimately at work in our lives: 'Not a day passes but that a portion of every human being becomes mine' (166). The strange colloquy with Death that closes the narrative is an index of Jane's liminal state. As she has felt the steady approach of her death, she has remarked to herself, 'Like Columbus, I foresee and know that I am approaching a world that is not yet visible' (164).

In his discourse, the phantom objects to the ways in which he has been 'stigmatised with many injurious names' (165) and justifies his periphrastic title 'THE UNIVERSAL FRIEND' (167), leading his keen disciple through an assortment of arguments designed to dispel not just our fear of death, but our misrepresentations of it as well. He expatiates on the benefits he bestows on human beings both individually and collectively, and even engages Jane in an unconventional thought experiment that draws on Thomas Malthus's theory on population. At the same time, he responds to Jane's allusion to Mary Shelley's *The Last Man*, recommending a more instructive subject for contemplation and literature than that novel's: the 'unutterable horrors [that] would curse an immortality of ever-increasing never-ending old age, an eternity of disease and anguish' and the universal consequence of this absence of death, a nightmare world of 'starving, yet undying races ... wag[ing] an universal war for the means of subsistence' (166). Death's novel auto-encomium decisively severs the Gothic associations from death.

While the positive assurance of immortality informs the dialogue between Death and Jane, the emphasis is on death itself. When Jane tells the phantom-angel, 'you have now rendered it so attractive' (166), the antecedent of 'it' is not immortality but death. Subsequently, the Divine is virtually eclipsed by Death in Jane's final thoughts and last words. As Jane rapturously embraces her 'momentous transformation', she fervidly professes her newfound faith, 'I know that death is the all-sufficing recompense for life' and calls on the still 'mysterious stranger' to 'prove that [he] deserve[s his] title of "THE UNIVERSAL FRIEND"', imploring him, 'grant me my inheritance, my precious birthright – the grave – the grave!' (167). While 'grave' may be a metonym for 'heaven', it also elides it. It is true that Jane expires marvelling at 'glorious visions' (167), but this more orthodox detail seems almost an afterthought on Smith's part. Smith may have designed this death scene to give a universal and non-sectarian cast to his transvaluation of death, but the ending's glorification and even sacralisation of death overshadow the fundamental tenets of Christianity.

If there is at times an intriguing torsion in Smith's novel between Gothic and the novel of faith, the triumphant close of Jane's life subsumes the Gothic traits of the narrative, and yet the strangeness and the residual heterodoxy of Jane's peculiarly focused clairvoyance and her unique communion with death are not dissipated. In a very brief coda to the story of Jane's exemplary life and her final beatitude, the narrator steps back from the account to affect some degree of dubiety. He refers to Jane's 'strange mental history' and wonders whether she had actually 'obtain[ed] a partial glimpse into' the invisible world and held 'communion with its spiritual occupants', or rather had 'been excited into a delusion, a hallucination, a monomania' (168). Smith thus in the end gives voice to the irresolution that Tzvetan Todorov sees as the defining feature of the genre of the fantastic and, in doing so, seems to attempt to return the novel to the province of the Gothic. The retrospective gesture, however, is belated, perfunctory, and unconvincing. Formally and as a motif, the recurrent preternatural appearances of a mysterious phantom dressed in black that both foreshadow the approach of death and signal its occurrence participates in the Gothic, but the affective charge of these moments in the text is anything but Gothic. If, as Elisabeth Bronfen remarks, Gothic fiction can 'articulate both an anxiety about and a desire for death' (2009: 115), Smith's novel, through a homeopathic infusion of Gothic, completely dissolves the anxiety and hyperbolises the desire.

Notes

1 Pat Jalland comments: 'Thousands of didactic deathbed scenes in nineteenth-century Evangelical tracts and journals attested to the zeal to save souls by showing people how to die. Death was a primary concern of Evangelical theology, since the doctrines of sin, assurance, and atonement emphasised Christ's sacrifice on the Cross to save people from their sins' (1997: 21).
2 In contrast to the situational and familial-historical mysteries affecting earlier Gothic heroines, these mysteries are generic, existential and spiritual.

References

Ariès, P. (1981) *The Hour of Our Death*, trans. H. Weaver (New York: Alfred A. Knopf).
Bennett, A. and N. Royle (2009) *An Introduction to Literature, Criticism and Theory*, 4th edn (Harlow: Pearson).
Botting, F. (1996) *Gothic* (London: Routledge).
Bronfen, E. (2009) 'Death', in M. Mulvey-Roberts (ed.), *The Handbook of the Gothic* (New York: New York University Press), pp. 113–16.

Jalland, P. (1997) *Death in the Victorian Family* (London: Oxford University Press).

Joseph, G. and H. F. Tucker (1999) 'Passing on: Death', in H. F. Tucker (ed.), *A Companion to Victorian Literature and Culture* (Oxford: Blackwell), pp. 110–24.

Larkin, P. (2013) 'Aubade', in S. Greenblatt, et al (eds), *The Norton Anthology of English Literature: The Major Authors*, vol. 2 (New York: W. W. Norton), pp. 1439–40.

May, T. (2009) *Death* (Stocksfield: Acumen).

O'Gorman, F. (2010) 'The dead', in F. O'Gorman (ed.), *The Cambridge Companion to Victorian Culture* (Cambridge: Cambridge University Press), pp. 255–71.

Shelley, M. (1990) 'On ghosts' [1824], in B. T. Bennett and C. E. Robinson (eds), *The Mary Shelley Reader* (Oxford: Oxford University Press), pp. 334–40.

Smith, H. (1846) *Love and Mesmerism* (New York: Harper and Brothers).

The Book of Common Prayer (1662) (London: John Baskerville). Available at: http://justus.anglican.org/resources/bcp/1662/baskerville.htm. Accessed 25 April 2015.

Todorov, T. (1975) *The Fantastic: A Structural Approach to a Literary Genre*, trans. R. Howard (Ithaca, NY: Cornell University Press).

Part II

Gothic revolutions and undead histories

4

Emma Galbally and Conrad Brunström

'This dreadful machine': the spectacle of death and the aesthetics of crowd control

The French Revolution's culture of spectacle focused on a machine, a device for separating heads from bodies in a fashion that managed to be both efficient and theatrical – the guillotine. Traditionally, the Revolution is figured as the supreme demonstration of Enlightenment, demolishing Gothic structures of thought and offering the light of reason to challenge tyrannical institutions that relied on obscurity. Yet in literary terms, this same Revolution became the apotheosis of Gothic, an intensification of the fearful excitements that had been raised by decades of Gothic literature preceding the events of 1789–1815. The Revolutionary Gothic offers the return of the repressed alongside a new mechanisation of terror, thereby reinforcing the reality that nothing more effectively dramatises darkness and obscurity than a cult of enlightenment. Enlightenment is nothing without a darkness to enlighten.

No author typifies the paradoxes of the Gothic energies of the French revolutionary era better than Edmund Burke. His sympathetic engagement with the body in pain was the inspiration for the reworking of the political sphere into the personal/domestic sphere contained within the Gothic novel. Notably, when attacking the Revolution, Burke deploys the language of colonialism and, when attacking British rule in the Bengal (in a speech supporting Charles James Fox's 1783 East India Bill), he declares that British India 'sustains, almost every year, the miseries of a revolution' ([1793] 1968: 379), revolution being a word that was undergoing critical resignification during this period. Throughout the eighteenth century, the word retained its older sense of 'rotation' and did not imply any grand Hegelian dialectic or the systemic reimagining of the political system. Authors might refer to 'the late revolution in affairs', meaning nothing more than a rotation of offices, the replacement of an in-group with an out-group. Similarly, when Burke uses 'revolution' in an Indian context, he is referring to the rapid turnover of imperial pillagers. He also declared, however, that, 'All circumstances taken together, the French Revolution is the most astonishing that has hitherto happened in the world' ([1790] 1969: 60). At this point of semantic flux and uncertainty in which newer and older uses of the word 'revolution' uneasily coexisted, the Revolution can be feared as something ancient and modern simultaneously.

Nothing is more simultaneously ancient and modern than the mechanisation of theatrical death enacted by the guillotine. Thanks to the Revolution, the public execution no longer represented the redress of the absolute power of the monarchy, but instead a 'body politic' in which the king was just another subject. The merciful celerity of this mechanism created a celebration of death that required quantity in order to sustain its public fascination. The guillotine was conceived of as an enlightened guarantor of transparent equivalence between sentence and execution. Superseding the unwieldy contingencies of rope and axe, the guillotine could guarantee a perfect result every time; the inexorable laws of gravity offered a thirty-two feet per second squared acceleration that would cut flesh and bone in a fraction of a second. Thus, the guillotine reinterpreted the role of public execution. It did not redress the balance of power between servile subject and the absolute power of sovereignty; it reactivated power for the new state. Known by jaunty epithets such as 'the scythe of injustice' and 'the popular ax' (Palmer, 1960: 455), the guillotine was imagined surgically as a scalpel that cut the rot from revolutionary France, at least until the Reign of Terror. Ronald Paulson (1983, 23) considers the role of the guillotine at the beginning of the Revolution as promoting the myth that the 'people' brought about the Revolution and each execution authenticated a version of 'popular justice'. However, Julia Kristeva, in her survey of artistic renderings of severed heads notes that

> the claims of a painless technique and democratic equality immediately merged with metaphysical speculation in the minds of those in charge. In solemn, sacramental speeches, they ennobled the unconscious, depressive, and erotic power of decapitation and interpreted it implicitly as a 'black work': since only what is high and celestial is attacked at the head, to bring down that head would mean to prepare another 'beyond'. (2014: 92–3)

A self-consciously modern and 'scientific' mode of execution cannot help but induce a sense of quasi-religious obscurity, affirming a sense of divine headship at the very moment of that divinity's truncation. To cut off the Head of State privileges even as it desecrates an ideal of 'Headship'. The guillotine's role in public execution was therefore to offer a symbol of irrevocable finality, alongside a necessarily incalculable element of terror (Paulson, 1983: 23).

The precision and predictability of the guillotine leant itself easily to representation. Simon Schama (1989) records that it was the relentless normality of the spectacle that most shocked witnesses. By democratising the right to a swift and dignified execution for the common criminal and privileged orders alike, the guillotine's effectiveness fuelled the blood lust of the crowds that gathered to watch the execution of King Louis XVI just nine months after the guillotine's adoption, dipping handkerchiefs and pens into the blood of the monarch, and in one instance, even tasting it (1989: 670). Meanwhile, Londoners who felt short-changed by a purely narrative description of its effects in the newspapers were given the chance to experience something far more visually dramatic, as this advertisement indicates:

EXECUTION OF THE KING OF FRANCE
Now exhibiting at No. 28, Hay-Market.
LA GUILLOTINE:
Or The Beheading Machine,
From Paris,
By which the late KING of FRANCE suffered.
And an Exact Representation of the Execution.
   The unhappy Fate of the SOVEREIGN of a Neighbouring Kingdom having excited universal Compassion in this Country, it is presumed the Curiosity of the Public will be gratified by the View and the Effect of an Instrument like that by which he suffered.
   Accordingly, a GUILLOTINE has been constructed under the immediate direction of a Gentleman, who very minutely examined the Original, which is exactly similar in every respect: And in Order that the Effect of the Machine may be the better conveyed to the Spectator, the Execution is performed on a Figure as large as Life; the Head is severed from the Body by the tremendous Fall of the Axe, and the Illusion is complete.
   To be seen this and every Day (Sunday excepted) from Eleven o'Clock in the Morning, till Five in the Afternoon.
ADMITTANCE ONE SHILLING. (Richard Twiss, a single-page advertisement, London, 1793)

The healthy market for fake executions of Louis XVI provoked another advertisement offering a rival spectacle on Oxford Street. These

spectacles prided themselves on the exactness with which the decapitation was copied. Mechanisation facilitates a form of guaranteed reproduction that would be impossible to achieve by someone wielding an
axe. Whereas spontaneous mob violence defies any effort of representation, clinical state violence lends itself to repetitive mimetic confidence. The Oxford Street advertisement runs as follows:

> No 45. OXFORD-STREET, new NEWMAN-STREET.
> LA GUILLOTINE,
> OR
> Beheading Machine,
> From
> PARIS.
>   SOME imperfect odels of the original Machine having been offered for public
> inspection, the Proprietor of this GUILLOTINE, in order fully to gratify the curios-
> ity of the public, had it constructed under the immediate direction of an ingen-
> ious gentleman, who had the exact dimensions of the original, and was present at
> the late Execution in PARIS.
>   The Public may, therefore, rest assured, that THIS MACHINE, together with the
> representation of the Execution, is in every respect compleat: indeed, the general
> satisfaction it has given to people is a proof of its superiority.
>   In order to imprint on the feeling mind a true idea of the manner, in which this
> dreadful Machine acts upon the human body, the execution is performed upon
> a figure as large as life; – the tremendous fall of the axe instantly severs the head
> from the body, and illusion seems reality.
>   The sympathetic tear gently steals down every cheek in commiseration for a
> puissant Monarch, endowed with every moral virtue, doomed to an ignominious
> death by a banditti of murderers and assassins.
>   *Admittance, – Ladies and Gentlemen, 1s. – Tradesmen and Servants, 6d.* (Single
> Page Advertisement, London, 1793)

It does not take a cynical imagination to recognise that morbid curiosity rather than compassion might have been the dominant incen-
tive to journey to either address and watch the decapitation of the
king's effigy. Unlike the Haymarket exhibit, the Oxford Street version
is priced to permit the lower orders to behold the monarch's death. It
is unknown how many Londoners witnessed this spectacle that made
such protestations of verisimilitude. If indeed, as advertised, 'illusion
seems reality', it is because a working model of a guillotine is, in fact,
a guillotine. Each performance would have lasted only a few minutes
and many performances would have been squeezed into each day. This
effigy of the French king, however, would not have been truncated in
front of a huge crowd but in front of a small group, roughly comparable
to those witnessing a modern execution within the United States. The

effect, had a wax model Louis been dispatched in front of a packed house in Drury Lane, might have been very different, or at least far more dangerous. Controlling the political meaning of death during the revolutionary period is, to a significant extent, a problem of crowd control, a concern with the logistics of directive sensibility. A packed theatre audience for the fake execution would have been an imitation not merely of a particular death, but of the power of those masses who had initiated and not merely witnessed revolutionary political events.

The nature of execution as mass entertainment concerned authorities in England as well as France. Following the Gordon Riots of 1780, the spectacle of execution had been considerably weakened in England, with the procession down Oxford Street to Tyburn replaced by a considerably more limited viewing area outside Newgate. The reason for this change was not a more squeamish public morality, but concern regarding the impact of a large massing of people on any account whatsoever.

The guillotine's commanding height makes it a more efficient signifier of death than Tyburn's triangular gallows, the so-called 'triple tree'. The guillotine represents perfectly the inevitability of death. Its mechanical insouciance illustrates a death that cannot be reasoned with or frustrated. However, although visitors to the Haymarket and Oxford Street exhibitions gained a frisson of voyeuristic realism, they were denied not only the death of a real monarch, but also the powerful sense of collective identity that participation in a Parisian execution crowd would have conferred. London re-enactments of the death of the king recreated the cynosure only, while removing the metaphor of the guillotine as the scalpel of the body politic, the 'scythe of injustice', thereby reducing it to a mere spectacle of mechanisation. From a policing point of view, a display of mechanism proved far less exceptional than a spectacle of political justice.

If political executions are a form of theatre, then theatre itself lends itself to a readily politicised culture of spectacle. All Gothic theatre, and perhaps all theatre, concerns itself with the uses and abuses of power. The issue of how to accommodate yet sanitise spectacle can be explored by considering two lavish stage entertainments of the late 1790s: *Aurelio and Miranda* (1798) – James Boaden's adaptation of Matthew Lewis's *The Monk* (1796) – and George Reynolds' *Bantry Bay* (1797).

Boaden had originally titled his play *Ambrosio*, after Lewis's main character, but was forced by the Examiner of Plays, John Larpent, to

change it to *Aurelio*, creating greater distance between the play and its
controversial source material (Wozniak, 2008: 82). Boaden's adaptation of *The Monk* is censored to the point of being virtually unrecognis-
able. The novel was published in 1794, and the play was not staged until
late December in 1798, not long after the Irish Rebellion had broken
out, with all that a Franco-Irish rising might entail for Britain. Boaden
had previously adapted several Gothic novels for the stage such as
Fountainville Forest (1794), *The Secret Tribunal* (1795), *The Italian
Monk* (1797), and others, and was arguably the most experienced
playwright to handle material as combustible as *The Monk*. Given the
context of Pittite repression, it is unsurprising that Ambrosio's stage
counterpart is much less threatening than Lewis's original monk, and
more predisposed to be reassimilated into society. Significantly, the
bowdlerisation of Lewis's story applies not merely to the onstage representation of the novel's content, which would test the sensibilities
of many twenty-first-century audiences, but also to the offstage events
that are merely reported by actors. Even an offstage mob must be
diverted from its violent purpose.

> Christoval: Haste, reverend Aurelio to the Convent!
> The people furiously assail the walls,
> And nothing but your presence can restrain them.
> Aurelio: Be ready to resist them, if I fail!
> Though there is virtue in their sympathy,
> Yet violence is not the march of justice.
> Where there are laws, the laws alone should punish. (Boaden, 1799: 64)

Boaden's play references the idea of popular insurrection only to dissipate it. Britain, even at its most repressive – especially at its most
repressive – continually invoked the concept of rule of law, therefore
dissolving the justification for insurgency. In Lewis's original novel,
mob violence is an inevitable but indiscriminate instrument of purga-
tive violence that confounds the innocent with the guilty. The rage
directed at the convent when it is discovered that the Prioress is guilty of
murder knows no limits. It cannot be curbed or redirected. In Boaden's
version, however, the authority of a wiser Aurelio is sufficient to reduce
the mob to sober obedience. Boaden's mob is not inherently violent or
retributive and a modest expression of law and order satisfies everyone.

The assumption that most people – uninfluenced by French
sophistry – prefer law, order, and the status quo, is central to anti-
Jacobin literature of the period. Most famously, Hannah More's *Village
Politics* (1792) preaches that the lower orders should stay out of poli-

tics, and yet she cannot help but engage the lower orders in political discussion. Her tract is a dialogue that concludes with a rejection of reactive terror and a disavowal of mob violence even as an instrument of state authority. Rustic 'Tom' has been persuaded of his own political unhappiness by reading Paine's *Rights of Man* (1791). 'Jack' reasons Tom back into political quiescence, including a rejection of violent anti-Painite reaction:

> Tom sings: "O the roast beef of old England!"
> Jack: Thou art an honest fellow, Tom.
> Tom: This is Rose and Crown night, and Tim Standish is now at his mischief; but we'll go and put an end to that fellow's work.
> Jack: Come along.
> Tom: No; first I'll stay to burn my book, and then I'll go and make a bonfire and –
> Jack: Hold, Tom. There is but one thing worse than a bitter enemy, and that is an imprudent friend. If thou woud'st shew thy love to thy King and country, let's have no drinking, no riot, no bonfires; but put in practice this text, which our parson preached on last Sunday, "Study to be quiet, work with your own hands, and mind your own business."
> Tom: And so I will, Jack—Come on. (More, 1792: 23–4)

More's purpose is avowedly didactic whereas Boaden merely seeks to make a dramatic spectacle palatable. Boaden's adaptation of Lewis's novel was self-censored because of the feared passions of a dangerous collective audience response. Yet plays could still be produced under the guise of a Gothic adaptation that expressed muted revolutionary or anti-revolutionary ideas. The 'Gothic' tends to explore the issue of repression, a concept that is hard to rid of political baggage.

Boaden's Aurelio, unlike Lewis's Ambrosio, learns to repent his dogmatic religious rigour before he can explode in an orgy of depravity:

> Our passions are the fairest gifts of Heav'n!
> Their just indulgence is our proper joy:
> 'Tis their perversion only makes us wretched. (Boaden, 1799: 67)

Aurelio, unlike Ambrosio, overcomes his repressive upbringing and becomes a far less austere individual before reaching breaking point. Thus, Aurelio's un-Hegelian revolution can be framed as a safe and complete rotation, a restoration of a prior state of calm rather than any irreversible transformation.

In the novel, mob rule is allowed to overwhelm the repressive institutions that have defined the cruelty of the plot as a whole. The rage that overtakes the monastery is depicted not as a wise measure of retribution but as merely another modification of terror, an anarchy reminiscent of the September Massacres that is as frightening as the terror it seeks to displace. The character of Aurelio is distinctive in that he is both victim and aggressor. Lewis's original Ambrosio is immediately recognisable as pre-Revolutionary Gothic while Catholicism is offered as a repressive 'old regime', anachronistic and antiquated. However, when viewed through the prism of counter-revolutionary allegory, Catholicism can embody the chivalry associated with established monarchies, and the monk's blasphemous overreaching can evoke the horrors of the Terror in Gothic costume. As exemplified by Lewis's protagonist, the concepts of individual autonomy, liberty, and freedom become pathways to incestuous rape, matricide, sororicide, and eternal damnation. The novel can be read as a form of allegory for the inevitable failure of the Revolution. Specifically, Ambrosio's revolution of mind and body may serve as an allegory for Robespierre's Revolution of bloody rebirth and eventual downfall. The character serves a dual purpose – representing both Robespierre and the new public man that was born of the Revolution.

The immediate context of Boaden's stage version was the suppression of Jacobinism in Britain and Ireland. In December of 1796, 15,000 French troops attempted to invade Britain through Ireland, but the plan had to be abandoned due to bad weather (Elliott, 1989: 324–33; Pakenham, 1992: 17–19). The thwarted Bantry Bay landings also created a brief window of opportunity for one of the more unusual counter-revolutionary entertainments of its age. The pastoral ballad opera *Bantry Bay* (1797) is a loyalist fantasy in which the courage of the Irish peasantry is restated in terms of their loving devotion to the British crown. This fantasy had an effective life of around seventeen months. Military historians calculate that had the French army landed in 1796, there was no British force capable of resisting its successful march on Dublin. The attitude of the Irish peasantry would therefore have been critical. Reynolds' loyalist romp is intended to reassure a London audience of Irish fraternal affection while flattering Irish public opinion into a version of the heroic loyalism represented onstage. A matter of months would demonstrate that 'the page of history' would offer a narrative very different from that imagined by Reynolds in 1797. Catholicism is key to Reynolds' message. In a narrative unthinkable a decade earlier, a religion synonymous in the English imagination with disloyalty and treason has become the principal means of securing the counter-revolutionary affections of the most proximate and unstable of colonies. Correspondingly, France is no longer to be feared for its

Catholicism but for its atheism, a factor that creates loyalists out of peasants such as O'Laughlin:

> O'Laughlin. … if a single man of them got among us, he'd never get back to tell who hurted him – Since ever I heard they pulled down the Irish colleges, and murdered the priests, it's by much ado I cou'd keep my hands from them, though the sea was between us. (Reynolds, 1797: 8)

The anti-clerical French have enraged the entire (fictitious) Irish people, yet the Irish peasantry remains essentially non-violent. The 'violence' of their loyalty remains rhetorical rather than actual, since mob rule, even in the service of the crown, may have unforeseen consequences. As a result, the Irish victory over the French is not only bloodless but compassionate as evidenced by the Justice's directive, 'Take care of the prisoners for this night; and let them, and our gallant volunteers, be regaled with strong beer and the best beef in the county of Cork' (Reynolds, 1797: 17). Reynolds follows More in affirming the central role of beer and beef-eating in the political demonstration of anti-Jacobin sentiment. The French prisoners are conquered by a display of conspicuous Irish hospitality. The 'spectacles' both of bloody insurrection and of counter-revolutionary reprisal are checked by a spectacle of festivity. Death is noteworthy for its absence.

Significantly, British sponsorship of Irish Catholicism is referenced when the question of who is to officiate at a wedding is raised. 'Nelly', the proud mother of four sons, three of whom are in the British armed forces and one of whom is a freshly minted priest, speaks up:

> Nelly: I hope your honour will put in a good word for my little *gossoon*, Father Barney; he is just come home from the college of Maynooth; and there is not his fellow in the county of Cork, for a job of this kind. (Reynolds, 1797: 26)

The seminary of Maynooth was only two years old when this pageant was mounted (suggestive of a somewhat truncated ordination syllabus), the result of lobbying by Edmund Burke. In the paranoid 1790s, the prospect of Irishmen travelling to continental Europe to train for the priesthood was troubling to a government that deplored voyaging to continental Europe for any reason. Having referred to the closure of Irish colleges by the French government, the audience is reminded that the British government has opened an Irish college and in a newly enforced ecumenical context, is now the sponsor rather than the enemy of Catholicism. The Catholic priesthood, invoked in the context of a Bantry Bay wedding, is no longer redolent of sterility and sexual repression but is instead an enabler of fertility, a marital aid rather than a celibate despot. The relaxation of the Penal Laws, apparently, creates a climate of mass national gratitude:

> Justice: … I am confident, that whether old or young, poor or rich, there is not a true-born Irishman who would not shed the last drop of his blood for his King and country. (Reynolds, 1797: 30)

Less than eighteen months after the landings of Bantry Bay, Irish blood was shed in quantities unimaginable by Reynolds in resistance to the forces of George III. The symbol of the 1798 Rising would be the pike rather than the guillotine given the extra-judicial quality of the bloodshed. Pikes, both French and Irish, were charged with considerable symbolic resonance. Regina Janes has noted the coexistence of the pike alongside the guillotine throughout the 1790s:

> For contemporaries, both the guillotine and the pike symbolised the Revolution, but they also occupied distinct, though overlapping, semantic space. Heads on pikes were the product of primitive, popular violence (or justice); the guillotine was the mechanism of revolutionary, institutional violence (or justice). Pike or guillotine shared the multiple, culturally determined meanings that belong to the public display of severed heads. Both evoked contradictory responses – horror in some quarters, relish in others – with the usual continuum in between, fascinated horror, queasy relish, and the shrug of indifference. But the guillotine was new. It was an instrument of public order, and almost at once it acquired a spectacular history that knotted it inextricably to the most controversial period of the Revolution. (1991: 21)

As the guillotine, apparently, supersedes the pike, the state's monopoly on violence is reimposed. The pike remains, however, as a potent palimpsest. The Revolutionary Gothic dramatises the uneasy alliance of the old and the new, between a form of decapitation associated with unpredictable mob violence and a form of decapitation associated with the totalising of modern state authority enforced by a symbol of complete predictability. And, as 1798 illustrated, the triumph of the guillotine over the pike, the state over the mob, was anything but stable or irreversible. The guillotine and the pike together symbolised revolutionary terror in its totalitarian as well as anarchist manifestation. The pike would be the chief weapon of the insurgent United Irishmen in 1798 and the pike therefore symbolises a version of revolutionary terror on 'British' soil in the 1790s.

Gothicism thrives on temporal anomalies. The very 'pastness' of the past demands the injection of modernity in order to express itself. Gothic theatricality served to provide a useful means of political propaganda; as a malleable form of expression, presumptions and agendas were narrated through the appropriation of existing Gothic tropes. The heightened emotional and experiential aspects of Gothic are traceable to ideological and political repression during the eighteenth century.

'Monk' Lewis himself enjoyed a keen sense of the value of a dramatic killing in *The Castle Spectre* (1798), a spoof Gothic melodrama. The dramatic spectacle of death is both acknowledged and diffused by the comic epilogue as performed by Mrs Jordan (mistress of the Duke of Clarence):

> And all perforce, his crimes when I relate,
> Must own that Osmond well deserved his fate,
> He heeded not papa's pathetic pleading;
> He stabbed mamma – which was extreme ill-breeding;
> And at his feet for mercy when *I* find,
> The odious wretch, I vow, was downright rude,
> Twice his bold hands my person dared to touch!
> Twice in one day! – 'Twas really once too much!
> And therefore justly filled with virtuous ire,
> To save my honour, and protect my sire,
> I drew my knife, and in his bosom stuck it;
> He fell, you clapped – and then he kicked the bucket! (Lewis, 1798: vi)

Monk Lewis was available in the late 1790s both as an original playwright and through the adaptation of his most famous novel. *The Castle Spectre* contains many elements of intentional comedy (unlike Boaden's *Monk* adaptation). This epilogue suggests that the tragic medieval Earl Osmond's crimes are so heinous that he deserves to be killed more than once. Like Prometheus, he must be restored to life just so that he can be stabbed nightly over a period of weeks. Popular righteous outrage demands such severity which, not coincidentally, can only be enforced by a long and profitable run of performances. The desensitising and accelerating effects of dramatic repetition are significant. Osmond dies every night but is nightly restored, just as wax Louis is recapitated on an hourly basis. The epilogue, therefore, advertises the salutary spectacle of death while diffusing its political danger with effective comedy. The necessity for such deflations is evidenced by Lewis's footnoted remark that the inclusion of the phrase 'titles which are absurd' was treated by some in the opening night audience as evidence of the author's dangerous egalitarian philosophy (1798: 47).

The anxieties caused by the huge new theatre at Drury Lane are themselves the paradoxical product of theatre censorship. The restrictive policy of theatre patents dating back to the Restoration, and further limited by the 1737 Theatre Act, had resulted in just two venues for

'legitimate' theatre to serve the swelling metropolis.[11] Stage representations on this massive stage, therefore, threatened to reproduce some
of the culture of public spectacle fostered by revolutionary France.
Attempts to limit the political impact of theatre sixty years earlier had,
paradoxically, created a 'mass audience' capable of staging a disturbing
version of popular sovereignty. The immensity of the 1790s theatre
encouraged a culture of spectacle and raised expectations of visual
extravagance at the very moment when all points of mass spectacle
were, by definition, politically suspect.

From a reactionary perspective, even a loyalist mob risks advertising
the power of the mob. Famously, the Duke of Wellington objected to
being cheered by his troops, since a cheer was an impertinent legitima-
tion of an 'opinion' among the lower ranks (Howarth, 1971: 42). Such
'opinions', even when carefully solicited, are notoriously difficult to
predict or control. Audiences in London in the late 1790s could witness an angry mob onstage or they could witness a fake regicide, but
they were not permitted to witness both. Contemporary offerings of
death without a crowd or a crowd without a death illustrate the need
for a carefully policed culture of spectacle to acknowledge the dramatic
appeal of events across the channel – but only up to a (sharp) point.

Note

1   The most detailed account of the political context of the 1737 Act is provided by
    Liesenfeld (1984).

References

Boaden, J. (1799) *Aurelio and Miranda, A Drama in Five Acts* (London: J. Bell).
Burke, E. (1969) *Reflections on the Revolution in France* [1790], ed. C. Cruise O'Brien
    (Harmondsworth: Penguin).
Burke, E. (1968) 'Speech on Fox's East India Bill' [1783], in P. J. Stanlis (ed.), *Selected
    Writings and Speeches of Burke* (Gloucester: Peter Smith).
Elliott, M. (1989) *Wolfe Tone: Prophet of Irish Independence* (New Haven, CT: Yale
    University Press).
Howarth, D. (1971) *A Near Run Thing: the Day of Waterloo* (London: History Book
    Club).
Janes, R. (1991) 'Beheadings', *Representations*, 35 (Special Issue): 21–51.
Kristeva, J. (2014) *The Severed Head: Capital Visions*, trans. J. Gladdings (New York:
    Columbia University Press).
Lewis, M. (1798) *The Castle Spectre, A Drama in Five Acts* (London: J. Bell).
Liesenfeld, V. J. (1984) *The Licensing Act of 1737* (Madison, WI: University of
    Wisconsin Press).

More, H. (1792) *Village Politics. Addressed to All the Mechanics, Journeymen, and Day Labourers, in Great Britain*, 2nd edn (London: F. and C. Rivington).

Pakenham, T. (1992) *The Year of Liberty: the History of the Great Irish Rebellion of 1798* (London: Orion Books).

Palmer, R. R. (1960) 'Popular democracy in the French Revolution', *French Historical Studies*, 1.4: 445–69.

Paulson, R. (1983) *Representations of Revolution, 1789–1820* (New Haven, CT: Yale University Press).

Reynolds, G. (1797) *Bantry Bay, or The Loyal Peasants, a Comic Opera in Two Acts* (London: R. White).

Schama, S. (1989) *Citizens: A Chronicle of the French Revolution* (Harmondsworth: Penguin Books).

Twiss, R. (1793) *Execution of the King of France Now Exhibiting at No. 28, Hay-market* (London: Printed for Richard Twiss).

Wozniak, H. A. (2008) 'Brilliant Gloom: The Contradictions of British Gothic Drama, 1768–1823' (PhD dissertation, University of California Los Angeles).

5

Yael Maurer

Undying histories: Washington Irving's Gothic afterlives

Washington Irving's reimagining of history as a Gothic site is most evident in his best-known tales 'The Legend of Sleepy Hollow' (1820) and 'Rip Van Winkle' (1819). In both texts, the incessant return of the past manifests itself in the forms of ghosts or revenant figures. Irving returns to the American Revolutionary War in 'The Legend of Sleepy Hollow' and to the more distant history of the Dutch settlers before the War of Independence in 'Rip Van Winkle' to demonstrate how the past never rests in peace but continues to interfere in the narrative present. Irving's texts locate the ghostly as a central feature of nation-making. The strategy of (re)telling foundational historical events as 'ghost stories' signals Irving's commitment to the stories of nations as always already 'haunted' by history. As Avery Gordon has argued in *Ghostly Matters: Hauntings and the Sociological Imagination*, haunting 'describes that which appears to be a seething presence, acting on and meddling with taken-for-granted realities' while the ghost is the 'sign' of this presence (2008: 8). Thus the ghost is 'not simply a dead or missing person, but a social figure whose investigation leads us to that dense site where history and subjectivity make social life' (8). Irving's tales engage with hauntings and ghosts that shape both the personal and collective experience of 'history' and 'social life' in the new American nation. His stories thus locate sites of rupture, places where the historical meets the ghostly, creating a disturbing view of glorified events and complicating the narratives of freedom, victory, and national emergence.

However, I suggest that Irving's 1824 tale, 'The Adventure of the

German Student' adds another dimension to his treatment of the American Revolution in 'The Legend of Sleepy Hollow' and 'Rip Van Winkle'. Whereas the two tales relate to a foundational event in American history, 'The Adventure of the German Student' returns to the French Revolution as a site of historical horrors. Shifting the scene to the bloody aftermath of the French Revolution offers Irving a different historical setting, as well as the most fitting emblem of the Gothic nature of history: the guillotine. Nowhere is the exposure of history as a deathly 'instrument' more evident, it would seem, than in the Reign of Terror that contravened the French Revolution's noble ideals of liberty, equality, and brotherhood with a scene of mass slaughter. Irving's tale of a young German student, whose encounter with a woman at the foot of the guillotine undoes his already fragile sanity when it is revealed that she was executed the night before, presents the 'historical' as a site of confusion and madness. The frame of the story further emphasises a potentially unreliable narrator. The narrator insists that his story is not to be doubted as he had it on good authority from the student in a madhouse. Such a tale of historical madness could only be told by a madman in an asylum. It seems, therefore, that everyone loses their heads in Irving's text, either literally – like the unnamed woman – or figuratively, like the student and possibly even the narrator of the tale. Irving thus employs the Gothic to allegorise the notion of personal and collective madness. The student's discovery of the (already dead, but seemingly alive) woman at the foot of the guillotine signals this dramatic presence of 'death-in-life'. In true Gothic fashion, it becomes hard to differentiate between the living and the dead.

Irving's tales of the historical repressed returning to haunt the present moment are part of the American Gothic mode which, as Teresa Goddu elucidates in her seminal study, exposes 'history's horrors' (1997: 3). Unlike other critics' focus on the psychological aspects of the American Gothic mode at the expense of a historicised account, Goddu claims that 'the gothic tells of the historical horrors that make national identity possible yet must be repressed in order to sustain it' (12). Irving's tales are prime examples of the ways in which the Gothic 'exposes the cultural contradictions of national myth' (10), revealing how those myths are 'haunted by history' (14). Irving locates the ghostly presence of the historical past at the centre of his texts. His protagonists come face to face with ghostly reminders and gruesome embodiments of the past in the form of ghosts and severed heads looking for their bodies, like the Hessian trooper in 'Sleepy Hollow', or the unnamed and headless woman at the foot of the guillotine in 'The Adventure of the German Student'. These encounters have a profound effect on Irving's protagonists, thus showcasing the dramatic effects 'history' has on the individual and the collective psyche. As Goddu reiterates, the Gothic mode is not an escapist one but 'an integral part of a network of historical representation' (2). The Gothic does not 'flee' reality but rather 'registers its culture's contradictions, presenting a distorted, not a disengaged, version of reality' (3). Irving provides us with this 'distorted' view of historical reality, making his tales prime examples of the Gothic mode's engagement with historical horror.

Following Leslie Fiedler's famous formulations, Eric Savoy and Robert K. Martin note that there is a 'dialogic relation between the American national symbolic and the tendencies of the Gothic' (1998: viii). As Fiedler has shown, this dialogic relation is ironic. American culture is 'essentially gothic', being ironically produced by a civilisation determined 'to be done with ghosts and shadows' (quoted in Savoy and Martin, 1998: viii). Irving's tales engage in this ironic dialogue between the need to get rid of ghosts and shadows and the insistent, almost obsessive need to tell 'ghost stories'. Thus Irving's texts often borrow the generic disguise of legends or folk tales. Despite this generic disguise, the texts nevertheless gothicise history, making it the site of horror and the return of the repressed, providing what may be called counter histories that enact, in their plot and form, how a seemingly dead history returns to haunt the living. As Michelle R. Sizemore suggests in 'Changing by Enchantment', Irving's tales 'not only map out liminal regions between reality and fantasy but also advance new ways of thinking about time and historical processes' (2013: 158). Sizemore names this literary device 'enchantment' and claims that it 'produces a temporal arrangement that problematises historical thinking founded on linear progressive time' (158). 'The Legend of Sleepy Hollow' and 'Rip Van Winkle' both engage with the notion of historical narratives in a way that is not 'linear' but rather, as Sizemore notes, 'draws together multiple chronologies' (159). Sizemore's notion of 'enchantment' takes centre stage in 'The Adventure of the German Student', where dreams and visions become all too 'real' in the overly sensitive mind of the young student. If we relate this to Sizemore's notion of dislocation, we shall see how the events of the plot also enact an unusual chronology. The woman at the foot of the guillotine, the reader discovers at the story's end, was executed the night before, yet the student believes she is alive and takes her home with him. It is only when the fragile link between head and body are finally severed, and the woman's head rolls on the floor, that the student loses his own 'head' and ends up in the madhouse. The narrative present, however, returns to a cozy communal setting where the narrator regales his companions with a 'ghost story', thus assuring the readers of the kind of stable linear progression denied by the tale itself.

It is in 'Rip Van Winkle', however, where Irving's manipulation of narrative time is a feature of both the plot (Rip falls asleep for twenty years and wakes up to a new historical reality) and the narrative situation (Rip becomes a chronicler of the past after his return from this long 'sleep' and the narrative ends with a return to an even more distant past in American history). 'Rip Van Winkle' is thus a tale of a man who is 'ripped' from history. The comic 'hero', who never does any work unless it is to help someone else, is the perfect vehicle for Irving's exercise in historical irony. When Rip encounters his ancestors, the rough bunch of Hendrick Hudson's men, they are only seen as 'strange' by virtue of their antiquated clothing. Rip does not recognise the past, after awakening from his twenty-year sleep, to be an altered historical reality; he also fails to see the present other than by noting the sartorial and physical changes in his new environment. Rip finds an altered reality where the signposts of the familiar regime (King George of England) are replaced by another in the form of George (Washington) and the American flag, which is seen by his unaccustomed eyes as a strange piece of cloth hanging from the once familiar inn. The two 'Georges' are doppelgängers rather than manifestations of a foundational change in national history, one 'Head' being replaced by another of the same name. This doubling gesture is also a highly ironic one when we consider the author's own biography; Washington Irving was born in 1783 and named after the hero of the American Revolution, George Washington. Irving's text, however, questions this glorification of the national hero. Irving places the personal at the centre at the expense of the political. The first name ('George') takes precedence over the national/political role ('King' or 'President'). Thus Irving's protagonist, Rip, a man more concerned with his personal well-being than with the public sphere, is the one who 'wins' by the end of the tale.

Irving's representation of historical change as a confused and alienating experience shifts the terms of the historical story. Rip's skewed vision of 'History' may be the more sane option as the tale ends with Rip as a happy man liberated from his wife's tyranny. The death of a personal 'tyrant' has meaning, whereas the removal of another 'tyrant' from the historical landscape does not. Irving subverts the national view of the War of Independence as a tale of freeing the nation from the oppressive yoke of British rule. In his wry description of the new Americans as a lean and angry bunch, unlike the more relaxed and comfortably 'plump' old regime, he qualifies history as the story of the victorious.

Irving's narrator, moreover, turns to an even more distant past in the postscript to the story – namely, the Native American tales of the Catskill Mountains where Rip met his forefathers. In this legend, the mountains' spirit is a Native American feminine element that rules the world and punishes evil-doers: This 'old squaw spirit … [was] said to be their mother. She dwelt on the highest peak of the Catskills, and had charge of the doors of day and night to open and shut them at the proper hour' (Irving, [1819] 2008: 42). This feminine spirit can also be less benevolent: 'If displeased, … she would brew up clouds black as ink, sitting in the midst of them like a bottle-bellied spider in the midst of its web; and when those clouds broke, woe betide the valleys!' (42).

The 'fairy mountains' (Irving, [1819] 2008: 27) that open the tale of a return to history, also end the tale, taking the reader back to the (pre) history of the narrative present. The evocation of the mythical history of the Native Americans whose presence remains as yet another 'ghost' in the layered histories of Irving's tale might, as Michelle Sizemore notes, amount to 'an act of appropriation that results in partial omission of Native American subjects and histories' (2013: 174). However, I would suggest that Irving's evocation of the feminine spirit might also reproduce the frightening female figure in his tale, Dame Van Winkle, as well as register how historical tales are always-already imbricated in the mythical landscape that is 'America'. By invoking this female spirit who is both vengeful and benevolent, Irving offers an alternative to the despotic figure of Dame Van Winkle, the earthly woman who made Rip's life a living hell. The Native American spirit at the end of the tale demonstrates the possibility of a feminine element that predates 'History' while also showing how the 'historical' tale of Rip's ancestors has much deeper roots in the 'pre-history' of 'America', a mythical past that overtakes the present. The Catskill Mountains and the spirits who dwell there will always stay the same, political changes notwithstanding.

In 'The Legend of Sleepy Hollow', the figure of the Hessian trooper who haunts the drowsy stillness of Sleepy Hollow in search of his head, which was lost in the American War of Independence, signals a different kind of historical rupture. The severed head of the German soldier, conscripted to fight a foreign war away from his native land, dramatises the inextricable links between the gruesome nature of war, its deathly consequences for the personal body as well as the 'body politic', and the inability to return to the 'whole' (and the 'whole-some') after the devastating impact of war. The tales of the Headless Horseman join the other 'glorified' (and fictive) tales of heroic conduct in war that the inhabitants of Sleepy Hollow enjoy repeating in a cozy domestic setting. Ichabod Crane, the itinerant schoolteacher, is another foreign element who, like the Headless Horseman, still haunts the region long after his mysterious disappearance. Ichabod Crane is finally undone by the ghost of the region's past since he so firmly believes in the historical legacy of his Puritan forefathers as represented in his favourite book, Cotton Mather's *History of Witchcraft*, as well as in the region's ghost tales. It is this idea of the Gothic nature of reality that transforms him into yet another ghost by the end of the tale. Crane 'haunts' Sleepy Hollow, becoming another uncanny figure of difference, while the inhabitants of the region continue to accept the authority of 'the old country wives' who are 'the best judges on that matter' (Irving, [1820] 2008: 24) of ghosts and shadows. The region's peaceful existence during the day gives way to the terrors of the evening when its troubled history resurfaces in the form of multifarious ghosts. The 'ghost' lingers on, reminding the inhabitants of a very 'present' past that will never rest in peace.

The most glorious event in American history thus turns in Irving's tale to a site of gruesome rupture. The American Revolution becomes the prime site of this enforced separation of head and body, emblema-tised in the figure of the Headless Horseman. The failed attempt to restore unity by putting the head back in its rightful place may also demonstrate the failed attempt to return to a past where the 'Head' (the King of England) ruled over the American colonies. As Regina Janes elucidates in *Losing Our Heads*, the severed head reappears 'when a discourse is in crisis' (2005: xiii). The severed head is thus a floating signifier assigned specific codes within each culture: 'Beheading is the body's catachresis: a violation of the rules of the body's grammar that generates a sensation of dismay, horror, delight, or absurdity' (12). 'The Legend of Sleepy Hollow' indeed generates mixed reactions of horror, delight, and absurdity. Irving is careful not to solve the mystery of Ichabod Crane's disappearance, providing his readers with both the 'supernatural' and the 'realistic' solutions as possible answers to an unresolved problem or, as Janes puts, it a representational 'crisis'. The 'severed head' may be a mere pumpkin used by Brom Bones to trick Ichabod Crane into thinking it is the Headless Horseman's head, but we shall never be certain. Unlike the inhabitants of the region who trust the authority of the old wives, we are left pondering the supernatural option while Irving's narrator slyly winks at us reassuring us that this is a mere 'legend'. It is in 'The Adventure of the German Student', however, where this decidedly Gothic inability to separate the living from the dead, the 'head' from the 'body', 'reason' from 'madness', becomes even more pronounced, making it a far more disturbing tale about the lethal impact of 'History' on mind and body alike.

The bloody engine: Irving's Gothic technologies

Irving's tale, published in 1824, functions as a vehicle for a historical return to a recent past, revisiting the Reign of Terror following the French Revolution to question the implications of the Age of Reason's decline into revolutionary fervour and personal, as well as collective, frenzy and madness. The German student's enthusiastic nature is seen as the seed of his final undoing. By implication, Irving suggests that it is this historical 'enthusiasm', the 'Spirit of the Age', that brings about madness. This becomes evident at the end of the story when the student, so wrapped up in his own delusions, takes the (apparently dead) woman home with him and 'marries' her. It would seem that the only thing that had kept the woman's head in place is the broad black band around her neck, described as her 'only ornament' (1824: 78). This detail assumes significance at the very end of the tale, demonstrating how the woman's seeming 'wholeness' and corporeality is a mere delusion. The guillotine had already beheaded her before the fatal encounter with the student. The nameless woman is thus doubly beheaded, first by the guillotine and then by the tale that unmasks her seeming 'wholeness' as a mere façade. Irving thus evokes, yet again, the inability to distinguish the living from the dead, a central feature of his Gothic tales.

'History', then, is reimagined and estranged. The bloody nature of past wars destabilises comfortable notions of a historical narrative that would assure an ordered tale of citizenship and national pride. In 'The Legend of Sleepy Hollow', this incessant need to tell the tale of the Horseman and, later, of Ichabod Crane's mysterious disappearance, stems from what Robert Hughes calls 'a matter of history' (2005: 11). In other words, the need to tell the tale, to make the 'ghost' more 'comfortingly familiar', or 'dressed in a little becoming fiction' only 'restages the essential, traumatic confusion of identity between the living and the dead' (12).

Hughes notes that 'The Adventure of the German Student' would feature another headless (and now plainly supernatural) ghost situated provocatively between love and history' (2005: 24). Irving locates his pair of lovers at the foot of the guillotine and mocks the nature of their undying love as being always already 'dead': the love object is, after all, a beheaded woman. As Regina Janes notes,

> the guillotine is linked with a sexually inviting female body. Such depictions emphasise the parallels between female anatomy and guillotine geometry and set up a tense oscillation between desire and destruction. If the desiring male reaches for the body, he chooses his own castration. More wisely, he chooses decapitation for the desirable female whose body is obtruded. (2005: 86)

The guillotine is thus an engine of symbolic castration and is linked to the fear of woman as castrator. In Irving's text, the erotically enticing woman at the foot of the guillotine is metonymically linked to the place where the student finds her. She *is* the guillotine and the student is first drawn to her allure much as he was first enticed by the Revolution. Only when the woman's severed head manifests itself does this link become clear and the student's 'head' become forever lost to madness.

The tale thus enacts the troubling inability to tell apart the living and the dead, as well as the inability to distinguish truth from fiction, a recurring theme in Irving's Gothic tales. In the figure of the 'dead bride' at the foot of the guillotine, we find a prime example of such a confusion of categories. Wolfgang is obsessed with visionary philosophy and is described as a ghoulish figure in the no less ghoulish 'catacombs' or libraries: 'He was, in a manner, a literary ghoul, feeding in the charnel-house of decayed literature' (1824: 72). Wolfgang, then, like Ichabod Crane in 'The Legend of Sleepy Hollow', has an unhealthy appetite for books. His 'ghoulish' pursuits are linked to the notion of 'decayed literature' suggesting that the power of tales in 'dead' books by 'long departed authors' is a contagion, a disease that affects both body and mind. Wolfgang's solitary visions soon become erotic. His mind is in an 'excited and sublimated state' and he dreams repeatedly of 'a female face of transcendent beauty' (73). This image 'haunts' him by day and by night. Irving's narrator comments on Wolfgang's mental state thus: 'in fine, he became passionately enamored of this shadow of a dream'

(73). This evocative term melds the 'ghost' (shadowy presence) and the 'dream' that conjures up this ghost and makes it 'real' and 'present' for the dreamer. Irving identifies this mental state as the root cause of the student's later madness, but it is also a *shared and collective* traumatic state in the face of unimagined and ungraspable historical horrors.

Wolfgang is at first infected by the 'popular delirium' and 'captivated by the political and philosophical theories of the day' (71). But this soon changes with the advent of the Reign of Terror. Facing the Terror's horrors results in a traumatic shock to the student's 'sensitive nature' (72) and his final madness. The student's infatuation only comes about as a result of this shock to the system in both senses of the word: personal and political systems are shocked and the result is personal and collective madness.

Wolfgang's fatal encounter takes place in front of the 'dreadful instrument of death' that 'had that very day been actively employed in the work of carnage' (1824: 74). This 'instrument of death' is also the instrument that propels the narrative. Just as the disgusted Wolfgang, whose heart 'sickens' at this grim site, is preparing to walk away, he sees the 'shadowy' form of the woman of his dreams, revealed to him in 'a succession of vivid flashes of lighting' at the foot of the scaffold (74). He recognises the woman's face as 'the very face that has haunted him in his dreams' (75). His 'violent and conflicting emotions' (75) at the sight of her, suggest that his 'dream' is actually a nightmare. The presence of the woman at this deathly scene and her intimate proximity to the guillotine evokes the 'femme fatale', a cultural figure that was most popular in the early and mid nineteenth century. As Heather Braun notes in *The Rise and Fall of the Femme Fatale*, the 'changeable figure of the femme fatale has long embodied increasing fears about the mutability of gender and class. Throughout the nineteenth century, the fatal woman was a ready symbol for a variety of cultural concerns including sex, aggression, disease, madness, foreign contagion, and social degeneration' (2012: 2). The meeting between the student and the unnamed woman embodies these concerns and fleshes them out. The student's erotic dreams are realised when he meets the woman. But the ominous meeting place and the student's reactions to seeing the woman of his dreams are ambivalent. This unnamed and unknown woman is a stranger and yet somehow known to the student. She is found at the most terrifying scene and yet the student is drawn to her, almost despite himself, in the same way that he is drawn to the scene of carnage symbolised by the guillotine. She is thus an embodiment of his frustrated erotic dreams and of his worst fears at one and the same time.

In this brief and fatal meeting, the woman points at the guillotine 'with a gesture of dreadful signification' (75). This gesture marks the woman as belonging to the guillotine, a 'femme fatale' who is linked to death by her very positioning. However, following Heather Braun's rereading of this cultural figure, we might note that 'the nineteenth-century femme fatale can also be ambivalent about her powers of destruction and therefore reluctant to accept her fatal allure' (2012: 3). Thus, although the femme fatale may 'attempt to warn [her] victims not to surrender their power; their warnings only serve to increase the destructive effects of desire' (2012: 3). This is the case in Irving's text. The student does not heed the femme fatale's warning gesture and misinterprets the woman's following words: 'I have no friends on earth!' said she. 'But you have a home', said Wolfgang to which she responds, 'Yes – in the grave!' (75–6). Instead of horror, these words melt the student's 'sick' heart. He offers her his humble home and his love in what the narrator wryly describes as 'the infatuation of the moment', further commenting that: 'Wolfgang was too much of a theorist not to be tainted by the liberal doctrines of the day' (79). Colouring the most 'irrational' of acts with the cloak of liberal, eighteenth-century Enlightenment rhetoric, the student's 'taint' here seems to be aligning him with thinkers and poets of the eighteenth century, like Wordsworth, who was initially an enthusiastic supporter of the noble ideals of the French Revolution and who later became 'disgusted', much like Wolfgang, by the attendant atrocities.

Wolfgang offers the lady, repeatedly described as the 'stranger', his undying love: 'I pledge myself to you forever' (1824: 80). In response to the stranger's solemn querying, 'Forever?', Wolfgang repeats the word 'Forever!', suggesting that this love is intended to continue to the grave and beyond. When Wolfgang returns to his 'bride', he finds that 'her face was pallid and ghastly. In a word, she was a corpse' (80). The 'bride' becomes a 'corpse bride' and Wolfgang is rudely awakened from his 'Romantic' dream. This rude awakening culminates in another instance of a headless body, much like the Headless Horseman in 'The Legend of Sleepy Hollow'. The headless woman and the headless horseman are both 'strangers' whose names are never revealed to us. Their function in these tales is to dramatise the horror of the historical moment, be it the nameless battle in which the Hessian trooper lost his head, or the moment when the nameless woman was beheaded by the guillotine.

Regina Janes offers a possible reading of 'History' as a force much like the guillotine: 'Impersonal, indifferent, and inevitable, history is a blade that cuts whatever interposes. Nor are its cuts to be questioned. They are only to be rationalised and understood' (2005: 93). In Irving's tale, history's 'cutting' force is made literal in the figure of the guillotine, while also retaining the symbolic meanings Janes suggests. It is the force of 'History' which Irving's protagonists have to encounter in one form or another. While Rip 'sleeps' through the historical change, Ichabod is either 'beheaded' by it or escapes it, depending on one's reading of the tale's unresolved ending; and Wolfgang, the ultimate 'stranger', a German student in Paris, is completely undone by 'History' as he faces historical horrors beyond his control. Robert Hughes rightly notes that 'history remains a crucial and unresolved problem' (2005: 6) in Irving's stories. The unresolved problem of the historical as ghostly and vice versa is at the centre of Irving's texts. As Avery Gordon notes, the experience of being haunted 'draws us affectively, somewhat against our will … into the structure of feeling of a reality we come to experience, not as cold knowledge but as a transformative recognition' (2008: 8). Irving's tales, despite their seemingly comic nature, draw us into this 'transformative recognition' of the ways we relate to a national history. Is 'History' an undying force that 'haunts' us with its insistence on forever repeating itself as a 'ghost story'? Teresa Goddu offers a very apt formulation about the relations between the gothic and the historical: the gothic is 'a complex historical mode: history invents the gothic, and in turn the gothic reinvents history' (1997: 132). In other words, American history is always – already – 'gothic'. The gothic tales serve to highlight this inextricable connection between the horrors of history and the gothic story. 'The Adventure of the German Student', 'The Legend of Sleepy Hollow', and 'Rip Van Winkle' all engage in historical reinvention. As this chapter underscored, Irving insists on the 'problem' of history. His open-ended tales do not attempt to solve this problem. The presence of death and ghostly figures at the heart of foundational historical moments makes the telling and retelling of the historical tale a fraught endeavour. Thus, although the tales are comic in nature, it would seem that Irving offers a much more radical rethinking of history than we may be led to believe by the tales' generic disguise. Irving's seemingly harmless 'ghost stories' told in a cozy domestic setting, turn out to be radical reinventions of 'History' as a constant problem to be grappled with in the here and now.

References

Braun, H. (2012) *The Rise and Fall of the Femme Fatale in British Literature, 1790–1910* (Plymouth: Fairleigh Dickinson University Press).

Goddu, T. (1997) *Gothic America: Narrative, History and Nation* (New York: Columbia University Press).

Gordon, A. (2008) *Ghostly Matters: Haunting and the Sociological Imagination*, 2nd edn (Minneapolis, MN: University of Minnesota Press).

Hughes, R. (2005) 'Sleepy hollow: Fearful pleasures and the nightmare of history', *Arizona Quarterly*, 61.3: 1–26.

Irving, W. (2008) 'The Legend of Sleepy Hollow' [1820] and 'Rip Van Winkle' [1819], in *The Legend of Sleepy Hollow & Other Stories*, ed. J. B. Kapoti (New York: Dover Publications), pp. 1–26; 26–42.

Irving, W. (1824) 'The Adventure of the German Student', in *Tales of a Traveller by Geoffrey Crayon, Gent* (Paris: L. Baudry), pp. 70–82.

Janes, R. (2005) *Losing Our Heads: Beheadings in Literature and Culture* (New York: New York University Press).

Savoy E. and Martin, R. K. (1998) *American Gothic: New Interventions in a National Narrative* (Iowa City, IA: University of Iowa Press).

Sizemore, M. (2013) '"Changing by enchantment": Temporal convergence, early national comparisons, and Washington Irving's *Sketchbook*,' *Studies in American Fiction*, 40.2: 157–83.

6

Adam White

Deadly interrogations: cycles of death and transcendence in Byron's Gothic

In its study of death, Byron's verse drama *The Two Foscari* (1821) mobilises a number of Gothic modalities, tropes, and themes: the fatal pressure of ancestral, hereditary, and familial forces; incarceration and torture; and a concern with texts and their capacity and propensity to generate a bleakly imagined afterlife. The Gothic scenarios and vocabularies in *The Two Foscari*, like Byron's *The Prisoner of Chillon* (1816) also under discussion in this chapter, are central to a study of how that which is loved and familiar becomes a source of pain and death. Jacopo Foscari repeatedly desires to return to Venice where his father the Doge (Francesco Foscari) and the Council of Ten persecute him; Jacopo's double role is of willing his own death and having a death-in-life imposed upon him. The Gothic situation and scenario of incarceration, persecution, and death again aligns *The Two Foscari* with *The Prisoner of Chillon*, where the prisoner witnesses repeated familial deaths. A central question dramatised in these works, and in Byron's *Manfred* (1817) and *Sardanapalus* (1821), is whether the persecuted and tortured psyche can break free from, or go beyond, the tyrannical burden of the ancestral past. What the reader witnesses in these works, especially *The Two Foscari* and *The Prisoner of Chillon*, is the repetition of death with the possibility of – and here Byron can be seen to be Romantic and to move away from the Gothic – transcending death and death-like conditions. Yet in *The Two Foscari*, Jacopo's longing and desire to return to Venice and the various avenues of transcendence that he associates with it – ranging from childhood memories to the idea of Venice as a liberating maternal figure – are such that he appears to invite his own torture and death in order to realise these possibilities, pointing to something ultimately neither Gothic nor Romantic but distinctively Byronic in the play's treatment of death.

The repeated events in these works (for instance, Jacopo Foscari's torture) and the language of repetition as connected to the deaths represented in them invites some critical analysis based on Sigmund Freud's *Beyond the Pleasure Principle* (1920), the most thorough-going study of death and repetition and a recurrent focus in recent Gothic scholarship. In a reading of 'Gothic's Death Drive', for instance, Gary Farnell (2011) contends that Horace Walpole's *The Castle of Otranto* (1764) stages the first physical death in Gothic fiction in the form of the death of Manfred's son Conrad. The novel ends with the death of Manfred's daughter Matilda. Death, then, is a repeated event that Farnell cites as a catastrophic version of Freud's idea of the death drive's basis in a 'compulsion to repeat' (Freud, [1920] 2003: 57, 61).

The Two Foscari is broadly in the tradition of Walpolean Gothic in being about '*sons* and *fathers*' (author's emphasis) (V.i. line 199), but in Freud's terms, the 'compulsion to repeat' was a person's working over and through troubling and traumatic experiences with the aim of restoring, or returning to, a prior state. This led Freud to posit the exist-ence of the death drive in *Beyond the Pleasure Principle*, where he states that '*the goal of all life is death*' (author's emphasis) ([1920] 2003: 78) and that 'the organism wants only to die in its own particular way' to return to an inorganic state (79). Freud's essay is in many ways a key text for reading Byron's Manfred and Sardanapalus and Jacopo Foscari, who all seek to die in their own fashion or, to put it another way, on their own terms.

The Prisoner of Chillon and *The Two Foscari* are each explicitly studies of – in a phrase Byron uses in both works and adapts from Milton's 'a living death' in *Samson Agonistes* ([1671] 1971: 578, line 100) – 'a living grave' ([1816] 1986, line 114; [1821] 1991, III.i. line 81). Byron's Venetian drama opens with Jacopo Foscari in what seems like a state of living death: his gaolers and members of the Council of Ten spare him a 'few brief minutes for his tortured limbs' (I.i. line 6) after another application of the strappado. *The Prisoner of Chillon* also begins with a direct focus on the corporeality of limbs as a symbol and sign of the prisoner's proximity to death:

My limbs are bowed, though not with toil,
    But rusted with a vile repose,

For they have been a dungeon's spoil,
    And mine has been the fate of those
To whom the goodly earth and air
Are bann'd, and barr'd—forbidden fare;
But this was for my father's faith
I suffered chains and courted death;
That father perish'd at the stake
For tenets he would not forsake;
And for the same his lineal race
In darkness found a dwelling-place;
We were seven—who now are one,
    Six in youth, and one in age,
Finish'd as they had begun,
    Proud of Persecution's rage. (lines 5–20)

'Mine has been the fate of those' indicates that death is a repeated event. Here, death has its root cause in the sins of the father who 'would not forsake' his religious beliefs; the phrase 'for the same' acts with a double valence in the sense that the sons are from the same line as the father and all but one (the prisoner) suffer the same fate as him. 'Three were in a dungeon cast' (line 25) also anticipates *The Two Foscari* and the Doge's reminder to his son Jacopo about his 'three goodly brothers, now in earth' (IV.i. line 113). *The Prisoner of Chillon* is in fact very specific about the number of deaths that occur. The father and brothers originally made 'seven' in number (line 17); three brothers remain and are imprisoned in one of 'Chillon's dungeons' (line 28), a place of 'seven pillars of gothic mold' (line 27). The deaths of two of the brothers here leaves the prisoner captive alone. The prisoner's dungeon, then, is an explicitly Gothic space, made more so by its conditions of living death: [the dungeon] 'was as is a new-dug grave' (line 362). The seemingly paradoxical state of the prisoner's bowed *and* rusted limbs fixes his state of submission. 'Finish'd as they had begun' also suggests a death-in-life or, rather, a birth that is already a death – a social death resulting from defiance in the face of persecution. Death, then, repeats:

One on the earth, and one beneath—
My brothers—both had ceased to breathe:
[…]
    I know not why
    I could not die,
I had no earthly hope—but faith,
And that forbade a selfish death. (lines 219–20, 227–30)

The alliterated 'b' draws attention to 'beneath', 'breathe' (the vowels resonate with 'ceased'), and 'brothers', indicating kinship, the familial

confronted by death. The prisoner suggests that he is trying to die himself but fails, a contrasting situation to Manfred's who claims in Byron's
play that ''tis not so difficult to die' (III.iv. line 151). The prisoner's
wish to escape his incarceration is expressed in the Christian metaphor of 'earthly hope'; this complex phrase is immediately qualified by
'faith': the only hope, then, lies in the beyond. In one sense, this signals
Byron's departure from the Gothic because it represents or holds out
– however remotely or obliquely – the possibility of transcending life
through faith, and the death all around the prisoner (his two deceased
brothers are buried nearby). In contrast, the Gothic novel *The Monk*
(1796) by Matthew Lewis, a favourite author of Byron's, treats torture
(of the monk Ambrosio) and death by closing down the possibility of
their producing transcendence:

> the Inquisitors ordered the Monk to be put to the question. … Nor was He
> released till fainting from excess of pain, insensibility rescued him from the hands
> of his Tormentors. … nor could [he] hide from himself, how justly he ought to
> dread Heaven's vengeance. … Even this resource [the possibility of Ambrosio
> taking 'refuge in the gloom of Atheism' and denial of the 'soul's immortality'] was
> refused to him. (Lewis, [1796] 1998: 424–5)

The repeated negative constructions in these paragraphs by way of
the word 'nor' indicate that death is a state that prohibits any form of
release. Indeed, critics have often interpreted the Gothic treatment of
death as shutting down transcendence, as with Fred Botting's claim
that, particularly in Ann Radcliffe's fiction, death 'is presented as the
absolute limit, a finitude which denies any possibility of imaginative
transcendence into an awesome and infinite space' (1996: 48).

In contrast, Byron's prisoner of Chillon often seems able to move
beyond his state of incarceration; for instance, by thinking directly
about the bird which is such an important, Christian symbol – 'A visitant from Paradise' (line 284) – in the poem (lines 252–70) – and
which is also represented in the prisoner's contemplation of the death
of one of his brothers as 'the human soul tak[ing] wing' (line 177).
Despite the conditions of carceral restraint, with the imprisoned brothers repeatedly described as being 'fettered' (lines 55, 106, 373) and
associated with 'earth' (lines 9, 57, 151, 160, 219, 245, 299), there is
an emphasis here on the mind's and body's capacity to make and form
their own worlds that is Romantic: 'And it was liberty to stride / Along
my cell from side to side' (lines 306–7). The creative potential of the
human mind is also evident in the prisoner's sensitive, imaginative
apprehension of the Alpine grandeur that lies tantalisingly outside the

dungeon's walls (lines 330–8); this, at least in part, leads the prisoner to a realisation of his own power over life and death in relation to the creatures (spiders and mice) that inhabit his cell (lines 381–90). Again, there are avenues of transcendence gained from the fact of death here in a way that signals Byron's departure from the Gothic even as he delineates a distinctly Gothic space in the poem.

Like the prisoner of Chillon, Jacopo Foscari is at the limits of the liminal. The torture of, for instance, Ambrosio in *The Monk* suggests that these scenarios of often extreme physical pain and distress in carceral spaces in Byron's works are fundamentally Gothic. *The Two Foscari* was not written for the stage but we hear Jacopo's cries and groans in Byron's terse directions (I.i. lines 228, 232). Jacopo is physically tortured in the 'terrific chamber' (I.i. line 179) of the Ducal prison, described by Marina (Jacopo's wife) as a space where 'none who enter there return / As they have enter'd' (I.i. lines 256–7). Marina's use of 'return' is also one of a number of instances where death is described in terms of repetition and return in Byron's play: 'resumption'; 'rejoin'; 'recall'; 'repeated'; and even '[r]eposing' are also used (I.i. lines 1–8).

Jacopo repeatedly voices his desire to return permanently to Venice following his repeated torture for treasonable correspondence with the Duke of Milan (I.i. lines 15–16) and after an earlier banishment to Crete. One way of reading these events is that Jacopo's treasonable correspondence invites detection by the Council of Ten so that he will be prosecuted and brought back to Venice; this might help to explain the strangeness of Jacopo's declaration that he feels 'Like a boy—Oh Venice!' (I.i. line 93) immediately following another application of the rack: for him, torture (and death) is a price worth paying for being in Venice and, as here, for the transcendence he associates with it.

Indeed, we first encounter Jacopo rhapsodising on his childhood feats, his memory of his eagerness and joy at many times and on many occasions swimming and plunging into the Grand Canal in Venice. The idea of a retrieval, reattainment, or refinding of a previously held object is a repeated action central to Jacopo's desire for mastery over death; he describes how those watching him in his 'childish race' in the waters 'wax'd fearful' (I.i. lines 96, 115) that he might have drowned, but that he 'oft' navigated the current to retrieve ('Returning with my grasp') 'such tokens' of 'shells and sea-weed' (I.i. lines 111–16).

Jacopo's drive towards death has a double focus by its concern with – as well as Venice's waters – 'earth' (the word is also resonant in *The Prisoner of Chillon*):

> Guard: And can you so much love the soil which hates you?
> Jacopo Foscari: The soil!—Oh no, it is the seed of the soil
> Which persecutes me; but my native earth
> Will take me as a mother to her arms.
> I ask no more than a Venetian grave,
> A dungeon, what they will, so it be here. (I.i. lines 140–5)

Jacopo's compulsion to repeat – his repeated desire to 'return' to Venice after periods of exile and further sentences (III.i. line 13; IV.i. line 101) – can be read as a manifestation of the Freudian version of the death drive. Death here is represented as a drive towards an origin, a return to a place once and already known. In *Beyond the Pleasure Principle*, Freud reads drives as fundamentally 'conservative' ([1920] 2003: 77–81) in their bid 'to restore a prior state' (76, 77, 81, 100). This is productive for reading both the Gothic (for example, the return of the 'dead mother' figure in Ann Radcliffe's novels, including *A Sicilian Romance* (1790)) and *The Two Foscari*. Jacopo voices the repeated desire to return to Venice and die rather than live: 'better / Be ashes here than aught that lives elsewhere' (I.i. lines 138–9). In these lines, the preference for death over life is figured in the image of the feminine embrace and, specifically, the maternal. The metaphor of the son returning to Venice as a child returning to the arms of his mother indicates that, as delusional as Jacopo's death drive may be, the mother offers and enables a potential transcendence of death by her capacity for returning Jacopo to a child-like state: Venice 'Will take me as a mother to her arms' (line 143). The transcendence offered by the maternal figure is also a restoration of that prior state of things (Jacopo's 'my native earth / Will take me' suggests an equilibrium brought about by the return of the body to a state of inorganic matter) that Freud associated with death and the death drive. Indeed, the complexity of Jacopo's lines quoted above is that they capture Freud's sense of the death drive as both returning to a state of nothingness *and* going 'beyond' life; Jacopo's declaration that 'my native earth / Will take me as a mother' is an image of burial (and so death) and also the maternal embrace, which is explicitly described ('will take me') as an escape from persecution.

Jacopo's incarceration is clearly Gothic but this moment of transcendence moves Byron's play away from the genre; Jacopo's drive towards an object of love that is also a place of death evidences something distinctively Byronic. In fact, Jacopo's resolution, his longing to return to Venice, is voiced almost in terms of an invitation to the state, and so to his father, to punish him precisely so that he can obtain or realise these moments of transcendence. In this, Byron again departs from Gothic convention because he dramatises Jacopo seeking out his own death: at the very least, Jacopo invites torture here in a way that seems at odds with the many persecution scenarios found in the Gothic novel, where this inimical pressure is certainly not deliberately willed or invited.

After further sentence of banishment, Jacopo again insists on returning to Venice:

> Jacopo Foscari: Ah, father! though I must and will depart,
> Yet—yet—I pray you to obtain for me
> That I once more return unto my home,
> Howe'er remote the period. Let there be
> A point of time as beacon to my heart,
> With any penalty annex'd they please,
> But let me still return. (IV.i. lines 99–105)

A 'beacon to my heart' suggests something visible on or over the horizon, a point of hope even in the midst of death ('any penalty annex'd'). Jacopo also earlier acknowledges that 'death' is 'the imprecation of despair! / And yet for this I have return'd to Venice' (III.i. lines 5–6). His obsessive reiteration of the desire to return looks forward to the significance of Freud's study of what, as he acknowledges, is the perplexing striving 'to return' to a previous or 'old' state in *Beyond the Pleasure Principle* ([1920] 2003: 78). Notably, Freud connects such drives to masochism (94–5), and there is something of this masochism in Jacopo's willed return to punishment, torture, and death in Venice.

Death in Byron's play is also a result of the ancestral past's refusal to die. The two Foscari are decimated by the present impact of two prior political deaths: Jacopo Foscari's fiercest persecutor is Loredano, a member of the Council of Ten who believes that Francesco Foscari was responsible for the deaths of his father and uncle, whose spectres 'stalk' him (IV.i. line 332). An exchange between Loredano and the Doge on hereditary and familial relations (II.i. lines 207–22) suggests that death itself is a form of perverse return reaching – by its intergenerational sway or hold – into the present as a form of ancestral repetition from the past. This is a form of repetition over which 'we' have no control, as made evident in the Doge's Shakespearian and Marlovian speech on death – his response to Marina's questioning of his identity as father presiding over the fate of his imprisoned son:

> Doge: So, we are slaves,
> The greatest as the meanest—nothing rests

Upon our will; the will itself no less
Depends upon a straw than on a storm;
And when we think we lead, we are most led,
And still towards death, a thing which comes as much
Without our act or choice, as birth, so that
Methinks we must have sinn'd in some old world,
And *this* is hell: the best is, that it is not
Eternal. (II.i. lines 357–66)

Byron's response to death is bleakly existential here, based on a view of the human condition as always reducible to the base state of the 'universal heritage' (II.i. line 346) of passions and appetites, of small and great forces beyond control, and, moreover, on sinful repetition from different worlds.

Jacopo's actions in effectively provoking the state to imprison him work in opposition to his father's statements about the human will, though perhaps this is the Doge's point; in their actions, both Foscaris lead 'still towards death', the father as judge and persecutor and the son as patriotic subject compelled and transfixed by his desire to return to torture in Venice. In the Doge's view, death is the irresistible, ironic answer to the vanities of life, but he also reiterates the theme of death resting on the repetitious, tyrannical hold of the past on the present, of the 'sins' of a previous generation or life exerting an inimical, pernicious, and inescapable force now, in the present. Death is specifically understood as an event that operates like a 'birth', but whereas this had a partly positive orientation when associated with the mother figure earlier in the play (I.i. lines 140–5), here it is a form of origin that is also at the same time a sinful inheritance and heritage.

The Doge introduces the metaphor of human life – or, at least, man – as a book or 'volume' (II.i. line 335). There is a wider pattern here in terms of Gothic precedents where, according to Michael Macovski, 'the kinship metaphor in the age of Byron' is both a matter of ancestral heritage and textual inheritance and 'is most pronounced in Romantic revisions of Gothic primogeniture' (2001: 32). The found, often fragmented, manuscripts that form the basis of many Gothic works and, for instance, the numerous poems excerpted in Ann Radcliffe's novels, suggest that the Gothic is peculiarly concerned with textuality. Life as a book is a metaphor with a genealogy beyond the Gothic, but Byron invests it with a Gothic orientation in the Doge's reference to 'gifted spirits, who have studied long / That loathsome volume—man, and pored upon / These black and bloody leaves his heart and brain / But learn a magic which recoils upon / The adept who pursues it' (II.i. lines 334–8). This expresses the idea of each life setting the stage for the history of the next generation, though the Doge reads man as a Gothic body composed of 'Those black and bloody leaves his heart and brain' (II.i. line 336), and the textual transmission is again one of repeated, futile actions (II.i. lines 350–7). The Doge's interpretation of man as always going 'still towards death' (line 362) is given heightened dramatic and physical import when Jacopo faces his dungeon wall, seeing the past as a grim, metonymic text and sepulchral tableau:

Jacopo Foscari [*solus*]:

What letters are these which
[*Approaching the wall*
    Are scrawl'd along the inexorable wall?
    Will the gleam let me trace them? Ah! the names
    Of my sad predecessors in this place,
    The dates of their despair, the brief words of
    A grief too great for many. This stone page
    Holds like an epitaph their history,
    And the poor captive's tale is graven on
    His dungeon barrier, like the lover's record
    Upon the bark of some tall tree, which bears
    His own and his beloved's name. Alas!
    I recognize some names familiar to me,
    And blighted like to mine, which I will add,
    Fittest for such a chronicle as this,
    Which only can be read, as writ, by wretches.
               [*He engraves his name* (III.i. lines 14–28)

Simile structures this passage, signifying repeated forms that record epitaphic, death-like history. The carceral and 'sad' condition is 'like the lover's record'; the familiar and loved is once more aligned in the play with pain and suffering, and Jacopo sees those who are 'captive' as each being a type of historical text joined by death. The play is concerned with the repetition of a deadly and deathly past, which is 'blighted' and a blight on the present. Jacopo's phrase 'my sad predecessors' joins his name and his tortured state – his death-in-life – to a second order that pre-dates his time and temporality but defines it for him. The paradoxical (dead and living) 'stone page' records ghostly presences, asking a current, tortured, and imprisoned subject to define himself in relation to that deathly past. This is a different form of writing from 'the charter / Left by our fathers' (II.i. lines 398–9), the ancestral inheritance of law operative in Venice that the Doge defends but that also makes Jacopo's fate 'inexorable' (IV.i. line 271). Rather than death being an 'absolute disconnection from any form of order', which Botting argues is a dominant pattern in the Gothic (1996: 52), death in *The Two Foscari* is a kind of irreversible order from political and ancestral tyrannies (the 'names familiar to' Jacopo might be familial), part of the 'intergenerational compulsion to repeat the past' that is at the same time, as Eric Savoy argues, fundamentally Gothic (2002: 172).

Marina, for instance, repeatedly identifies the Council of Ten in Gothic terms, as fiendish (I.i. line 264; IV.i. line 173), ghoulish 'demons' (IV.i. line 176), a half-dead species. These 'old human fiends, / [have] one foot in the grave' (II.i. lines 108–9) and so connect living and dead, and are obsessed with a 'Variety of torturing' (I.i. line 265). Under this pressure of torture, death is a form of repetition driven to, but made bearable by – as the Miltonic echoes in Jacopo's speech below suggest – the human mind and its connection to 'liberty' (III.i line 84):

> Jacopo Foscari: That has a noble sound; but 'tis a sound,
> A music most impressive, but too transient:
> The mind is much, but is not all. The mind
> Hath nerved me to endure the risk of death,
> And torture positive, far worse than death
> (If death be a deep sleep), without a groan,
> Or with a cry which rather shamed my judges
> Than me; but 'tis not all, for there are things
> More woful—such as this small dungeon, where
> I may breathe many years. (III.i. lines 85–94)

Death as a sleep, as allegory, holds out the possibility of some form of transcendence, while the precise word 'nerved' points to Jacopo's own agency in his living death – his preparing for and tempting of death – which he claims is not the worst of possible conditions for man, even as the repetition of 'mind' and 'death' signals that death is for him now the dominant actuality. Jacopo's corporeal sufferings under repeated torture lead him to a split position on the human body: the mind offers man the capacity to endure, but cannot quell the materiality of captivity at the hands of the state and his father, which, to him in his present condition, seems to be the greater part of existence. The 'mind' may help the body to endure torture and eventual death, but it also allows the body to exist for a long time in the conditions of imprisonment. This dual nature is part of a wider pattern in Byron's work. Here a corporeal and material existence exists alongside a mental faculty that is variously said to imprison or liberate that matter. Such a position on death demands a comparative reading with *Manfred*:

> Manfred: I bear within
> A torture which could nothing gain from thine:
> The mind which is immortal makes itself
> Requital for its good or evil thoughts—
> Is its own origin of ill and end—
> And its own place and time—its innate sense,
> When stripp'd of this mortality, derives
> No colour from the fleeting things without,
> But is absorb'd in sufferance or in joy,
> Born from the knowledge of its own desert. (III.iv. lines 127–36)

'Requital' means return – reward, punishment, or retaliation. Unlike Jacopo Foscari's repeated 'torture positive', Manfred's 'torture' might be said to be perpetuated primarily from within, from the mind. Manfred is here at the point of death. Earlier, he defiantly told the Abbot that his condition of 'tortures' and 'despair' is 'remorse without the fear of hell' (III.i. lines 70–1), so the reader must be cautious about ascribing a Christian position to these lines while still acknowledging that Byron's source is Milton's Christian epic *Paradise Lost* ([1674] 1971: 257, I. lines 254–6). Manfred's description of the mind as being 'its own origin of ill and end' suggests that it produces both beginnings and endings. The conditional 'When' suggests a process that either definitely does happen, or a process that might happen in the future: both are part of the transcendent possibilities of suffering or of joy that affirm that 'mortality' is a burden which can be removed or 'stripped' away. The condition of immortality is a condition of making, of self-making, and this situating of the mind (see also III.i. line 106) at the centre of such possibilities marks out the verse drama's clearest move away from the Gothic concern with death as a finite state.

If Manfred appears to arrive at the affirmation of the existence of an immortal mind, then *Sardanapalus*, published with *The Two Foscari* and *Cain*, is, while a no less complex articulation, more explicit in the focus on death and 'mind':

> Myrrha: I know no evil death can show, which life
> Has not already shown to those who live
> Embodied longest. If there be indeed
> A shore, where mind survives, 'twill be as mind,
> All unincorporate: or if there flits
> A shadow of this cumbrous clog of clay,

Which stalks, methinks, between our souls and heaven,
And fetters us to earth—at least the phantom,
Whate'er it have to fear, will not fear death. (IV.i. lines 54–62)

Sardanapalus is another study of ancestral tyranny; Sardanapalus, the last king of Assyria (in Byron's play, Myrrha is his chief favourite), 'dreams of life or death' (IV.i. line 73), and of being visited by his ancestors Nimrod and Semiramis, the latter described as a 'bloody-handed, ghastly, ghostly thing' (IV.i. line 105). Myrrha's 'Embodied longest' is a perplexing phrase, but a 'shore, where mind survives' appears to argue for an afterlife based on the existence of mind alone, outside or separate from the body. Myrrha qualifies this through a very distinctive take on the idea of the body imprisoning the soul: the mind will be released from the body, but the body is a 'clog of clay' that in turn might act as a ghostly presence that in some form binds or keeps the mind from total transcendence into a heavenly afterlife, while at the same time making death no source of fear. As John Ehrstine argues, 'death becomes not so much a consummation devoutly to be wished as a transcendent state energetically to be lived and earned. The Gothic "labyrinth" of this life, even of this cosmos, produces death' (1974: 101).

   'The Gothic labyrinth' is a choice phrase for the claustrophobic, deathly spaces of *The Two Foscari* and *The Prisoner of Chillon*, but endurance offers, in particular, Jacopo 'many years' of suffering. Like the prisoner, Jacopo repeatedly quantifies his grotesque, Gothic levels of 'Double, / Triple, and tenfold torture!' (IV.i. lines 156–7). Close to death, however, Jacopo expresses another, central possibility about this state – namely, the Christian hope that his tortures on earth will 'keep … [him] from / A like hereafter' (IV.i. lines 169–70). In this sense, death in *The Two Foscari* is a form of release. In his final speech, Jacopo reiterates and repeats his desire to return permanently to Venice: 'bear me' / Dead, but *still bear* me to a native grave' (author's emphasis) (IV.i. lines 146–7). Jacopo's insistence on being dead voices a position in which death is Venice-driven and a condition more merciful than life; to express this, Byron retains the Gothic vocabulary of Jacopo's tortured, 'lacerated' condition (IV.i. line 150), but he also imagines, memorably, the waters around Venice propelling Jacopo's return home to go beyond the corporeality and suffering of the human body and 'mingle with the sands which skirt / The land I love' (IV.i. lines 133–4).

   Unlike Jacopo, the prisoner of Chillon survives, and makes a defiantly philosophical statement that such proximity to death is a form

of communion that 'tends / To make us what we are' (lines 392–3).
Jacopo's absolute willingness to die – figured in *The Two Foscari* by
an insistent language of 'return' – poses perversions of normative cultural, political, and social values that are Gothic in their extremity and
extremities, while also dramatising ancestral, familial, and textual forms
as destructive and death-bringing. But while Byron deploys the Gothic
in the language, setting, and atmosphere of *The Prisoner of Chillon*,
Manfred, *Sardanapalus*, and *The Two Foscari*, the title characters in
these works also find moments of transcendence through death that
show a clear move beyond the Gothic's limits. In the Gothic, death is
often a state to be feared and resisted, but Manfred, Sardanapalus, and
Jacopo Foscari all strive and will towards death, and each dies on his
own terms.

References

Botting, F. (1996) *The Gothic* (London: Routledge).
Byron, G. G., Lord (1991) *Sardanapalus* [1821] and *The Two Foscari* [1821],
    in J. J. McGann and B. Weller (eds), *Byron: The Complete Poetical Works*, vol. 6
    (Oxford: Clarendon Press), pp. 15–129; pp. 129–227.
Byron, G. G., Lord (1986) *The Prisoner of Chillon* [1816] and *Manfred* [1817], in J.
    J. McGann (ed.), *Byron: The Complete Poetical Works*, vol. 4 (Oxford: Clarendon
    Press), pp. 4–16; pp. 51–103.
Ehrstine, J. W. (1974) 'Byron and the metaphysic of self-destruction', in G. R.
    Thompson (ed.), *The Gothic Imagination: Essays in Dark Romanticism* (Washington,
    WA: Washington State University Press), pp. 94–108.
Farnell, G. (2011) 'Gothic's death drive', *Literature Compass*, 8.9: 592–608.
Freud, S. (2003) *Beyond the Pleasure Principle*, in *Beyond the Pleasure Principle and
    Other Writings* [1920], trans. John Reddick (London: Penguin), pp. 43–102.
Lewis, M. (1998) *The Monk* [1796], ed. H. Anderson (Oxford: Oxford University
    Press).
Macovski, M. (2001) 'Revisiting Gothic primogeniture: the kinship metaphor in the
    age of Byron', *Gothic Studies*, 3.1: 32–44.
Milton, J. (1971) *Complete Poetry*, ed. John T. Shawcross (New York: Doubleday).
Savoy, E. (2002) 'The rise of American Gothic', in J. E. Hogle (ed.), *The Cambridge
    Companion to Gothic Fiction* (Cambridge: Cambridge University Press), pp. 167–88.

Part III

Gothic apocalypses: dead selves/dead civilizations

7

Jennifer Schell

The annihilation of self and species: the ecoGothic sensibilities of Mary Shelley and Nathaniel Hawthorne

Midway through the second volume of Mary Shelley's futuristic novel *The Last Man* (1826), the eponymous hero, Lionel Verney, attempts to describe the emotional impact of the plague on the citizens of England. He comments:

> Nature, our mother, and our friend, had turned on us a brow of menace. She shewed us plainly, that, though she permitted us to assign her laws and subdue her apparent powers, yet, if she put forth but a finger, we must quake. She could take our globe … and cast it into space, where life would be drunk up, and man and all his efforts for ever annihilated. (Shelley, 2004: 185)

Here, Verney employs ecoGothic language, emphasising the sublime aspects of the natural world. Personifying nature as a powerful feminine force endowed with agency, he stresses that all of humankind is destined for destruction. For Verney, the plague produces terror, inspires awe, and inaugurates a significant shift in the relationship between human beings and the natural world.

Not coincidentally, Nathaniel Hawthorne also used ecoGothic imagery to chronicle the extinction of the human race. In the story 'The Ambitious Guest' (1835), the narrator describes a catastrophic landslide that kills a rural, mountain family as 'a cataract of ruin', which 'overwhelmed the whole vicinity, blocked up the road, and annihilated everything in its dreadful course' (Hawthorne, 1974: 333). Much like Verney, Hawthorne's narrator underscores the sublime aspects of natural forces to indicate that humankind – metaphorically represented by the family – is powerless to resist the natural disasters destined to cause its extinction.

Adopting a transnational mode of analysis that traces the circulation of scientific ideas throughout the Atlantic World, I argue that
Shelley's and Hawthorne's writings reflect an acute fear of extinction
prevalent in British and American culture throughout the nineteenth
century. This apprehension stemmed from an important scientific
development of the era: the acceptance of Georges Cuvier's claim that
species extinction was a reality. Although it threatened long-standing
theocentric beliefs about the inviolability of the natural world created
by God as described in Genesis, this idea eventually gained credence
among nineteenth-century natural historians who began to notice that
increasing numbers of animals were poised on the brink of extermination. Some – the dodo bird and Steller's sea cow – had already been
pushed over the edge. These observations confirmed Charles Lyell's
even more troublesome theory that extinction could be caused by
anthropogenic, or human-driven, factors (1832: 156). Though Lyell
was not necessarily bothered by this idea, many of his contemporaries
grew concerned about the toll humanity exacted on other species. They
also worried about the future of humankind, itself.[1]

Certainly, this scientific development and its religious implications
contributed a great deal to nineteenth-century fears about extinction.
These feelings were exacerbated, however, by the fact that extinction
represents a particularly extreme form of death. While the decease
of an individual is a frightening occurrence, the death of an entire
species is an infinitely more terrifying loss because of its irrevocabil-
ity. According to Tim Flannery and Peter Schouten, extinction creates 'a gap in nature' that will never again be filled in quite the same
way (2001: 1). This absence has a disorienting, fear-inducing effect on
those humans confronted by it. As the anonymous author of 'Ghost
Species: Geographies of Absence and Extinction' explains, 'absence is
powerful – it reverberates through landscapes and memories ("gone
but not forgotten") and disturbs the "when" of spatiotemporal experience and the "how" of perception' (2014).

Products of this cultural climate, Shelley and Hawthorne use eco-
Gothic language to elaborate on these fears, imagining a completely
secular vision of the demise of humanity. In so doing, they adapt some of
the more traditional tropes of Gothic writing – its investment in excess,
its fascination with horror/terror, its emphasis on the sublime, its preoccupation with death – to emergent scientific concepts and environmental contexts. Although excess is manifest in many different aspects
of *The Last Man* and 'The Ambitious Guest', it is especially important to

their evocations of the sublime and their discussions of extinction. This is because, as Fred Botting observes, 'sublimity present[s] an excess that [can]not be processed by the rational mind' and 'confront[s] the individual with the thought of its own extinction' (2005: 37). By shifting the emphasis from the individual to the species, Shelley and Hawthorne amplify the scientific and environmental import of their meditations on death and create a specifically ecoGothic and godless form of *memento mori*.[2]

The transnational ecoGothic

My decision to juxtapose and examine Shelley's and Hawthorne's writings about extinction has been influenced by the scholarship of Monika Elbert and Bridget M. Marshall who explain 'the Atlantic world is connected through numerous networks – cultural, economic, and social' (2013: 7). These often tangled and convoluted routes allowed the circulation of goods and ideas throughout the Atlantic realm, forging connections among disparate places and people. According to Mark V. Barrow Jr, scientific theories about the reality of extinction developed in a transatlantic context, as American colonists discovered fossils and sent them to European scientists for further study (2009: 15–46). Across the eighteenth and nineteenth centuries, the individuals engaged in these networks of exchange – Cotton Mather, Thomas Jefferson, Georges Cuvier, Charles Lyell, to name just a few – generated theories about species extinction, publishing them in various American and European print culture venues where they were read by all manner of interested individuals.

Extinction had other transnational dimensions given the dramatic expansion of British and American territorial possessions. As these two empires grew, so did their environmental impact. Settlers brought invasive species and epidemic diseases to the places they inhabited. They also hunted animals, felled trees, dammed rivers, and slaughtered native peoples.[3] All told, these activities caused indigenous animal and human populations in the British colonies and the American West to diminish dramatically. Worried about extinction, numerous nineteenth-century British and American authors wrote compelling scientific treatises about endangered animal species. They also composed poignant elegies to the indigenous inhabitants of the United States, Canada, and Australia and wrote a good deal of apocalyptic fiction about the demise of humankind, much of it in the ecoGothic mode (Brantlinger, 2003: 1–16; Stafford, 1994: 197–231).

Over the past five years, the use of the term 'ecoGothic' has prolifer-ated among scholars interested in environmental writing that addresses the more terrifying/horrific aspects of the natural world. Importantly, it has been used to describe both a type of analysis and a mode of writing. According to David Del Principe, 'an EcoGothic approach poses a challenge to a familiar Gothic subject – nature – taking a non-anthropocentric position to reconsider the role that the environment, species, and nonhumans play in the construction of monstrosity and fear' (2014: 1). Here, I want to highlight Del Principe's claim about environmentally based fears, an idea that reinforces my argument about nineteenth-century authors and their responses to the problem of extinction.

In '"Deep into that darkness peering": An essay on Gothic nature', Tom J. Hillard suggests that the ecoGothic 'functions more as an adjec-tive describing certain *aspects* of the texts' than as a generic category or an analytical approach. He further contends that this formulation of the ecoGothic enables scholars 'to trace the Gothic qualities found in representations of nature throughout history, whether those represen-tations are found in Gothic fiction or not' (2009: 689). These observa-tions open up the category of the Gothic and, in so doing, they furnish a critical lens through which to examine the environmental aspects of *The Last Man* and 'The Ambitious Guest', texts more typically regarded as science fiction – or proto-science fiction – and historical fiction, respectively.

Extinction and death

My conceptualisation of extinction as a particularly pronounced, anxiety-inducing form of death has been influenced by the writings of both conservation scientists and psychoanalytic thinkers. Although extinction is a scientific idea, it is fraught with feeling for those who study and contemplate it. As Richard Leakey and Roger Lewin astutely observe, 'Many of the attitudes that govern discussion on extinction reflect emotional as well as scientific viewpoints' (1995: 48). In their conclusion to 'Conservation biology: Its scope and its challenge', an otherwise objective meditation on the discipline of conservation biol-ogy, for example, Michael Soulé and Bruce Wilcox (1980) express their views of extinction in vivid, emotional terms. With powerful verbs and striking adjectives, they warn, 'The green mantle of Earth is now being ravaged and pillaged in a frenzy of exploitation by a mushrooming mass of humans and bulldozers' (1980: 7).

Leakey and Lewin (1995) and Soulé and Wilcox (1980) suggest that emotional responses to the problem of extinction revolve around concerns about death. While the former posit that the feelings stem from worries about the vulnerability of the human race, the latter contend that extinction is frightening and terrifying because it represents 'an end to birth' (Soulé and Wilcox, 1980: 8). Though different, both claims have merit, especially when viewed in the light of Ernest Becker's and Robert Jay Lifton's theories about human responses to death and dying. According to Becker 'the fear of death … is the basic fear that influences all others, a fear from which no one is immune, no matter how disguised it may be' (1973: 15). He goes so far as to describe this fear as a 'terror' that is both 'universal' and 'all-consuming' (1973: p. 15). Lifton, meanwhile, suggests that humans cope with these fears by embracing various forms of 'symbolic immortality', two of which are particularly important to mark with respect to the issue of species extinction (1979: 17). As he explains, many individuals achieve 'a sense of endless biohistorical continuity' by producing children, thereby passing their genetic material on to their descendants (18). He notes that others experience symbolic immortality through their affiliation with seasonal cycles of birth and death that take place in a natural environment perceived as 'limitless in space and time' (22).

Importantly, extinction threatens to interfere with these two forms of symbolic immortality. As Lifton himself notes in his discussion of twentieth-century fears of nuclear apocalypse, 'Imagery of extermination does not eliminate any of these modes of symbolic immortality, but casts all of them into doubt' (1979: 345). Though certainly relevant to the nuclear age, this observation also pertains to other chronological periods because some of the most disruptive and terrifying features of extinction are timeless. Insofar as it prevents a species from producing offspring, extinction threatens biological forms of symbolic immortality. Insofar as it irrevocably alters the natural world, extinction also interferes with environmental forms of symbolic immortality. Thus this particular form of death deprives humans – including nineteenth-century British and American authors just beginning to accept it as a scientific reality – of some of their most important coping mechanisms. This is precisely what made extinction so terrifying to contemplate for both Mary Shelley and Nathaniel Hawthorne.

The Last Man and the literal extinction of mankind

Because of its twenty-first-century setting and its prescient depiction of such environmental issues as climate variability, global pandemic, and species extinction, *The Last Man* has received a good deal of attention recently from such ecocritics as Michael Page, Siobhan Carroll, and Lauren Cameron. Though thoughtful and perceptive, most of this scholarship focuses on Shelley's scientific interests, not her adaptation of Gothic tropes to ecoGothic contexts. Because it takes into account both the form and function of Shelley's writing, the latter approach yields more insight into *The Last Man* and its completely secular articulation of the extinction of humankind.

Gothic excesses appear everywhere in *The Last Man*. They are most evident, however, in Lionel Verney's depictions of the plague, the ecological and biological catastrophe that eventually destroys humanity. These passages abound with a surplus of figurative expression and descriptive detail. Over the course of the novel, Verney refers to the plague as an 'invader', a 'destroyer', a 'desolater', a 'fiend', an 'archfiend', a 'serpent-head', and an 'invincible monster' (Shelley, 2004: 199–318). He also consistently personifies the plague as feminine, a strategy that serves to underscore the natural aspects of the epidemic. In one particularly striking instance, Verney couples gendered pronouns with an archer metaphor: 'Summer advanced, and, crowned with the sun's potent rays, plague shot her unerring shafts over the earth' (220). This implicit allusion to Artemis, the Greek goddess of the hunt, serves to foreground the deadliness of the disease.

Metaphorically speaking, Verney also compares the plague to an earthquake, opening a 'deep and precipitous' fissure 'under our very feet', and a Juggernaut 'crushing out the being of all who strew the high road of life' (Shelley, 2004: 218; 318). Tellingly, he reiterates certain similes as the novel progresses, augmenting and intensifying them in the process. When the epidemic first reaches England, Verney describes the Lord Protector, Ryland, as warning his subjects that 'there is no refuge on earth, it [the plague] comes on us like a thousand packs of wolves' (193). A bit later, he repeats the comparison, adding the phrase, 'howling through the winter night, gaunt and fierce' (213) to stress the increasingly terrifying aspects of the illness.

Toward the end of the novel, Verney employs an excess of supernatural imagery, describing France as a desolate landscape filled with 'spectres', 'ghosts', and 'appalling shapes' (Shelley, 2004: 326). Shortly thereafter, he characterises a delirious opera-dancer as a 'goblin' and an infected French nobleman as an 'apparition' (327–8). Though it might seem out of place in a secular story about the scientific reality of species extinction, this supernatural imagery serves an important purpose insofar as it represents the mental and emotional extremes to which Verney and his fellow refugees have been driven. For them, the destructive force of the plague is so frightening that the supernatural begins to permeate the natural, and reality begins to blur into unreality.

In *The Last Man*, Verney's profusion of figurative language and supernatural imagery is accompanied by an excess of graphic, gory detail designed to incapacitate readers with feelings of horror. At their most extreme, these moments rival those in Matthew Lewis's *The Monk* (1796). Of one of the plague's victims, Verney says, 'he lay on a heap of straw, cold and stiff; while a pernicious effluvia filled the room, and various stains and marks served to shew the virulence of the disorder' (Shelley, 2004: 206). In the next chapter, he describes a village whose 'paths were deformed by unburied corpses' (221). When he arrives in France, he observes, 'sights far worse, of the unburied dead, and human forms which were strewed on the road side, and on the steps of once frequented habitations' (319). A useful way of understanding the function of these grotesque passages is furnished by Fred Botting, who describes horror as a 'response to an excess [death] that cannot be transcended' (2014: 69). With their focus on the physicality of post-mortem corporeal deterioration, these images serve to convey the horrors of a disease-ridden, secular world in which death represents 'the absolute limit, a finitude which denies any possibility of imaginative transcendence' (Botting, 2014: 69).

Although the epidemic drives the extinction of humankind in *The Last Man*, it is not the only factor. Humanity also endures numerous other catastrophic natural disasters, all of which Verney describes using another discourse of excess popular with Gothic authors – that of the Romantic sublime. Stressing human frailty and powerlessness, he details England's extreme temperatures, wild windstorms, and sudden floods, as well as Mexico's famines and Ecuador's earthquakes (Shelley, 2004: 183–6). According to Verney, a strange astronomical event terrifies the inhabitants of Asia and Africa: 'a black sun arose: an orb, the size of that luminary, but dark, defined, whose beams were shadows, ascended from the west; in about an hour it had reached the meridian, and eclipsed the bright parent of day' (178). Later, Verney witnesses another sublime celestial phenomenon:

three other suns, alike burning and brilliant, rushed from various quarters of the heavens towards the great orb; they whirled round it. The glare of light was intense to our dazzled eyes; the sun itself seemed to join in the dance, while the sea burned like a furnace, like all Vesuvius alight, with flowing lava beneath. (296)

These passages all contain an excess of descriptive detail designed to inspire terror, not horror, in readers. According to Botting, terror differs from horror in that the former 'activates mind and imagination, enabling an overcoming of fears and doubts' while the latter 'freezes human faculties, rendering the mind passive and immobilising the body' (2014: 68–9). Coupled with his horrific images of decaying bodies, these passages add complexity and dimension to Verney's representations of humanity's shifting relationship to the natural world.

Of all the ecological catastrophes occurring in *The Last Man*, none is as rife with sublimity as the prospect of the extinction of humankind. At one point, Verney attempts to explain why he is so terrified of this scientific eventuality: 'we [humans] call ourselves lords of the creation, wielders of the elements, masters of life and death, and we allege in excuse of this arrogance, that though the individual is destroyed, man continues for ever' (Shelley, 2004: 184). Here, Verney elaborates an idea very similar to Lifton's concept of symbolic immortality. He adds, 'Thus, losing our identity, that of which we are chiefly conscious, we glory in the continuity of our species, and learn to regard death without terror. But when any whole nation becomes the victim of the destructive powers of exterior agents, then indeed man shrinks into insignificance, he feels his tenure of life insecure, his inheritance on earth cut off' (184). Much like Lifton, Verney emphasises that humans deal with death by symbolically embracing the 'continuity of our species'. For him, extinction is terrifying because it completely disrupts this coping mechanism.

While it meditates on death and indulges in all manner of excesses, Shelley's ecoGothic *memento mori* does not elaborate traditional generic themes involving the vanity of earthly pleasures or the prospect of the afterlife. It also refuses to address such typical Gothic concerns as deviance, depravity, divine retribution, scientific boundary-crossing, or the 'sins of the father' (Botting, 2014: 13, 45, 51). Verney may offer some general observations about humanity's arrogant attitudes toward nature, but he does not discuss the specific transgressions of particular individuals or societies. Over the course of the novel, he advances a purely secular vision of global apocalypse driven by powerful but indifferent natural forces, not a vengeful and punitive God (Page, 2012: 98–101). As such, all of the individual characters in the novel, Verney included, appear to be innocent victims of unfortunate circumstances. In the end, *The Last Man* offers no lessons about the appropriate limits of scientific knowledge or the moral failings of human beings. Influenced by the recent discovery of the reality of species extinction, the novel does, however, offer something infinitely more terrifying – namely, a scientifically and environmentally grounded ecoGothic vision of the utter insignificance of *Homo sapiens* in the grand scheme of a godless universe.

'The Ambitious Guest' and the metaphorical extinction of mankind

Even though many of Hawthorne's tales address important scientific and environmental issues, including extinction, ecocritics have paid scant attention to his writing. In recent years, a handful of scholars – Robert A. Abrams, John Gatta, and Aaron Sachs – have begun to remedy this oversight. Importantly, they elect to focus on the more positive, albeit ambivalent, depictions of nature that appear in Hawthorne's writing. For this reason, they tend to ignore the representations of nature that contain ecoGothic elements. By examining precisely these aspects of Hawthorne's 'The Ambitious Guest', I seek to address a noteworthy gap in this steadily growing body of scholarship.

Significantly, 'The Ambitious Guest' reimagines a famous natural disaster, a landslide that claimed the lives of the entire Willey family in Crawford Notch, New Hampshire in 1826. According to John F. Sears, this devastating event satiated the American 'appetite for catastrophe' (1982: 359–60). Many Americans responded to the disaster in print, some even comparing it to the flood in Genesis. Building on Sears's research, I maintain that Hawthorne's story represents a secular version of the biblical catastrophe, revolving around natural rather than divine forces, and culminating in the metaphorical demise of humankind. To this end, it adapts traditional conventions of the European Gothic – descriptive excesses, supernatural imagery, sublime nature – to American environmental contexts. Thus, Hawthorne, like Shelley, expresses the fears of a culture consumed by the idea of extinction.

In the first paragraph of 'The Ambitious Guest', the narrator describes the anonymous family's mountain home using language reminiscent of that employed by European Gothic authors to portray remote, foreboding castles. First, he sketches a portrait of a rustic family cosily clustered around a roaring fire on a September night. Then, he disrupts this image of domestic bliss, explaining that the cottage is located in 'the bleakest spot of all New-England' where the wind is 'sharp throughout the year, and pitilessly cold in the winter' (Hawthorne, 1974: 324). Foreshadowing the demise of the family, he notes that 'a mountain towered above their heads, so steep, that the stones would often rumble down its sides, and startle them at midnight' (324). For added effect, he observes that they burn 'the splintered ruins of great trees, that had come crashing down the precipice' (324). With striking imagery and pointed contrasts, these sentences endow nature with sublime characteristics and establish an atmosphere of Gothic dread.

To impart a sense of the supernatural to the story, the narrator personifies the wind as 'wailing' and 'moaning' in a ghostly, funereal fashion (Hawthorne, 1974: 325). When a mysterious young stranger arrives, the supernatural imagery intensifies. As soon as he takes a seat by the fire, 'something like a heavy footstep was heard without, rushing down the steep side of the mountain, as with long and rapid strides, and taking such a leap, in passing the cottage as to strike the opposite precipice' (326). Shortly after the appearance of this metaphorical giant, the wind takes on a 'deeper and drearier sound', a noise which the stranger characterises as 'the choral strain of the spirits of the blast, who, in old Indian times, had their dwelling among these mountains, and made their heights and recesses a sacred religion' and which the narrator describes as the 'wail' of a funeral procession (331). Figuratively speaking, this passage – and its spectral imagery – links the family to the extinct, or nearly extinct, indigenous inhabitants of New England. An implicit invocation of the Gothic theme that the 'sins of the father' are visited upon the next generation, it foreshadows the death of the family and plays upon the fears of Americans complicit in the genocide of the native peoples of the New World.

As the story progresses, the narrator continues to amplify the disturbing supernatural imagery. Just before the fatal landslide occurs, the grandmother informs the family of a morbid superstition: 'if anything were amiss with a corpse, if only the ruff were not smooth, or the cap did not set right, the corpse, in the coffin and beneath the clods, would strive to put up its cold hands and arrange it' (Hawthorne, 1974: 332). Although her family reacts with revulsion to this 'ghastly conception' of animated corpses and vivisepulture, she nevertheless makes a request of her children: 'when your mother is drest, and in the coffin – I want one of you to hold a looking-glass over my face' so that 'I may take a glimpse at myself, and see whether all's right' (332). Terrified and 'engrossed' by these remarks, the family and their mysterious guest fail to hear the 'deep', 'awful', terrible' sound of the landslide as it advances swiftly down the mountain toward them (332).

Significantly, the narrator depicts the catastrophe that destroys the family – and by metaphorical extension, humankind – as a sublime act of nature. To stress the mind-boggling terror of the unfortunate event, he highlights the family's initial response to it: 'young and old exchanged one wild glance, and remained an instant, pale, affrighted, without utterance, or power to move' (Hawthorne, 1974: 332). Warning readers that 'the simplest words must intimate ... the unutterable horror of the catastrophe', he explains that the family members quickly recover themselves and quit the cottage, fleeing 'right into the pathway of destruction' (333). What makes this event particularly striking – and ironic – is that the cottage is left untouched by the massive 'cataract of ruin' that 'annihilated everything in its dreadful course' (333). Had they stayed where they were, they would have lived. As it is, they are all killed by the powerful onslaught of nature.

In his evocations of the sublime and the supernatural, Hawthorne – much like Shelley before him – adapts Gothic conventions to environmental contexts in order to meditate on the potential extinction of humankind. Thus he too advances a kind of ecoGothic *memento mori*. Significantly, 'The Ambitious Guest' differs markedly from *The Last Man* insofar as it elaborates more traditional themes having to do with earthly vanity and cosmic justice. Over the course of the story, the mysterious stranger proves to be a Mephistophelean tempter, whose 'high and abstracted ambition ... not to be forgotten in the grave' is both infectious and irresistible (Hawthorne, 1974: 327). After hearing these words, the father expresses a wish for his life to be commemorated with a personalised headstone and the grandmother articulates a desire to control her physical appearance after her death (329–32). Instead of rejecting worldly vanities, these characters cling to them as a way of assuaging their fears of death and achieving symbolic immortality. Though a secular rather than a divine event, the landslide serves as a punitive force that obliterates these vain individuals, and by metaphorical extension, all of humanity.

As this evidence suggests, 'The Ambitious Guest' is much more traditionally Gothic than *The Last Man*, particularly with respect to the themes it elaborates. In the former, nature represents an avenging force that exacts cosmic justice for humanity's historical crimes and moral failings in God's stead. In the latter, nature is an indifferent, uncaring entity that operates according to laws unfathomable to humans. Although disturbing, Hawthorne's vision of the natural world – and humanity's place in it – is not as bleak and nihilistic as Shelley's. For this reason, Hawthorne's brand of ecoGothic writing would prove to be extremely popular with later authors and filmmakers, who would elaborate upon the revenge-of-nature motif and adapt it to different environmental contexts in such books and movies as *The Birds* (1963), *Jaws* (1974), *Frogs* (1972), and *Prophecy* (1979).

Notes

1 Numerous scholars have traced the history of scientific ideas about extinction. See Stafford (1994) and Barrow (2009).
2 Twenty-first-century scholars continue to adapt Gothic tropes to their discussions of extinction. Mark V. Barrow Jr. (2009: iii) calls extinct species 'Nature's Ghosts', while the University of Cambridge's Department of Geology dubs them 'Ghost Species'. Meanwhile, the phrase, 'specter of extinction' has become an academic cliché.
3 Numerous scholars have recorded the environmental impact of colonial endeavours and frontier settlement. See Crosby (1986) and Taylor (2009).

References

Abrams, R. A. (2004) *Landscape and Ideology in American Renaissance Literature: Topographies of Skepticism* (Cambridge: Cambridge University Press).

Barrow, M. V., Jr. (2009) *Nature's Ghosts: Confronting Extinction from the Age of Jefferson to the Age of Ecology* (Chicago: University of Chicago Press).

Becker, E. (1973) *The Denial of Death* (New York: Free Press).

Botting, F. (2014) *Gothic*, 2nd edn (London: Routledge).

Brantlinger, P. (2003) *Dark Vanishings: Discourse on the Extinction of Primitive Races, 1800–1930* (Ithaca, NY: Cornell University Press).

Cameron, L. (2012) 'Mary Shelley's Malthusian objections in *The Last Man*', *Nineteenth-Century Literature*, 67.2: 177–203.

Carroll, S. (2013) 'Crusades against Frost: *Frankenstein*, polar ice, and climate change in 1818', *European Romantic Review*, 24.2: 211–30.

Crosby, A. W. (1986) *Ecological Imperialism: The Biological Expansion of Europe, 900–1900* (Cambridge: Cambridge University Press).

Del Principe, D. (2014) 'Introduction: The ecoGothic in the long nineteenth century', *Gothic Studies*, 16.1: 1–8.

Elbert M. and B. Marshall (eds) (2013) *Transnational Gothic: Literary and Social Exchanges in the Long Nineteenth Century* (Farnham: Ashgate).

Flannery T. and P. Schouten (2001) *A Gap in Nature: Discovering the World's Extinct Animals* (New York: Atlantic Monthly Press).

Gatta, J. (2004) *Making Nature Sacred: Literature, Religion, and Environment in America from the Puritans to the Present* (Oxford: Oxford University Press).

'Ghost Species: Geographies of Extinction and Absence' (2014) (Cambridge: Department of Geography, University of Cambridge). Available at: http://geog.cam.ac.uk/research/projects/ghostspecies/. Accessed 27 June 2015.

Hawthorne, N. (1974) *Twice-Told Tales* (Columbus, OH: Ohio State University Press).

Hillard, T. J. (2009) '"Deep into that darkness peering": An essay on Gothic nature', *Interdisciplinary Studies in Literature and Environment*, 16.4: 685–95.

Leakey R. and R. Lewin (1995) *The Sixth Extinction: Biodiversity and Its Survival* (New York: Doubleday).

Lifton, R. J. (1979) *The Broken Connection: On Death and the Continuity of Life* (New York: Simon and Schuster).

Lyell, C. (1832) *Principles of Geology* (London: John Murray).

Page, M. (2012) *Literary Imagination from Erasmus Darwin to H. G. Wells: Science, Evolution, and Ecology* (Farnham: Ashgate).

Sachs, A. (2013) *Arcadian America: The Death and Life of an Environmental Tradition* (New Haven, CT: Yale University Press).

Sears, J. F. (1982) 'Hawthorne's "The Ambitious Guest" and the significance of the Willey Disaster', *American Literature*, 54.3: 354–67.

Shelley, M. (2004) *The Last Man* [1826] (Ware: Wordsworth Editions Limited).

Soulé, M. E. and B. A. Wilcox (1980) 'Conservation biology: Its scope and its challenges', in M. E. Soulé and B. A. Wilcox (eds), *Conservation Biology: An Evolutionary-Ecological Perspective* (Sunderland: Sinauer Associates).

Stafford, F. J. (1994) *The Last of the Race: The Growth of a Myth from Milton to Darwin* (Oxford: Oxford University Press).

Taylor, D. E. (2009) *The Environment and the People in American Cities, 1600s–1900s: Disorder, Inequality, and Social Change* (Durham, NC: Duke University Press).

8

John Cameron Hartley

Death cults in Gothic 'Lost World' fiction

Early in the epistolary opening to Mary Shelley's three-volume 1818 edition of *Frankenstein*, the fledgling explorer Captain Walton, writing to his sister, describes his 'fervent and vivid' daydreams in which he imagines a 'region of beauty and delight' where 'snow and frost are banished', located somewhere at the North Pole (2008: 5). During that same year, John Cleves Symmes had published his theories regarding the hollowness of the Earth, and two years later, the pseudonymous Captain Adam Seaborn published an account of his penetration into a world within the world via Antarctica, in *Symzonia: A Voyage of Discovery* (1820). Some seventy years later the author of the document presented as *A Strange Manuscript Found in A Copper Cylinder* (1888), exploring the lost region at the other ends of the Earth from Walton, at the South Pole, seems to echo Shelley's explorer when he describes 'not a world of ice and frost, but one of beauty and light' (De Mille, 2011: 40).

Even as the world gradually opened up to exploration, colonisation, and indeed exploitation, fiction reflected a continuing desire that there might still be uncharted seas surrounding hidden lands and races. The physical manifestations of beauty encountered by literary explorers are often accompanied by a confrontation with peril, and with their own mortality. While 'travellers' tales' are a noted sub-genre of fantasy literature, the 'Lost World' is a distinctly late Victorian genre, with Lost World narratives harnessed for philosophical and political reasons, as emphasised by the allegorical, utopian, or dystopian cultures featured within them. Crucially, it is not the utopian visions that appear to have survived in the popular imagination, but rather those that invoke a Gothic dystopian setting. Within the fictional Lost World, where the era's hubristic anxieties regarding race, gender, the fragility of *fin-de-siècle* society, and personal mortality seem to have established their own dark empire, Victorian cultural certainties were challenged by divergent belief systems and the mystery and terror of death.

The corpse as topography

H. Rider Haggard introduced his hero Allan Quatermain in *King Solomon's Mines* (1885). 'Hunter' Quatermain, who has established a great reputation as an explorer and a slaughterer of elephants for ivory, is approached by Sir Henry Curtis and his friend Captain Good, to lead an expedition into the African interior to search for Curtis's brother who has been lost while seeking to make his fortune. This story and its follow-up *Allan Quatermain* (1887), along with the novel *She* (1887), pursue narratives promulgating the theories of cultural diffusion and survival as expounded by Haggard's friend, the anthropologist and critic Andrew Lang (Malley, 1997: 275–97).

King Solomon's Mines sees Quatermain and his companions, including the dispossessed King Ignosi, penetrate into the fertile valley of Kukuanaland after crossing a desert and scaling the mountain range of Suliman Berg. Having defeated the usurper King Twala the party is taken to the legendary mines by the ancient witch Gagool, Twala's adviser. Gagool incarcerates the companions in the mines but is herself killed in the act. William J. Scheik (1991) has not unconvincingly teased out a reading of the novel as a pornographic joke in that the map that leads Quatermain and his companions on their trek forms a representation of a female body; the mountains they cross are known as Sheba's Breasts and the mine opening itself, wherein lies the treasure, is depicted as a pit within a triangular region. Scheik sees this sexual sub-text as indicative of Haggard's implicit misogyny, as the treasure-seekers' penetration of the cavern almost results in their deaths. Aggressively gendered, Haggard's Lost World version of Africa is not passively waiting to be violated; in fact it threatens to consume its male interlopers, revealing the primal male anxiety underlying the misogyny. In Scheik's analysis, the fact that Gagool and the Kukuana maiden Foulata are killed, while the men escape in a version of the birth process, reinforces this reading, with the masculine imperative reborn into a world without women, or one in which the feminine can be removed. Gagool is crushed beneath a descending stone door operated by an ancient mechanism, a particularly cumbersome representation of the vagina dentata folk myth (1991: 19–30).

In *She*, Horace Holly is tasked with the guardianship of his only friend's son, Leo. Leo's birthright, apart from outstanding good looks, is an ancient inscribed sherd and corresponding documentation, which not only identifies Leo as the descendant of Kallikrates, an Egyptian priest, and his wife Amenartas, but passes on the obligation to seek out the female killer of Kallikrates with instructions on how to find her and ultimately to attempt to slay her in revenge. Despite the fantastical elements of a story two thousand years in the making, Leo and Holly accept the quest, penetrating into the African interior to discover the lost city of Kôr, and the Amahagger people and their white queen Ayesha or *Hiya*, She-Who-Must-Be-Obeyed.

The former inhabitants of Kôr died or fled the city due to plague. The Amahagger are the devolved descendants of the survivors, and Ayesha, whether she is immortal or just long-lived, has seen civilisations crumble. She now makes her home among the mummified remains of the former inhabitants of the city. Sandra M. Gilbert and Susan Gubar have extensively analysed Ayesha as a personification of the femme fatale and the New Woman, triggering curiously ambivalent sexual and political anxiety among the patriarchy of the late Victorian era, and beyond (1989: 3–46). Among other insights, they note that, as with Quatermain and his companions in *King Solomon's Mines*, the male explorers Holly and Leo are required to penetrate a 'melodramatically sexual' landscape when they enter Kôr (1989: 15). If the mine and the city of Kôr are gendered, indeed sexualised, landscapes then it must be noted they are also corpse-like. Kôr is a literal necropolis, King Solomon's Mine being disused or dead. Consequently, any symbolic penetration becomes an act of necrophilia. Haggard's explorers in both books violate a particularly rigid taboo and should in consequence be expected to pay the price, but retribution seems to fall elsewhere, on marginalised characters like Foulata and Holly's manservant Job, and ultimately upon uncanny occult figures like Gagool and Ayesha. These casualties of empire, become disposable substitutes for Quatermain, Curtis, and Good, and Holly and Leo, who all emerge from their incarcerations symbolically reborn. This seems to be an affirmation of the triumph of reason, with those characters bound by superstition perishing, while the pragmatic rationalists survive, although notably Horace Holly emerges with his worldview expanded by his experiences.

The corpse and the body politic

The archaeological discoveries of the *fin de siècle*, and the public enthusiasm for Egyptology, fuelled an intense fascination with lost civilisations, and a corresponding literature. The reader must approach these stories mindful of the postcolonial criticism advanced by such theorists as Edward Said, and by way of Patrick Brantlinger's positing of an 'Imperial Gothic' which, as defined by James Proctor and Angela Smith, 'tends to express anxieties over the failure of religion through a fall from civilisation into barbarism and savagery' (2007: 96). Alongside the superior attitudes and nationalistic racism of Western imperialism, these narratives are able to acknowledge the inevitable fragility of empires, and a fear of individual and national degeneration to a state of undifferentiated chaos at odds with the increasing organisation that defined society's material and cultural progress. Also present is a personal confrontation with mortality, as triggered by post-Darwinian scientific and rationalist challenges to Christian theology.

H. Rider Haggard was concerned with the expansion of the British Empire, and his work has seen him pinned with the same 'Jingo Methodist' label that Sir John Marriott testily noted had been applied to Rudyard Kipling. Like his friend Kipling, Haggard 'uttered a warning against vain-glorious boasting, [and] against those who trust over-much in chariots and horses' (Marriott, 1946: 286). Kipling's poem 'Recessional' which was composed for the occasion of Queen Victoria's Diamond Jubilee in 1897 appeared ten years after the publication of Haggard's *She* and was a meditation upon hubris, and the fragility of empires when spiritual faith is replaced by a faith in might alone. While Haggard's work seems to support the notion that Martini-Henry rifles are effective against most threats encountered by the representatives of civilisation, he also suggests that, faced with the depredations of time and moral decline, there is no defence.

This was the era of Max Nordau's *Degeneration* (1892), which at its most reactionary put Darwinism into full reverse and predicted a return to a pre-Enlightenment culture typified by social and personal disintegration. While Nordau found the decadence of the *fin de siècle* to be undoing established customs and morality, it is also arguable that an attachment to the past carries its own dangers. A central dynamic in traditional eighteenth-century Gothic literature is an intrusion from the past threatening the present; secrets or sets of behaviours emerge that are shown to be at odds with an enlightened rationalist culture.

Such intrusions are out of place or out of time, *unheimlich* in Freud's ([1919] 2003) construction of the uncanny. Equally uncanny are things that overstay their welcome, institutions or individuals, reeking of the past and bedecked with the trappings of superstition, and existing beyond their usefulness. Horace Holly, reflecting upon Ayesha's 'evil tendencies' concludes that her hardened cynicism is the result of her great antiquity. He observes that 'many of us are only saved by timely death from utter moral petrification if not moral corruption' (Haggard, 1994: 232). Ayesha is also uncanny because she is an anachronism having managed to ward off death. A classic Gothic Wanderer, like the Wandering Jew, she is bound to the earth by her murder of her lover Kallikrates and the constancy of her love for him. It is hard not to find some comparison between Ayesha and Britain's own Queen Empress Victoria. Already fifty years upon the throne upon the publication of *She*, Victoria had overseen imperial ambitions that Ayesha could only dream of (243–5). While Haggard used his imperial romances to consider the fragility of empires, he was clearly concerned with the physical and spiritual survival of the individual. Brian Aldiss (1975) claims that the core of the fantasies written between 1890 and 1920 were almost entirely personal, concerned with the salvation of the hero and his immediate circle and not the planet as a whole. Aldiss identifies Haggard, and the writers who followed him, as expressing 'a common anxiety about death', and using the fantasy genre as an acknowledgement and hence a safety valve for those anxieties (1975: 154–6). John G. Moss has argued that Haggard 'was terrorised by mortality but, unlike most, he had the imagination and the ability to confront his terror and make something out of it'. (Moss, 1973: 27).

Surviving the corpse

Alexandra Warwick (2007) in her essay 'Victorian Gothic' quotes Iain Sinclair's observations on the way that the Gothic escaped from the realm of fiction and achieved an independent existence. Warwick sees Gothic permeating 'every area of Victorian life: domesticity, the family, the streets, the empire, the future' (2007: 35). Stephen D. Arata (2000) cites Patrick Brantlinger in characterising the late Victorian reading public as fascinated by primitivism and the occult, fixations registered in the contemporary literature steeped in gothicism (2000: 162). An interest in spiritualism and the survival of consciousness after death is just one aspect of this fascination, one with great pertinence for Haggard.

In his autobiography, *The Days of My Life* (1926), Haggard recalls attending séances while at Scoones crammer prior to taking the Foreign Office entrance exam. While sceptical about intervention from the spirit world, he attributes the curious events he witnessed to some ultimately 'mischievous' mental phenomena, but does not wholly rule out the potential for communion 'with other souls that have passed from us'. In his chapter 'Psychical', Haggard recounts incidences of vivid 'dream pictures', which he suggests may be memories of personal past incarnations, racial memories, or simply the subconscious workings of his writer's imagination.

In *She*, and in *Ayesha: The Return of She*, Haggard seems to be making a powerful case for alternative teachings to Christianity, especially those that foreground reincarnation. In the final chapter of his autobiography, Haggard asserts his Christian faith and explains how he reconciles his putatively divergent beliefs. While acknowledging the similarities between the teachings of the Buddha and those of Jesus Christ, he expresses the view that Buddhism is 'a religion of Death, holding up cessation of mundane lives and ultimate extinction as the great reward of virtue', while Christianity offers eternal life (2014: ch. 23). Haggard has no wish to live again on the surface of the earth but 'like the Buddhists, I am strongly inclined to believe that the Personality which animates each of us is immeasurably ancient, having been forged in so many fires, and that, as its past is immeasurable, so will its future be' (2014: ch. 23). Impossible as it is to imagine the complete extinction of consciousness after death, Haggard asserts 'the almost universal instinct of mankind was to believe that death is but a gate of other forms of continued and individual Life'. Faced with the concept of a personal existence ruled by 'blind, black, brutal chance' and ultimately 'full-stopped with doom', he challenges the 'impenetrable darkness', and attempts to offer an alternative (Haggard, 2014: ch. 23).

The tragic death of the hero's son at the outset of *Allan Quatermain* (1987) instigates a deal of soul-searching. Quatermain is already a widower, and his friends and fellow mourners Curtis and Good propose a final expedition. Brian Aldiss has located the fantasy writing of the late nineteenth and early twentieth-century in 'its embodiment of a wish to escape from claustrophobic urban culture' (1975: 154). Quatermain has tired of the material comfort that the plundering of *King Solomon's*

Mines brought him, along with 'this prim English country, with its trim hedgerows and cultivated fields, its stiff formal manners, and its well-dressed crowds' (Haggard, 1955: 22).

Kelly Hurley (2001: 142–3) posits that the active embrace of barbarism, in combination with the escape from ennui, causes the narrator-hero to turn his back upon the debilitating influence of modern living and take his chances among the noble savages of the wilderness rather than the degenerate savages of metropolitan de-evolution. Allan Quatermain sees contemporary civilisation as 'only savagery silver-gilt' and, due to fall in its turn as did those in Egypt, Greece, and Rome. His philosophical world-weariness already sees little distinction between 'savage' and civilised man. Haggard shared these views with anthropologist Andrew Lang, who wrote, 'let civilisation die decently as die it must' (Haggard, 2014: ch. 10). The flight to a lost world from the conformity of modern society, even if it embraces the threat of extinction at the hands of death-dealing cannibals and priests of the occult, may be seen as an attempt to escape the entropy endemic in contemporary civilisation.

Allan Quatermain lacks the invention and ambiguity of *King Solomon's Mines* and *She*, and is interesting principally for killing off the eponymous hero. In an adventure that reads as a classic bit of colonial fiction, Quatermain, Curtis, and their companions Captain Good and the Zulu chieftain Umslopogaas discover the Zu-Vendi, a lost white race in the African interior, an act that accidentally initiates a civil war and involves their taking sides in the ensuing slaughter. Quatermain and Umslopogaas are able to choose the nature of their deaths, dying decently and with dignity after making a good account of themselves in battle. Quatermain has become disillusioned with society, and muses on his deathbed, 'How can a world be good in which Money is the moving power, and Self-Interest the guiding star?' (Haggard, 1955: 308).

Curtis, as King-Consort of Zu-Vendis, closes the only channel of communication with the outside world, to preserve the country's 'blessings of comparative barbarism' from 'gunpowder, telegraphs, steam, daily newspapers, universal suffrage' and 'speculators, tourists, politicians and teachers' (1955: 314–15). Curtis also hopes to unite the clans under a single central government, to put an end to civil war, and to sap the power of the priesthood to end their political interference and 'pave the road for the introduction of true religion' (1955: 314). Curtis has a selective approach to progress, viewing a future where some form of benevolent despotism combines with Christianity, in a society frozen in 'comparative barbarism', as preferable to the other dubious benefits of civilisation. The Gothic barbarity encountered in Zu-Vendis proves, with some modifications, entirely congenial to the Victorian empire-builder.

The corpse writes back

The ability to overcome death, through unnatural acts or occult pacts, is a characteristic of the Gothic 'Others' encountered by the heroes of these Victorian narratives. While Haggard's heroes travel to lost worlds where natural laws are not upheld, Victorian England is threatened by representatives of Gothic cultures who manage to bypass those same natural laws. Bram Stoker's *Dracula* (1897) and Richard Marsh's *The Beetle* (1897) both conjure threats from uncanny regions – Dracula from Transylvania and the sexually polymorphous Beetle from an Orientalist Sudan. *Dracula* and *The Beetle* are examples of the reverse colonisation narrative that Stephen D. Arata has posited as 'the period's most important and pervasive narrative of decline', whereby the nation's moral and spiritual stagnation renders it 'vulnerable to attack from more vigorous, "primitive" peoples' (2000: 162). Reverse colonisation imagines the victims of colonial oppression or their avatars wreaking havoc upon their degenerate former masters, and is just one aspect of a complex relationship established between England, as the representative of Eurocentric civilisation, and the foreign land or lost world, as the repository of all that is primitive and base.

H. Rider Haggard's writing is generally read as typical of Imperial Gothic where, as James Proctor and Angela Smith suggest, 'the colonised culture is given Gothic treatment as being itself the source of barbarism, temptation and horror' (2007: 96). In *She*, Haggard's heroes encounter the Amahagger, who are ultimately revealed to be a tribe of cannibals. Patrick Brantlinger has indicated that in the mid-nineteenth century, reports of cannibalism, which evidenced the barbarity and evolutionary inferiority of the African races, were used as part of the process to legitimise imperialism (1985: 84). Barri J. Gold suggests an alternative view of the Amahagger people; unfettered by the Gothic morbidity of the Englishmen, they are comfortable with the abject, recycling everything from funeral urns to drinking vessels, shrouds to clothing, corpses to candles and, unfortunately, living human beings to food (1995: 306). Despite his demonising of the Amahagger, Haggard glimpsed the savage beneath the skin of the civilised man. He regarded civilisation itself as a veneer and human nature as unmalleable. More pragmatically, Haggard viewed man's basic savagery as the essential part of his nature upon which he depended in an emergency, especially when faced with his own death (1955: 24).

The corpse as carnival

The document discovered in James De Mille's *A Strange Manuscript Found in a Copper Cylinder* (1888) is both a reference to Poe's *Ms. Found in a Bottle* (1833) and the basis for the novel's framing narrative. De Mille's story is worthy of critical attention as an early example of metafiction, replete with the staples of Lost World fiction, which it parodies to comment satirically upon Victorian society, its carnivalesque presentation subverting a genre that had barely become established. Its treatment of death provides a context and counterpoint to the work of Rider Haggard.

In February 1850, Lord Featherstone, his intimate friend Oxenden, and their friends Dr Congreve and Melick lie becalmed between the Canary and Madeira Islands in Featherstone's yacht *Falcon*, when they discover a copper cylinder containing a manuscript adrift in the ocean. The document comes from the hand of Adam More, the first mate on the ship *Trevelyan*, and purports to recount the strange adventures that befell the ship and crew after becoming lost in the seas surrounding the Antarctic. The four friends take it in turn to read the account, and comment learnedly upon the contents whilst arguing about its authenticity.

More encounters a degenerate race of cannibals, before escaping into the land of the Kosekin, a more advanced race that build cities and tame a variety of prehistoric creatures for husbandry and transport, but who also prove to practice human sacrifice and cannibalism in a ceremony known as the *Mista Kosek*. In discussion with their head man, the Kohen, More discovers that the Kosekin love the dark and hate the light, and worship and embrace death. The Kosekin also attempt to rid themselves of possessions and the trappings of rank, as poverty affords high status within their society; the Kohen's standing is a burden to him and he, like his fellows, craves death, as More discovers:

> For it must never be forgotten that the Kosekin love death as we love life, and this accounts for all those ceremonies which to me were so abhorrent, especially the scenes of the *Mista Kosek*. To them a dead human body is no more than the body

of a bird: there is no awe felt, no sense of sanctity, of superstitious horror, and so I learnt, with a shudder, that the hate of life is a far worse thing than the fear of death. (De Mille, 2011: 103–4)

Death for the Kosekin carries no sense of abjection; but the Kohen suggests to More that in some ways Kosekin society is not so very different from his own. Hypocritical Victorian society glorifies the imperial adventures that result in wholesale slaughter:

> Have you not told me incredible things about your people, among which there were a few that seemed natural and intelligible? Among these was your system of honouring above all men those who procure the death of the largest number. You, with your pretended fear of death, wish to meet it in battle as eagerly as do we, and your most renowned men are those who have sent most to death. (De Mille, 2011: 119)

More escapes being the victim in a ceremony of human sacrifice by shooting the chief priests. His ability to dispense instant death by means of his firearms sees him worshipped by the Kosekin, and he and his love interest Almah further elevate themselves in Kosekin society by the onerous sacrifice of accepting the riches of others, allowing the donors to attain their ambition of poverty. More ultimately conquers by assimilating the Kosekin philosophy and turning it to his own advantage. His cultural background, and the eagerness for battle noted by the Kohen, allows him finally to 'rule by terror – to seize, to slay, to conquer', and yet the death drive manifested by the Kosekin renders this a mutually acceptable compromise (De Mille, 2011: 29). De Mille's satire is located to an obvious Gothic space, better to imagine an inversion of values that highlights the hypocrisy of Victorian society while More's triumph establishes a cultural resonance between Victorian imperialism and the lost world of the Kosekin, with the trade in death being a grim but common currency.

The corpse as conundrum

In his influential essay on *The Uncanny*, Freud ([1919] 2003) notes that, for many, death is a primary source of the sensation of the uncanny. He was reluctant to deal with it from the outset, however, 'because here the uncanny is too much mixed up with the gruesome' ([1919] 2003: 148). Julia Kristeva identifies the source of this reluctance: 'The corpse, seen without God and outside of science, is the utmost of abjection. It is death infecting life' (1982: 4).

In *Beyond the Pleasure Principle* ([1920] 1922) Freud defines the 'death drive' as the action of the ego in impelling the organism to the quietus of death, as a means of resolving the tensions implicit in the fact of existence. He also notes that the organism will resist danger, and practice self-preservation, in order to secure a death of its own choosing (V: 7–9). Allan Quatermain has his own interpretation of this in *King Solomon's Mine*. In his view, 'The Almighty gave us our lives, and I suppose He meant us to defend them; at least I have always acted on that' (Haggard, 1979: 14). In his own book-length meditation on Freud's work, also entitled *The Uncanny*, Nicholas Royle (2004) devotes a chapter to 'the death drive' and identifies the association between this concept and 'the figure of a woman'. Citing Elisabeth Bronfen, Royle establishes woman's connection with death through the simple 'fact' of their shared uncanniness (Royle, 2004: 87). In 'The theme of the three caskets' ([1913] 1953–73), Freud also identifies the death drive with the feminine, and specifically with feminine beauty, by charting a transposition between the Goddess of Death (Atropos) and the Goddess of Love (Aphrodite). Freud claims that the Mother-goddesses of the ancient world 'all seem to have been both creators and destroyers – both goddesses of life and fertility and goddesses of death' ([1913] 1953–73: 295). Freud further identifies 'the three inevitable relations that a man has with a woman' in her capacity as mother, as mate, and as destroyer – or as mother, mother-substitute, and the Mother Earth that receives his corpse (300).

On his first encounter with Ayesha in *She*, Horace Holly feels he is 'in the presence of something that was not canny'. Ayesha's robes make her appear like 'a corpse in its grave-clothes', but, paradoxically, 'one could distinctly see the gleam of the pink flesh beneath them' (Haggard, 1994: 140). Ayesha, herself a Queen of the Underworld, combines the potential for life and death, and inspires love and fear in equal measure; if she at times appears fickle and unfathomable then the male characters display conflicting emotions too. Billali, Ayesha's *aide-de-camp*, quotes a 'proverb' to express his wariness: 'as for women, flee from them, for they are evil, and in the end will destroy thee' (1994: 110). He later explains the Amahagger's 'worship' of their womenfolk to Holly, saying 'without them the world could not go on; they are the source of life', a matter that had not struck Holly before (1994: 113–14).

Afterlife?

Just as the traditional Gothic of the eighteenth century seems freighted with a dark nostalgia for the superstitious extremes of a medieval past, even as it charted its distance from an enlightened present, so Haggard's fictional adventurers would seem to yearn for a wholesome barbarism, divorced from the complications of modernity, against which to pit their strength and wits. In fact, the Gothic Africa, and later Tibet, conjured by Haggard, is full of the ambiguity and ambivalence that defines the genre itself. Haggard's Gothic spaces both threaten death and offer a means to defeat it.

Ayesha's apparent demise at the end of *She* and her rapidly ageing transformation into something 'no larger than a big monkey, and hideous' seem to stress that natural laws may not be flouted by occult practice, and that death cannot be cheated (Haggard, 1994: 279–80). Ayesha's return, however, and the increasing mysticism on display in *Ayesha: The Return of She*, suggest that Haggard is attempting to reconcile his Christian belief in an afterlife with his assimilation of the divergent spiritual practices he has encountered on his travels.

Haggard's two great fictional heroes, Horace Holly and Allan Quatermain, are vessels for two different philosophical approaches. Both embark upon expeditions that ultimately become explorations of what Shakespeare astutely describes as 'The undiscovered country, from whose bourn / No traveller returns' (*Hamlet*, III.i line 86–7). Holly, an open-minded academic, has his worldview expanded by his uncanny encounter; Quatermain, pragmatic and down to earth, manages to maintain his beliefs intact.

The introduction to *Ayesha: The Return of She*, suggests that Horace Holly is reunited with Leo and Ayesha in the next world, or on another plane of existence, following an uncanny ceremony replete with hermetic trappings, a pagan stone circle, and an invocation to Isis (Haggard, 1978: 6–9). The manner of Holly's passing would seem to endorse some acceptance of occult belief counter to Christian theology, although Holly has not sought to extend his earthly existence by occult means. Holly's final acceptance of Ayesha's powers have caused him to believe that Ayesha will appear when he is about to die, and be his guide to the next life (333–5). Holly also appears to have found some philosophical compromise whereby he can reconcile his beliefs, when he considers the nature of Ayesha, 'ensouled alone, redeemable only by Humanity and its piteous sacrifice' (4).

This statement seems to hark back to the Christian concept of salvation.

Allan Quatermain, who has experienced equally strange adventures, has a more orthodox leave-taking and embraces a conventionally Christian concept of the afterlife, as his parting words to his expedition partners Sir Henry Curtis and Captain Good express: "'I am going on a stranger journey than any we have taken together. Think of me sometimes," he murmured. "God bless you all. I shall wait for you'" (Haggard, 1955: 311). Haggard's explorers encounter death in Gothic locations, and are offered the opportunity of some kind of immortality. The occult path to immortality, through the promise of reincarnation, while apparently efficacious, is shown potentially to bring tragedy and destruction. Immortality, as Haggard's works repeatedly suggest, is perhaps best enshrined in memory and deed.

References

Aldiss, B. (1975) *Billion Year Spree: The History of Science Fiction* (London: Corgi Books).

Arata, S. D. (2000) 'The occidental tourist: *Dracula* and the anxiety of reverse colonisation', in K. Gelder (ed.), *The Horror Reader* (Abingdon: Routledge), pp. 161–71.

Brantlinger, P. (1985) 'Victorians and Africans: the genealogy of the myth of the dark continent', *Critical Inquiry*, 12.1: 166–203.

De Mille, J. (2011) *A Strange Manuscript Found in a Copper Cylinder* (Richmond: One World Classics).

Freud, S. (2003) *The Uncanny* [1919], trans. D. McLintock (London: Penguin Books).

Freud, S. (1953–73) 'The theme of the three caskets', in *The Standard Edition of the Complete Psychological Works of Sigmund Freud, Volume XII (1911–13)*, trans. James Strachey (London: Hogarth Press and the Institute of Psycho-Analysis), pp. 289–302.

Freud, S. (1922) *Beyond the Pleasure Principle* [1920], trans. C. J. M. Hubback, (London and Vienna: International Psycho-Analytical).

Gold, B. J. (1995) 'Embracing the corpse: discursive recycling in H. Rider Haggard's *She*', *English Literature in Transition, 1880–1920*, 38.3: 305–27.

Gilbert S. M. and S. Gubar (1989) *No Man's Land 2: Sexchanges* (New Haven, CT, and London: Yale University Press).

Haggard, H. R. (2014) *The Days of My Life: An Autobiography* [1826], ed. C. J. Longman (Adelaide: The University of Adelaide).

Haggard, H. R. (1994) *She* [1887] (London: Penguin Modern Classics).

Haggard, H. R. (1979) *King Solomon's Mines* [1885] (London: Octopus Books).

Haggard, H. R. (1978) *Ayesha: The Return of She* [1905] (New York: Ballantine).

Haggard, H. R. (1955) *Allan Quatermain* [1887] (London: Collins).

Hurley, K. (2001) 'The Modernist Abominations of William Hope Hodgson', in A. Smith and J. Wallace (eds), *Gothic Modernisms* (Basingstoke: Palgrave), pp. 129–49.

Kristeva, J. (1982) *Powers of Horror: An Essay on Abjection*, trans. L. S. Roudiez (Ithaca, NY: Columbia University Press).

Malley, S. (1997) '"Time hath no power against Identity": historical continuity and archaeological adventure in Rider Haggard's *She*', *English Literature in Transition, 1880–1920*, 40.3: 275–97.

Marriott, J. (1946) *English History in English Fiction* (London: Blackie and Son).

Moss, J. G. (1973) 'Three motifs in Haggard's *She*', *English Literature in Transition, 1880–1920*, 16.1: 27–34.

Proctor, J. and A. Smith (2007) 'Gothic and empire', in C. Spooner and E. McEvoy (eds), *Gothic* (Abingdon: Routledge), pp. 95–104.

Royle, N. (2004) *The Uncanny* (Manchester: Manchester University Press).

Scheik, W. J. (1991) 'Adolescent pornography and imperialism in Haggard's *King Solomon's Mines*', *English Literature in Transition, 1880–1920*, 34.1: 19–30.

Shakespeare, W. (1909–14) *Hamlet* [c. 1600], ed. C. W. Eliot (New York: P. F. Collier and Son).

Shelley, M. (2008) *Frankenstein: or The Modern Prometheus, the 1818 Text* (Oxford: Oxford University Press).

Warwick, A. (2007) 'Victorian Gothic', in C. Spooner and E. McEvoy (eds), *The Routledge Companion to Gothic* (Abingdon: Routledge), pp. 29–37.

9

Matthew Pangborn

Dead again: zombies and the spectre of cultural decline

When Prince Conrad 'was dashed to pieces, and almost buried under an enormous helmet, an hundred times more large than any casque for human being, and shaded with a proportionable quantity of black feathers' in Horace Walpole's *The Castle of Otranto* (1764), readers of the Gothic were presented with a rather peculiar view of death ([1764] 2003: 74). Neither simple fact of human mortality nor opportunity for the *memento mori* lessons of *vanitas* painting and *carpe diem* poetry, death in the Gothic is presented as overwhelming spectacle, always gesturing toward some larger import than one individual's end. Indeed, the dependability with which death appears in the Gothic as an all-enveloping power, and the spread of this mood to texts more invested in communicating sense than stoking sensation, suggests we think of the Gothic less as a tightly constrained fictional genre and more as a medium through which death is conceptualised as looming over society as a whole. Only, two questions arise: What exactly is this 'death' the Gothic wants to bring to the reader's attention? And, given the otherwise bold extravagance of its language, why can it not name its topic outright?

Mary Wollstonecraft's *A Vindication of the Rights of Men* (1790), for example, while a political tract that critiques Edmund Burke's condemnation of the revolution across the Channel, also identifies a deathliness in its opponent's outlook:

> Man preys on man; and you mourn for the idle tapestry that decorated a gothic pile, and the dronish bell that summoned the fat priest to prayer. You mourn for the empty pageant of a name, when slavery flaps her wing, and the sick heart

retires to die in lonely wilds, far from the abodes of men. Did the pangs you felt for insulted nobility, the anguish that rent your heart when the gorgeous robes were torn off the idol human weakness had set up, deserve to be compared with the long-drawn sigh of melancholy reflection, when misery and vice are thus seen to haunt our steps, and swim on the top of every cheering prospect? Why is our fancy to be appalled by terrific perspectives of a hell beyond the grave? – Hell stalks abroad. ([1790] 1997: 95)

Certainly one death facing society in the passage is that of the Old World of the nobility with which the writer accuses Burke of allying himself. Yet Wollstonecraft enlists such Gothic themes as savagery, superstition, mourning, revenge, luxury, vice, murder, and hell to argue that even though the nobility is 'dead', it is still 'preying' on others. Burke notably identifies his opponents with the cannibalistic undead in *Reflections on the Revolution in France* (1790), the work to which Wollstonecraft is responding. His prophecy of a French regicide paints the revolutionaries' 'cannibal appetites' hardly 'gorged' as they 'hack that aged parent in pieces, and put him into the kettle of magicians, in hopes that by their poisonous weeds, and wild incantations, they may regenerate the paternal constitution, and renovate their father's life' ([1790] 2004: 249, 194). Leaving to one side the rhetorical purposes of the writers' flourishes, as it is not my aim to rehash their debate, what is striking is that both agree the defining moment of their era is one in which the dead threaten to consume the living.

One could dismiss this coincidence as a quirk of the era, except that both writers' images precisely reflect a current resurgence of the Gothic in the form of the zombie. Indeed, not just Wollstonecraft's imagery but also her repeated use of the epithet 'Gothic' in both *Vindications* parallels German social theorist Ulrich Beck's employment of the term 'zombie' to designate the startling persistence in the present day of outdated concepts from the past (Beck and Beck-Gernsheim, 2001: 202–13). According to Beck, people now cling to notions such as that of the family even though it clashes with the extreme individualism required by a hyper-mobile post-modernity; similarly, Wollstonecraft uses the term 'Gothic' to charge Burke with clinging to an aristocracy that makes no sense in a more modern era of republicanism. What is thus perhaps most remarkable about the language Wollstonecraft and Burke use is not their agreement about a strange diagnosis of their time but the utter familiarity of that diagnosis in our own. As in late-eighteenth-century England, the Gothic today has not confined itself to fictional genres but has spilled over into other modes of writing, with commentary on economics especially overrun not just by zombies but also by 'ghostburbs' and 'vampire squids'.[1] If, as I will argue, the Gothic is currently undergoing a rebirth thanks to the figure of the zombie, scrutinising the language that links the two periods at opposite ends of modernity helps us to identify the outdated ideas whose unaccountable persistence makes the death the Gothic evokes appear so all-powerful and overwhelming.[2]

A death more than death

One death imagined by both Burke and Wollstonecraft through their Gothic imagery is the disappearance of the quality each deems essential to human civilisation: for Wollstonecraft, the sympathy permitting people to share in another's misery and thus seek not to cause it, is already waning through cruel practices such as slavery; for Burke, the revolution is only one more example of theorists flouting the guiding force of custom like so many disobedient children. For each writer, too, the quality described as being at risk is distinctly modern, as its loss triggers the fall into a regressive history: in Wollstonecraft's excerpt, a fall conceived as a return to a superstitious Dark Age, and in Burke's, as the necromancy of classical Greek legend. The Gothic in Wollstonecraft's and Burke's texts thus functions to combine at least three effects of the decline their culture faces: one, the reversal of the modern conception of time as inevitably progressive, an assurance articulated, for example, in Immanuel Kant's definition of the Enlightenment as 'man's emergence from his self-imposed immaturity' ([1784] 1996: 58); two, the erosion of an essential psychological characteristic that separates Westerners from non-moderns, or 'cannibals'; and, three, its strange sparking in the minds of its contemplators a dramatic reframing of a rather theoretical political discussion in terms of an anonymous, distanced, and tortured body.

In pairing a concern for social stability with an imagistic emphasis on bodily violence, Wollstonecraft and Burke are hardly alone among eighteenth-century thinkers. Writing on recurring images of the body during that supposed era of the mind, Daniel Cottom remarks on the prevalence of the cannibal in historic reflections on society, suggesting 'cannibalism is commonly termed unthinkable' during the eighteenth century 'only because it is all too thinkable, all too compelling, as an image for the fundamental nature of social life' (2001: 150). Certainly abolitionists' arguments that the use of sugar grown on slave plantations was equivalent to drinking human blood, support the identification of the new global market with cannibalism.[3] Burke's image of rebellious children cooking their parents shows how close to the surface of the collective psyche is this idea of consumption, as the retributive justice imagined for the exploited 'body' of the masses is the consumption of its exploiters. The vengeance of such a body also appears in Walpole's *The Castle of Otranto* in the form of the return of a repressed disproportionality threatening the gentle observer, a helmet so big it might crush a prince, and legs so hulking they could trample a castle. This commonality of concern should not be surprising. In the 1790s, despite recent developments such as James Watt's steam engine, economic growth in Europe – the progress assumed distinctive of the modern West in proclamations such as Kant's – still depended on muscle power. The shared insight of Burke, Wollstonecraft, and Walpole is that they identify their culture's tenuous relationship, if only obliquely, with the body and its all-important motive force as potentially causative of crises that could end a period of booming productivity however much it might already be taken for granted as part of the West's natural superiority over savage Others.

Yet if Wollstonecraft and Burke alert their readers to the possible reversal of the narrative of progress through the loss of those all-important labourers by way of oppression or revolution, the fantastic language of the writers has at least one other function: self-sabotage. By damning the revolutionaries as dabbling in black magic, Burke relegates them to bogeymen in a children's tale. Similarly, although Wollstonecraft provides an example of sympathy's failure, she adds wings to the figure of slavery, making it into just another monster. Both writers thus undercut their own warnings rather than countenance fully the crises they have only begun to imagine. In fact, one might say this is the purpose of their use of the Gothic: to balance their audience precariously between a breakdown that seems unthinkable (perhaps because, following Cottom's logic, revolution makes it seem just around the corner) and a rejection of that same possibility as only fantasy.[4] It is precisely this space that the zombie has become so adept at inhabiting.

Raising the dead

Dead yet somehow living, unthinking yet intently focused on gobbling up that one substance Westerners are prohibited by taboo from considering food, the zombie is ideal for articulating self-contradiction. As such, it is the perfect figure with which our own time might confront a seemingly long-ago conquered fear, risen again to threaten our future. The discovery of other resources than muscle power, petroleum in particular, bore out Wollstonecraft's and Burke's confidence in the West's ability to dodge the fall they feared. Agricultural application of petrochemicals has allowed world population to soar. Today, oil supplies 95 per cent of the world's transportation, 95 per cent of its packaging, and 95 per cent of its food production and distribution; in food production and distribution alone, the average American 'eats' 400 gallons of oil per year (Urry, 2013: 1, 6–7, 50). The problem is the rate of cheap conventional extraction has peaked: in 1970, in the United States, and in 2005, globally. After those dates lie increasing costs of extraction that cannot be borne by oil consumers, no matter how low prices drop – and, eventually, these higher costs mean greater scarcity in those goods and services based on oil (Urry, 2013: 17–18, 100). As a power rising from the ground, today's zombie stands not just for that ancient, active 'dead' matter of petroleum; it also represents an earth whose very materiality, its having physical limits, makes it appear to believers in an inevitable human progress as a vengeful body whose greatest talent lies, as astrophysicist and science populariser Neil deGrasse Tyson has rather gothically opined, in the many ways it has of 'killing us' (2008). It is in this context of a threat to limitless growth that eighteenth-century images of a vengeful dead body have been resurrected in the work of George A. Romero.

Although the zombie may be found in earlier Hollywood films than Romero's seminal *Night of the Living Dead* (1968), in these movies – *White Zombie* (1932) and *I Walked with a Zombie* (1943), to name two of the better known – the figure belongs to the exotic ethnography of the Caribbean, and reflects little about American culture except its fascination with empire and discomfort with the legacy of slavery. With Romero's film, however, the zombie arrives freighted with the very pressing issues of the American present.[5] *Night of the Living Dead* was released twelve years after Shell geologist M. King Hubbert presented his famous paper predicting US peak oil production, and only two years before that peak arrived. It was filmed seventy miles away from the first major oil well drilled in the United States, in Titusville, Pennsylvania. And the film's plot reflects the consequences of the falling arc of oil production for American society. Beginning with a young brother and sister's car trip to their father's grave, the film opens with a sense of loss of some guarantee of stable societal order. As the young woman finds shelter with strangers in an abandoned farmhouse, this disorder only further degenerates into racially and generationally motivated factions that recall Abraham Lincoln's characterisation of the nation as a 'house divided'. Predictably, the group's hopes for escape revolve around finding a vehicle and enough gasoline to outrun the spectres of pre-Enlightenment cannibalism outside, who represent a past that should have been killed off by modernity's petroleum-fuelled triumph over natural limitations.[6]

One common concern that surely links the early Gothic's treatment of death with the contemporary zombie is the possibility that the cultured Westerner might be 'bitten back' by what she or he is consuming.[7] What stands to bite back the contemporary consumer of oil is a return of the dead past of pre-modernity with that substance's decline. Appropriately, resource scarcity is a common feature of films and television shows made in the mould of *Night of the Living Dead*. Yet, if the zombie is thus, as Sarah Juliet Lauro identifies it, 'inherently an ecological avenger', resource scarcity often functions to spotlight the brutality of humans against humans (2011: 235).[8] While the zombie is just as useful as the vampire for expressing, as Margot Adler puts it, how 'we are sucking the lifeblood out of the planet', this brain-dead figure is more pessimistic about our chances of surviving not only the planet's revenge but also our own murderous competition over the remainders (2014: 37). Moreover, if, as Nina Auerbach recognises about the figure of the vampire, they 'go where power is', the zombie differs from the vampire mainly in that its act of going to power follows after a human future has been graphically decided through apocalypse (1995: 6). The zombie's insightful reflection of contemporary society thus lies in its essential characteristic of a violent consumption that occurs past the point when it might gain any lasting benefit from what it devours, and when humanity should know better.[9] Zombie films and television shows thus demonstrate that if the mantra that motivates a modern Westerner is Kant's Enlightenment maxim 'Dare to know', then the contemporary West has an astonishingly zombie-like way of being able to act in ignorance of what it knows only too well.

How can you kill what is already dead?

Just as the supernatural nature of the cannibals figured by Burke and Wollstonecraft serves to undercut their warnings of cultural collapse, however, so too does the zombie reveal a desire to escape the problems confronted in its self-destructive consumption. In *American Zombie Gothic* (2010), Kyle William Bishop notes five 'peaks' at which the production of zombie horror films reaches a high point before falling off again. Three of them – 1973, 1979, and 2006 – mark peaks for serious horror films, and two of them – 1988 and 2010 – peaks for 'parodic' works, in which fears of looming apocalypse are treated as cause for zombie comedy, or 'zombedy' (Bishop, 2010: 14–15, 205). Comparing these dates against American and global oil production and consumption, one notices that the peaks of 'serious' zombie films coincide with oil shocks – the two OPEC embargoes of the 1970s, and the world conventional oil peak in 2005 – while the peak periods for zombie parody occurred when oil production made a recovery in the 1980s after successful drilling in areas such as Alaska's North Slope and the North Sea, and in the late 2000s through the practice known as 'fracking'.

The threat embodied by those creatures referred to in the television series *The Walking Dead* (AMC) as 'walkers' thus appears tied to the ready supply of cheap gasoline: when that supply is great, zombies are comedic figures; but when that supply dips, zombies again confront audience members with the terrifying prospect of finding their own alternate means of transportation. But even when the crisis might appear pressing, the zombie still allows the contemporary viewer the same opportunity to dismiss its nightmares that the Gothic offers to the readers of Wollstonecraft and Burke. *Night of the Living Dead*, for all of its grim depiction of real crisis, for example, still depends upon a rather far-fetched plot. And for every crowd of shuffling, car-less monsters in such films, there is always at least one survivor who enjoys a power and plenty proportionate to the death around him. Indeed, the genre's persistent flirtation with a celebration as well as a condemnation of the hyper-consumerism available in films such as Romero's *Dawn of the Dead* (1978), in which self-preserving survivors take shelter in a shopping mall and gorge themselves on its contents, has led Jennifer Proffitt and Rich Templin to equate the 'zombie apocalypse' with a 'libertarian paradise' (2013: 29–44). If the zombie serves as a substitute for oil itself, that ancient dead stuff given so much new life by modern know-how, it is significant that every work ruminates on its depletion through the imagining of deluge.

If the zombie genre evokes a crisis of resource depletion, it thus also serves to distance viewers from a decline already apparent in places like now-bankrupt Detroit, one-time global automobile-producing capital, where plans for a zombie theme park to rejuvenate the city's economy have stalled due to lack of funds.[10] While the zombie raises the spectre of an almost unimaginable horror (unimaginable, again following the logic of Cottom, because the utopian promise of the modern world has so often broken down into its hellish Other), what the zombie offers is comfort to a viewer who is able to identify its warnings with fantasy. The zombie thus demonstrates a conflicted desire to warn of an end to the model of limitless growth underlying Western modernity while yet preserving a narrative of progress. The final line of the Brad Pitt vehicle *World War Z* (2013) is instructive in the way it expresses this contradiction, as the fearful possibility of a reversal of American history back to an earlier period of world war is presented as an opportunity for yet another Greatest Generation of heroic individualists, for whom 'Our war has just begun'.

Dead beings on a dead planet

The zombie thus represents, as the undead did for Burke and Wollstonecraft, an almost unimaginable spectre of cultural decline. Indeed, the spectacular carnage involved with that event's imagining might even be read as distracting the audience from viewing decline as a realistic possibility. But if the figure shows such consistency across the centuries, it must be due to the zombie's expressing something essential about the thinking that links both eras, something even more terrifying than the loss of confidence in that progress that is supposed to define the modern West. The philosophical figure of the cannibal expressed anxiety about the age long before Wollstonecraft and Burke employed it, which is perhaps why they identify it as dead, something that should have long ago been laid to rest. In films such as *Night of the Living Dead*, too, the zombie is reliably depicted as that Other of modernity born out of modernity's greatest technological triumphs: it is, notably, the re-entry into the Earth's atmosphere of an irradiated NASA space probe that triggers the 'ghouls'' rise. What this consistency suggests is that, true to its form as walking contradiction, the zombie explores a 'primitiveness' not opposing the modern but one brought about *through* modernity.[11] Returning to Beck's use of the term (Beck and Beck-Gernsheim, 2001), one might even identify the zombie's savagery as connected to a specific idea – a link supported by every film and television zombie's vulnerability only to trauma to the brain – an idea that persists though it is no longer useful, and one that is familiar to every Gothic work: the notion that the human individual might be conceived as the isolated exception to his or her environment, the only real, self-assertive adult in a world Kant must assume is otherwise immature, undeveloped, unconscious – the sole living creature in a world full of, well, death.

As the social scientist and cyberneticist Gregory Bateson points out, 'the unit of survival is *organism* plus *environment*' (author's emphasis) because 'the organism that destroys its environment destroys itself' (Urry, 2013: 228). And yet, as the Indian environmental and political activist Vandana Shiva writes, the representative modern concept from Bacon and Descartes onwards is of the Earth as a 'Terra Nullius', an empty, 'dead' space inviting conquest by that same figure Kant describes as self-reliant, independent, and alone (Shiva, 2012). If zombies appear human but lack a certain human quality, a *je ne sais quoi*, therefore, it is only because modern humans in their relentless, blind consumption also seem to lack something.[12] What the modern human seems to lack is the awareness that it is a self-destructive absurdity if it assumes itself independent from the many systems necessary for its life. Perhaps this is the true cause of Wollstonecraft's and Burke's panic – not merely the revolution, but the light the crisis shines on themselves and their readers who seem to have no common characteristic except the imperative – call it duty or sympathy – that they identify and take responsibility for something or someone beyond themselves. This self-reflection is certainly at the heart of the panic in zombie works, as each involves the need to deny that nagging suspicion that an extractive, exploitative relationship with the world only brings ruin.

In almost every zombie work, a moment of separation is staged between a character and a loved one who has been infected, whose identity has been demonstrably shaped by forces beyond the boundaries of the skin.[13] In Romero's *Dawn of the Dead*, one such moment comes as Roger, bitten by one of the ghouls and thus fated to change into one himself, appeals to his good friend Peter:

Roger: You'll take care of me, won't you, Peter? I mean, you'll take care of me when I go.

Peter: Just try to get some sleep, man. Save your strength.

Roger: I don't want to be walkin' around – like that! Peter – Peter?

Peter: Yeah, I'm here, man!

Roger: Don't do it until you are sure I *am* coming back. I'm gonna try – not to – I'm gonna try – not to – come back. I'm gonna try – not to ...

The setting of a shopping mall in which they have been holed up for months, surrounded by ghouls, gives Roger resolve to fight whatever 'instinct' or 'memory' that compels the undead to Remain Calm and Shop On, a special poignancy. We know, in other words, his stance is the very definition of the lost cause. The moment is framed in close-up, which only intensifies its gloom, given the action-film genre's unspoken rules of restraint from affection between men. Yet what is Roger doing except pulling his friend closer, through those very bonds of sympathy and duty Wollstonecraft and Burke tell us are the essential human traits? And what is Peter's response, in ignoring Roger's loaded plea to 'take care of' him and in refraining from using his friend's name even as Roger calls on him three times – like some perverse echo of the apostle's denial of Christ – except pushing away his own vital emotional investment in the other man? This abstract self-distancing is the zombie's primal scene.

The image of modern humans with which we are left by our consideration of the zombie – and the Gothic – is thus much different than Kant's young adult confidently snatching the keys to the car that will take him far away from the natural limits of earth. It better resembles that image provided by contemporary news reports struggling to make sense of a humanity that keeps on going despite peaks in vital resources and a climate that will take decades to react fully to the pollution still being pumped into the atmosphere. In such stories, modern humans appear walking self-contradictions. They are present yet removed, sociable yet alone, rational yet homicidal. After spending so long imagining an escape from a world viewed as somehow separate from and insufficient for the self, modern humanity is finally confronted with the idea that such self-isolation and abstraction has profoundly self-destructive consequences. Fittingly, it is a similar lesson Walpole advances at the end of *The Castle of Otranto* when his hero Theodore takes possession of a tremendous power that has killed his lover and levelled his castle, leaving him only with a 'melancholy that had taken possession of his soul' ([1764] 2003: 165). Powerful but without love and a home, surrounded only by dead objects, what is he but an animate corpse?

Notes

1 Margot Adler similarly notes that the economic crisis of 2008 sparked references to vampires in Wall Street reporting (2014: 21). 'Ghostburbs' refers to suburbs abandoned after that crisis (Urry, 2013: 34). Matt Taibbi's phrase 'vampire squid' refers to Goldman Sachs' manipulation of the stock market (2010).

2 Jennifer Rutherford identifies an experience of death allowed by the zombie that is remarkably similar to the experience of death I have described as offered by the Gothic: 'Social thinkers have been telling us for over a century that the denial of death is intrinsic to modernity, but zombie fictions head contrariwise into an obscene, explosive and super-heated encounter with death' (2013: 84).

3 Sidney W. Mintz discusses the 'consumption' of slaves in the production of sugar but also the zombie-like 'gastro-anomie' of 'desocialised, aperiodic eating' (1985: 43, 213).

4 In this rejection of a real threat as fantasy, the Gothic reinforces what Slavoj Žižek calls 'ideological fantasy' – not 'an illusion masking the real state of things but … an (unconscious) fantasy structuring our social reality itself' (1989: 33).

5 As Kyle William Bishop enumerates this 'new paradigm' of the zombie, after Romero's film, '(1) [zombies] have no connection to voodoo magic, (2) they far outnumber the human protagonists, (3) they eat human flesh, and (4) their condition is contagious' (2010: 94).

6 Christine Heckman draws a similar conclusion about *The Walking Dead*'s expressing 'anxiety about the way in which American identity is simultaneously defined and threatened by a capitalist economic system that runs on fossil fuels' (2014: 96).

7 Urry comments, 'Resources can "bite back", since energy lies at the heart of much social life, hidden from view, but on occasion having dramatic consequences' (2013: 12–13).

8 As Kim Paffenroth asks, 'What are we, other than … slightly smart zombies, a tribe of deranged, self-destructive cannibals preying on one another?' (2006: 7).

9 Paffenroth observes, 'Zombies derive no nourishment from eating people … so the whole theme of cannibalism seems added for its symbolism' (2006: 4).

10 Indeed, donations are no longer being accepted for the project. For more information, see www.indiegogo.com/projects/z-world-detroit--3.

11 Thus I would disagree with Jerrold E. Hogle who describes the Gothic as contrasting 'vestiges of a waning past' with 'more modern' ideas (2010: 2), and with Bishop, who sees the zombie as having 'no established antecedent in written literature' (2010: 5, 12–13).

12 Rutherford interprets the zombie as a metaphor for a human-like entity lacking an indefinable '*je ne sais quoi*' (2013: 22). For Tony Williams, this estrangement of the human in *Night of the Living Dead* is definable as the 'deformations of human personality operating within a ruthless capitalist society' (2003: 21).

13 Rutherford, examining the choice offered to the protagonist to 'smash in the head of your husband, mother, sister, brother, child, or lover, or join with them in a zombie embrace', comments it is 'all too familiar to anyone who's been through a nasty divorce' (2013: 4). According to Shiva, each modern human has been through such a 'divorce': from a living planet (2012).

References

Adler, M. (2014) *Vampires Are Us: Understanding Our Love Affair with the Immortal Dark Side* (San Francisco, CA: Weiser Books).

Auerbach, N. (1995) *Our Vampires, Ourselves* (Chicago and London: University of Chicago Press).

Beck, U. and E. Beck-Gernsheim (2001) *Individualisation: Institutionalised Individualism and its Social and Political Consequences* (London: Sage).

Bishop, K. W. (2010) *American Zombie Gothic: The Rise and Fall (and Rise) of the Walking Dead in Popular Culture* (Jefferson, NC, and London: McFarland).

Burke, E. (2004) *Reflections on the Revolution in France* [1790], ed. C. C. O'Brien (London: Penguin Classics).

Cottom, D. (2001) *Cannibals and Philosophers: Bodies of Enlightenment* (Baltimore, MD, and London: Johns Hopkins University Press).

Darabonte F. (dir.) (2010–present) *The Walking Dead* [Television] (USA: AMC).

Forster, M. (dir.) (2013) *World War Z* [Film] (USA: Paramount Pictures).

Heckman, C. (2014) 'Roadside "vigil" for the dead: Cannibalism, fossil fuels and the American dream', in D. Keetley (ed.), *'We're All Infected': Essays on AMC's* The Walking Dead *and the Fate of the Human* (Jefferson, NC: McFarland), pp. 95–109.

Hogle, J. E. (2010) Foreword, in K. W. Bishop, *American Zombie Gothic: The Rise and Fall (and Rise) of the Walking Dead in Popular Culture* (Jefferson, NC, and London: McFarland), pp. 1–4.

Hubbert, M. K. (1956) 'Nuclear energy and the fossil fuels', *Shell Oil Company/American Petroleum Institute* (presented San Antonio, TX, 7–9 March). Available at: www.hubbertpeak.com/hubbert/1956/1956.pdf. Accessed 2 September 2014.

Kant, I. (1996) 'What is Enlightenment?' [1784], in Schmidt (ed.), *What Is Enlightenment?: Eighteenth-Century Answers and Twentieth-Century Questions* (Berkeley and Los Angeles: University of California Press), pp. 58–64.

Lauro, S. J. (2011) 'Afterword: Zombie (r)evolution', in D. Christie and S. J. Lauro (eds), *Better Off Dead: The Evolution of the Zombie as Post-Human* (New York: Fordham University Press).

Mintz, S. W. (1985) *Sweetness and Power: The Place of Sugar in Modern History* (New York: Viking).

Paffenroth, K. (2006) *Gospel of the Living Dead: George Romero's Visions of Hell on Earth* (Waco, TX: Baylor University Press).

Proffitt, J. M. and Templin, R. (2013) '"Fight the dead, dear the living": zombie apocalypse, libertarian paradise?', in M. Balaji (ed.), *Thinking Dead: What the Zombie Apocalypse Means* (Lanham, MD, and London: Lexington), pp. 29–44.

Romero, G. A. (dir.) (1978) *Dawn of the Dead* [Film] (USA: Laurel Group).

Romero, G. A. (dir.) (1968) *Night of the Living Dead* [Film] (USA: Image Ten et al.).

Rutherford, J. (2013) *Zombies* (London and New York: Routledge).

Shiva, V. (2012) 'Everything I need to know I learned in the forest', *Yes!*, 5 December. Available at: www.yesmagazine.org/issues/what-would-nature-do/vandana-shiva-everything-i-need-to-know-i-learned-in-the-forest. Accessed 2 September 2014.

Taibbi, M. (2010) 'The great American bubble machine', *Rolling Stone*, 5 April. Available at: www.rollingstone.com/politics/news/the-great-american-bubble-machine-20100405. Accessed 5 April 2015.

deGrasse Tyson, N. (2008) 'Interview on *Death by Black Hole and Other Cosmic Quandaries*', 19 February (New York: City Arts and Lectures). Available at: www.youtube.com/watch?v=h1iJXOUMJpg. Accessed 2 September 2014.

Urry, J. (2013) *Societies Beyond Oil: Oil Dregs and Social Futures* (London and New York: Zed Books).

Walpole, H. (2003) *The Castle of Otranto* [1764] and *The Mysterious Mother* [1768], (ed.) Frederick S. Frank (Peterborough, ON: Broadview).

Williams, T. (2003) *The Cinema of George A. Romero: Knight of the Living Dead* (London and New York: Wallflower).

Wollstonecraft, W. (1997) *The Vindications: The Rights of Men, The Rights of Women* [1790 and 1792], (ed.) D. L. Macdonald and K. Scherf (Peterborough, ON: Broadview.

Žižek, S. (1989) *The Sublime Object of Ideology* (London and New York: Verso).

Part IV

Global Gothic dead

10

Christina Petraglia

A double dose of death in Iginio Ugo Tarchetti's 'I fatali'

Italy's version of the Gothic novel and short story, known as the *romanzo* and *racconto nero*, have remained on the periphery of Italian fiction since the time of the fantastic's late arrival on the peninsula after the Unification in 1861, when the country was still struggling with modernisation and national identity (or the lack thereof), and when writers – tired of the historical novel, and the veneration of Alessandro Manzoni's *I Promessi Sposi* (*The Betrothed*) (1842) – were lamenting the absence of a powerful contemporary, national litera-ture.[1] Iginio Ugo Tarchetti bemoaned the sad state of the novel in Italy while simultaneously promoting a revitalisation of Italian narrative through thematic innovations and transcendence of the Manzonian model.[2] In *Idee Minime sul Romanzo* (*Minimal Ideas on the Novel*) (1865), Tarchetti poses the question: '*Perché l'Italia non ha romanzi? O almeno perché non ha romanzi originali?*' ('Why doesn't Italy have novels? Or at least why doesn't it have original novels?') (1967: I. 522),[3] before affirming that *I Promessi Sposi* pales in comparison to the fiction of other countries (1967: I. 528). Tarchetti, however, does not expound an explicit poetics of the modern Italian novel, nor of the narratives of the *Scapigliatura*, of which he is the most-renowned author. The Italian term itself connotes 'existential disheveledness or rebellion' (Del Principe, 1996: 23) and its proponents were known for anti-conformist, anti-military, and anti-bourgeois stances, as well as for expressing anxieties concerning modernisation and identity in texts that, like their European counterparts, depict the 'underside of realism' (Jackson, 1981: 25) and the 'underside of enlightenment and humanist values' (Botting, 1996: 2). The ephemeral, liminal literary period of the *Scapigliatura* (1860s–1870s), chronologically situated between Italian Romanticism and Decadentism, and existing during the digestion of French Naturalism by budding *verisiti* ('realists') shares thematic and stylistic affinities with the Gothic traditions of its European neighbours.[4] The works of the *scapigliati* are riddled with transgressions of normativity typical of the Gothic: death, disease, deformity, uncanniness, crises of consciousness, and the occult worlds of the supernatural and the psychical. The *Scapigliatura*, therefore, stands as the exordium of a modern Italian 'writing of excess' (Botting, 1996: 1), or a Gothic Italian-style. Inspired by such authors as Edgar Allan Poe and E. T. A. Hoffmann, Tarchetti pioneers a genre that continues to hover on the non-canonical periphery of Italian letters. He rejects the nationalistic propaganda of the historical novel, proactively supercedes Italy's version of realism known as *verismo*, and celebrates the occult realms of spiritism, superstitions, and parapsychology in stark contrast to the respective literary and cultural trends of naturalism and positivism of the late nineteenth century.[5]

Decades before psychoanalysis acknowledges the marriage of death and the double, the two take centre stage in the *oeuvre* of Tarchetti. His posthumously published volume *Racconti fantastici* (*Fantastic Tales*) (1869), which helped cement his reputation as the progenitor of the Italian fantastic, establishes its macabre tone with its inaugural *novella* 'I fatali', a fragmented narrative comprised of superstitions realised, hair-raising incidents, inexplicable illness and disaster, and vampiric figures in the form of noble foreigners, all of which concludes with a newspaper report of murder.[6] In the *novella*, an unnamed narrator recounts the story of Baron Saternez, who falls in love with Silvia, heiress to the fortune of a Milanese businessman. During their engagement, Silvia falls ill and her jealous ex-suitor Davide believes Saternez is to blame, for he seems to bring illness and accidents to those near him. We later learn that all of the Baron's brothers and sisters had died, and it is implied that perhaps his intrinsically fatalistic influence had something to do with their deaths. A legendary *fatale* and enemy of Saternez, Count Sagrezwitch, eventually arrives in Milan. After the mysterious stabbing of the young Baron, presumably at the hands of the Count, a newspaper article reveals his real name to be Gustavo Sagrezwitch and the reader is led to believe that the rivals were father and son. The plural title of 'I fatali', with its ambiguous meanings of 'the fatal ones' and 'the fated ones', underscores the motifs of death and duality that run throughout the *novella*, as two contrasting faces of Death are embodied in the enig-matic Count Sagrezwith and his estranged son, Baron Saternez.[7] The present chapter reads this deathly duo through a psychoanalytic lens as complementary doubles, each embodying a different face of fatal-ity; expounds upon the father–son rivalry in which mortality is always, already, present; and interrogates how Tarchetti portrays the spectacu-lar nature of death. His treatment of death in 'I fatali', as in all of his fantastic tales, reflects changing *fin-de-siècle* attitudes; it is not circum-scribed by established Christian notions of an afterlife or a 'tame death' that a reader finds, for example, in Manzoni's historical novel, nor by a 'beautiful death' dear to the Romantic sensibility (Ariès, 1981: 609–11).

The personification of death is an age-old trope, yet Tarchetti splits Death into two mysterious, aristocratic foreigners, each possessing dif-ferent wills while sharing the same lethal power. His choice of noble-men to act as deliverers of destruction could be interpreted as the author's critique of the aristocracy and the bourgeois insofar as these hegemonic classes contributed to the maintenance of a (dis)unified Italian State in which class, economic, and educational differences helped to keep the masses oppressed.[8] Sagrezwitch and Saternez are of Polish origin; so, the fear of and fascination with the foreign Other is coupled with anxieties concerning the Austro-Hungarian Empire that occupied parts of Poland, and that had ruled in much of Northern Italy before the Unification. In this Italian Gothic tale, the foreigner possesses an allure, yet poses a threat in his Otherness, as he does in other national Gothic literatures, such as the Count in Stoker's *Dracula* and Coppola in Hoffmann's *The Sandman*. Tarchetti's abstract figure of Death, embodied in Sagrezwitch and Saternez, undergoes the pro-cess of 'decomposition' often encountered in stories of the double, in which various attributes of a given character are uncoupled and distrib-uted amongst other characters, each endowed with one group of the original attributes, and each functioning as the others' double (Rogers, 1970: 12). In 'I fatali', however, the given 'character' – Death – comes from the extradiegetic universe, not from the story itself. From Otto Rank's seminal treatment of *der Doppelgänger* in his 1914 homony-mous treatise, to contemporary literary criticism on this inherently Gothic trope that deconstructs the limits between self and Other (and between self and self), the double shares an intimate relationship with death. In his various trans-cultural studies of identity, Rank traces the double's evolution as a pre-modern projection of the immortal soul to a post-Enlightenment, macabre omen of the self's finitude. With the progression of positivism and industrialism, and the death of God, the nineteenth-century double morphs into 'a reminder of the individual's mortality, indeed the announcer of death itself' (Rank, 1953: 76). He thereby instils a fear in the literary subject (and consequently in the reader), for as he looks upon himself in an Other, loses his sense of individuality and subjectivity, sees the imminent annihilation of the self, and is reminded of his inevitable mortality in a modern world where 'tame death' (Ariès, 1981: 603–5), which is accompanied by an afterlife, no longer necessarily exists. In his essay 'The Uncanny' (1919), Freud emphasises the modern shift in the double's meaning in relation to death: while in primitive times, the double was 'an assurance of immortality', in a secularised world, the double becomes 'the uncanny harbinger of death' (2003: 142). Tarchetti's uncanny harbingers of death and bringers of destruction are circumscribed by the modern family romance, as birth and death are associated with doubles; fathers and sons in literature may also be doubles for each other, insofar as the son stands as the father's duplicate (Rogers, 1970: 9). Moreover, a child, like the primitive double, serves as the father's guarantee against death, that is, as his only possibility, outside of the sphere of historical or artistic fame, for a completely secularised immortality because he lives on in his son. Saternez and Sagrezwitch are complementary doubles, for they are both capable of wielding harmful influences over others who often avoid them out of instinct (Tarchetti, 1967: II. 20). They are opposite in their appearances and attitudes toward their fates; Sagrezwitch seems to live his fatality with a sort of Nietzschean *amor fati*, while Saternez struggles against his innate role in the cosmos as a *jettatore*, a man with innate powers to inflict – either intentionally or unintentionally – harm and suffering on others. Saternez attempts to live a normal, bourgeois lifestyle, getting engaged, attending the Carnival and the opera, and walking the streets of Milan. Do his father and fate therefore chastise him for trying to transgress his authentic identity in the Heideggerian sense? Does his wish to live a life that for him is inauthentic result in the nullification of his existence and ultimate death? In other words, is he attempting to be someone that he is not? These questions, like the truth behind the duo's relationship and Saternez's murder, remain mysteries.

The father and son also differ in their respective characterisations as manly and effeminate, and the narrator's descriptions of them reveal their ties to language and the inexpressible, nonetheless upholding their common identification with different versions of Death incarnate.

Despite his repellent aura (Tarchetti, 1967: II. 11), Saternez attempts to insert himself into Milanese society. His girlish beauty and gentleness render him attractive to many, as if he were the peaceful, sleep-like death embodied in the mythical figure of Thanatos, the twin brother of sleep and the god of non-violent death. In contrast, Sagrezwitch's lethality is far-reaching, collective, and explosively violent, recalling the death associated with the ferocious, mythical vampiric sisters of Thanatos, the Keres. Saternez's delicate physicality and his 'something of the feminine' (1967: II. 11), combined with his blond hair, blue eyes, and thin stature, render him akin to the typical Petrarchan beauty, or even, as the narrator later specifies, 'a supernatural being' (II. 14).[9] His effeminate look, which is mentioned several times, coupled with his sentimentality, affiliates him with sensory, visceral space, apart from language, as he exudes emotions through physical reactions to stimuli. During a Carnival celebration, a boy who comes in contact with Saternez is hit by a carriage and when the Baron sees him unconscious and with a broken arm in a café, he turns pale and quickly leaves. After locking eyes with a girl at the opera who subsequently faints during the intermission, Saternez's face suddenly assumes the pallid look of a cadaver (II. 16). His passion when speaking of his love for his betrothed Silvia further associates him with the emotional. In proclaiming his great ability to recognise and remember faces (II. 33), he aligns himself with a knowledge that transcends language, one that is tied to images and memories, much like the realm of the Imaginary that proceeds from the feminine. The Baron's beauty is not merely womanly; it is also ineffably attractive (II. 11) and therefore recalls the Kristevan semiotic where the masculine symbolic code proves devoid of meaning. The Baron's effeminate aesthetic and seemingly unthreatening comportment replicate a death instinct unlike Sagrezwitch's outwardly turned aggression; rather, because Saternez's fatality is characterised by a gentleness and attractiveness, it reflects a death instinct that signals a return to non-existence, either to an inorganic state as depicted in the Nirvana principle (Freud, 2009: 71), or to a pre-natal world characterised by the womb/tomb dynamic.

Count Sagrezwitch's reputation as the most fatal man precedes him the world over; he is always present '*sul teatro delle calamità più terribili ... ai disastri più spaventosi*' ('at the theatre of the most terrible calamities ... at the most frightening disasters') (Tarchetti, 1967: II. 18).[10] He is a loner, and those who know his power avoid him, while those who do not ignore him out of instinct (II. 20). In short, he, like the cruel death he augurs, elicits fear and trembling from those around him. His association with grandiose and inexplicable natural disasters, like the infinite of the sublime, overwhelms our mind and confounds our perception of reality. The initial description of the Count and details of the catastrophes at which he is inexplicably present are overheard by the narrator; he does not witness them first-hand. The elder *fatale* remains a mystery throughout the tale, never speaking directly to the narrator; therefore, the reader never 'hears' his words, thus adding another level of sublimity to his persona, as the terror of the sublime works on the audience's inability to see and understand it. As Burke affirms, 'To make anything very terrible, obscurity seems in general to be necessary. When we know the full extent of any danger, when we can accustom our eyes to it, a great deal of the apprehension vanishes' (1990: 54). Should Sagrezwitch speak in the story and have his words transcribed, and should the narrator actually witness the disasters he influences, a great deal of his terrible mystique would dissipate. He does become more visible throughout the tale, however, after his arrival in Milan. The detailed description of him, recounted by an acquaintance of the narrator in Café Martini, offers an initial glimpse of this father figure, a middle-aged man who commands a confident wisdom, while his black hair indicates a youthful strength. In contrast to his son's white-blond tresses that seem to belong to a young boy (Tarchetti, 1967: II. 14) and his 'beauty, more feminine than masculine' (II. 27), Sagrezwitch's ebony beard, combined with his wicked look, signify a staunch virility.[11] His medium height and regular features align him with an Everyman. He also acts like everyone else, as an acquaintance of the narrator notes (II. 20). These characteristics suggest the common existence of those deadly forces and violent wishes in all of us that Freud will later identify as components of the death instinct. The Count could be classified as that death drive that partly expresses itself as 'an instinct of destruction directed against the external world' (Freud, 2011: 381). As a patriarch who gives life yet ultimately takes life from his son, he stands as an authority figure *par excellence*, assuming even god-like qualities in his power to influence or kill at will. As the father who seems fully aware of his fatality and pleased to exercise it (Tarchetti, 1967: II. 20), Sagrezwitch embodies the law, passes judgment on Saternez (perhaps for his refusal to embrace his role as a *fatale*), and finally stabs him in the heart. Sagrezwitch's act of filicide overturns the Freudian family romance in which we encounter parricide, a trope that is frequently tied to an appearance of the double in literature. In killing the son, however, the father also figuratively kills himself as his only remaining progeny – his only hope of immortality – is destroyed.[12]

Also noteworthy is the force of Sagrezwitch's gaze, which 'possesses a magnetic, inexplicable quality that virtually compels you to stare and greet him in spite of yourself' (Tarchetti, 1992: 128). The power of Sagrezwitch's '*sguardo*' (Tarchetti, 1967: II. 21) offsets the sweetness of his son's gaze as highlighted by the narrator (II. 28), and further enhances his status as an authority figure who watches and regulates the natural order of things. Roda argues that the eyes of the *fatali* are irrelevant in the story because, unlike the protagonist of Gautier's *Jettatore*, Sagrezwitch and Saternez do not explicitly kill with their eyes. The gaze itself, however, is indeed relevant even if the harm that emanates from the *fatali* does not necessarily originate in the eyes, for the gaze itself is tied to the spectacular nature of death as it emerges throughout Tarchetti's Gothic tale. The Count, as an incarnation of Death, attracts and repels the looks of those who surround him, and this feature recalls Death's representational roots in spectacle. In Italy, the body of a deceased person is laid out on display so that kin may say their final goodbyes. In the fifteenth century, the *Ars moriendi* instructed readers on the art of dying and the artistic motif of the *danse macabre* appeared, depicting dancing skeletons interacting with each other and the living. These paintings, drawings, and engravings remind the viewer of her own mortality. Other *memento mori* – objects that remind us that we shall surely die like everyone else, such as a skull on one's work desk – also possess that spectacular nature, as they are created for us to gaze upon, and to gaze back at us in return. If we consider this exchange of gazes through a Lacanian lens, death's returning stare reminds us that, like the *fatali*'s supposed victims of freak accidents, calamities, and disease, we too will meet our demise and be stripped of our subjectivity. In death, we will ultimately become the ungazing object gazed upon by another, like the corpse placed on display in its coffin.

Death is also the other side of Life, its complementary double. It follows no rules and does not discriminate. These two characteristics – lawlessness and liberality – are explicitly expressed once a year in Italy during Carnival festivities, which notably mark the first scene of Tarchetti's *novella*. It opens at the 1866 Carnival on the cosmopolitan streets of Milan. Carnival, like the fantastic itself, is endowed with the propensity to turn the world 'inside out' (Bakhtin, 1984: 122), to confound binary power structures and our notions of what is real and

imaginary. In fact, Tarchetti prefaces the story proper with an ideological frame in which he immediately deconstructs positivistic perceptions
of reality, and demonstrates an anti-conformist stint in his poetics. In
this frame, an unnamed narrator expounds a 'logical' argument 'prov-
ing' the existence of harmful or fatal forces even before he introduces
us to the deathly duo of Sagrezwitch and Saternez. Tarchetti seeks
to ground his supernatural short stories in the everyday world, and
demonstrate that the paranormal exists as transgressing rationalistic
views of this world. In Bonifazi's fundamental study of the fantastic
in Italian literature, he explains the double narration of fantastic texts
that must contemporaneously possess elements of verisimilitude and
inverisimilitude (1982: 10). Tarchetti's microcosm of 'I fatali', set in
the Milan of 1866 of cafés, bustling city streets, Carnival celebrations,
and opera performances, depicts the everyday world of his contemporary readers; however, it is also infused with veritable examples of
those occult figures – jettatori, or jinxes – that belong to the realm of
superstition. The narrator claims this superstitious belief in fatal forces
is so common amongst the masses that it essentially becomes a fact of
life: 'If I see a superstition seize the spirit of the masses, I say that deep
within it resides a truth, since we do not have ideas without facts, and
this superstition can issue only from a fact' (Tarchetti, 1992: 118).
Such a claim undermines the authority of the positivism in vogue at
the time, which posits the quantifiable and observable material world
as the only real world. His assertion that a superstition is a 'belief ...
virtually innate' (Tarchetti, 1992: 119) in the masses and, therefore,
deriving from a fact not only further disrupts rational conceptions of
the knowable, it also suggests the notion of collective knowledge, and
recalls both the Freudian uncanny in the return of the unfamiliar familiar and the Jungian collective unconscious. Referring to the phenomenon of fatality as both superstition and fact essentially disrupts the
traditional conception of each, and blurs the dividing line between the
two, recalling the liminal spaces so prevalent in the Gothic and in the
discourse of the double, while simultaneously overturning the positivistic order of things. The overturning of order continues throughout
the story proper and becomes further tied to the spectacle introduced
with the initial Carnival sequence: in a similar opera scene in which
Saternez's stare causes a young girl to faint; in the elegant and ordered
semblances of the fatali, capable of destruction and disorder; and in the
final wedding reception of Silvia and Saternez when the former disap-
pears with Sagrezwitch, never to return alive. The narrator describes

the '*spettacolo assai curioso*' ('quite curious spectacle') in which the Carnival-goers, those masked who are outnumbered by the unmasked '*spettatori*' ('spectators') (Tarchetti, 1967: II. 10), all observe and inter-act with each other. Ghidetti refers to the Milan cityscape as the theatre of the deeds of the *fatali* (1968: 222), and the first view we have of Saternez depicts him as the creator or the centre of a spectacle insofar as his repulsive powers have generated a circular void around him in the crowd. Italians and foreigners stare at him as if he were on display like the unclaimed corpses in the window of Paris's nineteenth-century morgue that were used to promote the spectacle of death, allowing visi-tors to directly experience the abject.[13] While the immobile Saternez in the opening scene is not a corpse, as a potentially fatal force, a natural *jettatore*, the crowd viscerally perceives his occult powers. At the con-clusion of the tale, however, the reader not only discovers Saternez's true name, Gustavo Sagrezwitch – a quasi-confirmation that he is indeed the Count's son, – she also gets a glimpse of his corpse with a knife immersed in his heart via the narrator's transcription of the newspaper article reporting his death. Just as the story of these fatal figures begins with the ultimate spectacle of the Milanese Carnival with Saternez encircled by a void in the crowd with the narrator and the readers 'looking' at him, so the tale ends with another great nineteenth-century vehicle of spectacle – the newspaper, which puts crimes and corpses 'on display'. The narrator's and the reader's gaze fall upon Saternez's corpse as it is described in print, and upon a dead Death incarnate.

The obscurity enveloping the father figure of Sagrezwitch, the uncer-tainty surrounding Saternez's death, and the uncanniness of their so-called powers, push the characters into the realm of the sublime. While we are certain that Saternez suffers because of his ill-fated powers and we know he accepts the confrontation with his father that leads to his death, we are left wondering whether Sagrezwitch ever experiences guilt for his lethal role as a *fatale*, and if he intended to kill his son. The reader can only assume – based on the narrator's hearsay – that the Count does not suffer because of his toxic powers. The veil of mystery shrouding the identities and purposes of the younger and elder *fatale* is never lifted. Moreover, we never know the details surrounding the father–son relationship between Saternez and Sagrezwitch, nor the cir-cumstances of the former's murder. Whether or not deadly beings exist may remain an enigma to an unconvinced reader, and whether or not the Count and the Baron are father and son remains inconsequential.

In fact, a level of uncertainty, or a willing suspension of disbelief creates that liminal state so pleasurable in both Todorovian fantastic discourse and the Burkean sublime. Both work within the milieu of the unseen, the unknowable, the unclear, and the incomprehensible, in which an obscure idea may be hinted at darkly. This Tarchettian tale leaves the reader in a state of sublime uncertainty as she has experienced the terror of fatality yet remains removed from it. She is also left in the realm of the Todorovian fantastic, even though she has witnessed the seemingly supernatural and the narrator has 'proven' the veracity of uncanny harbingers and bringers of death.

Notes

1 In 1983, Italo Calvino, often considered a writer of the contemporary fantastic, compiled an anthology of what he considered emblematic short stories of the 'visionary' (supernatural) and 'everyday' (uncanny) fantastic in the nineteenth century and refused to include Italian authors 'merely out of obligation', claiming that 'the fantastic is a minor element in nineteenth-century Italian literature' (1983: xvii). Ceserani affirms that the marginal position of the fantastic 'led many critics to judge this Italian output as in general qualitatively inferior to that of other European fantastic literatures' (1983: 42). Ceserani concludes that it remains uncertain exactly why the fantastic arrived so late in Italy, citing the peculiarities of Italian Romanticism of the early nineteenth century and the country's stunted modernisation as possibilities (1983: 42–3).

2 The 1842 definitive edition of Alessandro Manzoni's *I Promessi Sposi* (*The Betrothed*) laid the groundwork for the modern Italian novel. Reworked by the author in order to transform the language into standard Italian, the historical novel describes the struggles of the young lovers Renzo and Lucia, desperate to marry though prevented from doing so because of many outside factors, during the time of a great plague that struck Northern Italy between 1629 and 1631. Historical allusions, societal and ecclesiastical critiques that also applied to Manzoni's time, and the power of and resignation to God's will are just a few elements that comprise the narrative.

3 Translation mine.

4 '*Veristi*' is the name given to a group of mostly Southern Italian writers that were active after the Unification, between the Italian Romantics of the early nineteenth century and the Italian Decadents of the *fin de siècle*. The term *verismo*, from the adjective '*vero*' meaning 'true', connotes a certain realism that is wrought with psychopathology; existential crises, both individual and collective, as Italy was struggling to 'create' Italians or a national identity after the Unification; Southern cultural and linguistic nuances; and questions of progress, consumerism, and social mobility. Luigi Capuana's novelistic exordium, *Giacinta* published in 1879, ten years after Tarchetti's death, is considered the prototype of the *verismo* that flourished in the last two decades of the nineteenth century, especially in the works of Giovanni Verga, Federico De Roberto, Matilde Serao, and Grazia Deledda.

5 Del Principe situates Tarchetti and the other *scapigliati* within Gothic tradition, affirming their place, not as a 'footnote to Romantic sensitivities' of pre-1860 Italy, but as a 'new territory in which the thematics of dementia, psychosexuality, the Gothic, antibourgeois conformism, decadence and the avant-garde' emerge (1996: 13).

6 Bonifazi refers to Tarchetti as, 'the founder of the genre', observing that his fantastic tales were published about fifty years after the first appearances of the nineteenth-century fantastic in Europe, though they are contemporary to the resurgence of interest in the fantastic in France (1982: 79).

7 Ghidetti, editor of Tarchetti's collected works, rightly notes that death exists as '*il nucleo dell'arte tarchettiana*' ('the nucleus of Tarchettian art') (1967: 7); therefore, one translation of the title could be 'The fatal ones', even though the question of fate most certainly enters into discourses on death, especially considering that in mythology, the Fates spin, measure, and cut the thread of life. In fact, Lawrence Venuti, in his English translation of Tarchetti's *Racconti fantastici* chooses 'The fated' as the title of the collection's first *novella*. At any rate, the ambiguous connotation of the word 'fatali' further reiterates the motif of duality that runs throughout all of the fantastic tales.

8 In 1881, twenty years after Italian Unification, the national percentage of illiterate individuals remained very high; about 64 per cent of children between the ages of six and twelve, and 54 per cent of youth between the ages of twelve and twenty still remained illiterate (Turi, 2007: 159).

9 Translation mine.

10 Translation mine.

11 Translation mine.

12 Various psychoanalytic studies of the literary double discuss the father–son double in light of parricide. Ernest Jones examines *Hamlet* from the perspective of decomposition in which Hamlet exists as the decomposed part of a whole, for he represents the rebellious son of incestuous and patricidal impulses (Rogers, 1970: 12–13). In *Dostoevsky and Parricide*, Freud addresses one of the great authors of the double and the dominating trope of parricide in literature. Tymms discusses familial doubles (including that of father and son) in *The Brothers Karamazov* (1949: 99–106). In stories of the double, such as Hans Heinz Ewers's silent film *The Student of Prague* (1913), which is discussed at length by Rank (2001) in *The Double*, one of the personages of the dyad kills the other, yet in murdering his Other he realises that he has also killed himself.

13 See Martens (2008) for historical background on the Paris Morgue during the time of Dickens and Browning.

References

Ariès, P. (1981) *The Hour of Our Death*, trans. H. Weaver (New York and Oxford: Oxford University Press).

Bakhtin, M. (1984) *Problems of Dostoevsky's Poetics* [1963] (Minneapolis, MN: University of Minnesota Press).

Bonifazi, B. (1982) *Teoria del Fantastico e il Racconto Fantastico in Italia: Tarchetti, Pirandello, Buzzati* (Ravenna: Longo).

Botting, F. (1996) *Gothic* (London: Routledge).

Burke, E. (1990) *A Philosophical Enquiry into the Origin of our Ideas of the Sublime and Beautiful* [1757], ed. A. Phillips (Oxford: Oxford University Press).

Calvino, I. (ed.) (1997) *Fantastic Tales: Visionary and Everyday* [1983] (New York: Pantheon).

Ceserani, R. (1983) *La Narrazione Fantastica* (Pisa: Nistri-Lischi).

Del Principe, D. (1996) *Rebellion, Death, and Aesthetics in Italy: The Demons of Scapigliatura* (Madison, NJ: Associated University Presses).

Freud, S. (2011) *The Ego and the Id* [1923], ed. J. Riviere (Mansfield Centre: Martino Publishing).

Freud, S. (2009) *Beyond the Pleasure Principle* [1920] (Eastford, CT: Martino Fine Books).

Freud, S. (2003) *The Uncanny* [1919], ed. H. Haughton (New York: Penguin).

Freud, S. (1959) *Collected Papers*, ed. J. Strachey (New York: Basic Books).

Ghidetti, E. (1968) *Tarchetti e la Scapigliatura Lombarda* (Naples: Libreria Scientifica).

Ghidetti, E. (ed.) (1967), 'Introduzione', in I. U. Tarchetti, *Tutte le Opere I* and *II* (Bologna: Cappelli).

Jackson, R. (1981) *Fantasy: The Literature of Subversion* (London: Methuen).

Martens, B. (2008) 'Death as spectacle: the Paris morgue in Dickens and Browning', *Dickens Studies Annual*, 39: 223–48.

Rank, O. (2001) *The Double* [1914] (Chapel Hill, NC: University of North Carolina Press).

Rank, O. (1953) *Beyond Psychology* [1941] (New York: Dover).

Roda, V. (2007) 'The eye that kills: Notes on a fantastic theme', in F. Billiani and G. Sulis (eds), *The Italian Gothic and Fantastic: Encounters and Rewritings of Narrative Traditions* (Madison, NJ: Associated University Presses), pp. 59–79.

Rogers, R. (1970) *A Psychoanalytic Study of the Double in Literature* (Detroit, MI: Wayne State University Press).

Tarchetti, I. U. (1992) *Fantastic Tales*, trans. L. Venuti (San Francisco, CA: Mercury House).

Tarchetti, I. U. (1967) *Tutte le Opere I* and *II*, ed. E. Ghidetti (Bologna: Cappelli).

Todorov, T. (1975) *The Fantastic: A Structural Approach to a Literary Genre* (Ithaca, NY: Cornell University Press).

Turi, G. (2007) *Storia Dell'Editoria Nell'Italia Contemporanea* (Milan: Giunti).

Tymms, R. (1949) *Doubles in Literary Psychology* (Cambridge: Bowes and Bowes).

11

Katherine Bowers

Through the opaque veil: the Gothic and death in Russian realism

'Our life and the life beyond the grave are
equally incomprehensible and horrible ...
apparitions are terrible, but life is terrible, too.'[1]
Anton Chekhov

In the 30 April 1853 issue of the *Moscow Gazette*, a commentator remarked, 'Among current items of news, primacy must be accorded, without dispute, to that mystery which nature has hitherto hidden from men and whose traces are only now beginning to be discerned' (quoted in Vinitsky, 2009: 3). The 'mystery' in question here is life after death, and the author's suggestion that one can now 'discern traces' of what happens after death implies the possibility of looking through the 'veil' for a glimpse of the afterlife. A broader cultural impetus to understand death emerged in this period, and the question of whether an afterlife existed and its nature was a key point in scientific, philosophical, and theological inquiry and debate in the nineteenth century, which manifested not only in the rise of movements such as materialism and spiritualism, but also in increased scrutiny of both folk and religious belief systems. As a literary form that dealt 'with life and reality in their true light' (Belinskii, 1956: X. 16),[2] realism accommodated this cultural climate; realist writers, especially in the Russian tradition, actively engaged in these debates in their fiction.

Russian realism 'aims at conveying reality as closely as possible and strives for maximum verisimilitude' (Jakobson, 2001: 38) and one might assume it privileges a materialist worldview, but its form enabled exploration of varying philosophical stances. One of the most famous examples of this ability is Fedor Dostoevskii's *The Brothers Karamazov* (1880), in which the existence and nature of God is on trial and convincing arguments for both sides are embedded in the novel. Similarly, as the vogue for spiritualist activities such as séances came to prominence in the second half of the century, realism reflected and informed these debates and trends (Vinitsky, 2009: 3–13). While there is a distinction between the Gothic-fantastic, in which supernatural events might occur, and spiritualism, in which the supernatural is another aspect of the natural, Gothic language and narrative devices appear in realist texts that engage with the spirit world, as well as those that evince a materialist worldview.[3] Indeed, as Christine Berthin argues, the Gothic's engagement with spectral elements is at 'the crux of our modernity' (2010: 1).

The nineteenth-century rise of spiritualism and its attendant debates coincided and conflicted with the 'age of science', a period of intense scientific inquiry and progress. In Russia, scientific inquiry became a matter of national importance in the era of Great Reforms that followed the country's defeat in the Crimean War; thinker and revolutionary Aleksandr Gertsen emphasised the period's scientific momentum in his 1868 memoir *My Past and Thoughts*: 'Without the natural sciences there is no salvation for modern man. Without that wholesome food, without that strict training of the mind by facts, without that closeness to the life surrounding us ... the monastic cell [would remain] hidden somewhere in the soul, and in it the drop of mysticism which might have flooded the whole understanding with its dark waters' (1982: 88).[4]

Throughout the nineteenth century, scientific thought was bound up with philosophical and political positions, a coupling that manifested in literature. Ivan Turgenev's Bazarov, the nihilist and atheist hero of *Fathers and Sons* (1862), proudly holds scientific fact above all other considerations, even remaining stoic in the face of his own death, caused by an error made while performing an autopsy. In Lev Tolstoi's *Anna Karenina* (1877), Konstantin Levin proclaims himself an atheist, but is troubled by his inability to believe in an afterlife and the implications of that for his own life's meaning. Levin's (1935) concept of death manifests in scientific terms, taken from the natural science volumes he has been reading: 'In infinite time, in infinite matter, in infinite space, is formed a bubble-organism, and that bubble lasts a while and bursts, and that bubble is I.'[5] His inability to reconcile the meaning of his life with his inevitable death and subsequent nonexistence results in palpable terror and suicidal thoughts.

Irene Masing-Delic attributes this terror to the decline of Russian Orthodoxy as a doctrine in nineteenth-century Russia: 'Like other branches of Christianity, Russian Orthodoxy offers immortality only after death, in a spiritual dimension not to be found on earth ... But atheists and materialists from the 1860's onward did not find transcendental paradises material enough to be real. They dismissed these celestial realms and the immortality found there as fairy tales without any scientific foundation' (1992: 3). In Masing-Delic's analysis, this trend resulted in twentieth-century Russia's fascination with immortality, while in the nineteenth century, a move away from Orthodox doctrine in the upper classes arguably manifested in an increased emphasis on mortality in philosophy, pseudoscientific movements such as spiritualism, and explorations of man's relationship to his own demise in literature and the arts. Bazarov and Levin stand as characters who represent a particular philosophical stance, which is tested within their novels through narrative framing and perspective. Thus were realist writers able to access 'a full and authentic report of human experiences', encouraging readers to question their own assumptions and beliefs about death and the possibility of life beyond (Watt, 2001: 32).

This tendency of Russian realism lends its texts intensity through circumventing the 'careful distance' Sarah Webster Goodwin and Elisabeth Bronfen (1993: 3) observe in writings about death. Instead, Russian realist works tap into the idea of death as a 'collective experience', one that all face at life's end. Philippe Ariès identifies this collective mindset as pre-eminent in medieval Europe, observing moreover that 'death became the occasion when man was most able to reach an awareness of himself' (1974: 46). Ariès similarly observes this 'medieval' mindset among nineteenth-century Russian peasants who are able to die more authentically, without secrecy in Tolstoi's writings such as 'Three Deaths' (1859) and The Death of Ivan Il'ich (1880) (1981: 561–2, 567). This point resonates with G. P. Fedotov's argument that the Russian peasant lived in the Middle Ages through the nineteenth century (1960: 3). As Ivan Il'ich suffers, his family's inability to admit he is dying proves more torturous than his illness, and in the end he can only bear the presence of a *muzhik* whose peasant background enables him to speak frankly about death.

This chapter will examine the function and effect of Gothic literary devices in the treatment of death in two short Russian realist works, Turgenev's 'Bezhin Meadow' (1851) and Anton Chekhov's 'A Dead Body' (1885). These works stand as examples of writers working out how to write about death within the bounds of realism. As Alan Bewell notes, 'Since we cannot experience death and also describe it, it is necessarily primarily a product of representation' (1989: 187). Turgenev's anxiety surrounding death and Chekhov's realisation of his own deteriorating body lend vibrant urgency to their exploration of death's facets, and it is striking that both examine peasant belief systems within this context as well as turn to the Gothic.[6] The Gothic's forte is its expression of the mystery of death (Howells, 1982), but folk belief also provides insight into death through ritual. The Gothic becomes a mode that conveys the fear surrounding the unknown, and, through generic expectation and its subversion, manipulates reader response (Bowers, 2013). The Gothic simultaneously contrasts and resonates thematically with the folkloric beliefs of peasants, enabling a literary exploration of attitudes toward and fears surrounding death.

'Bezhin Meadow' and 'A Dead Body' take a similar theme – fear of death – and setting – a traveller encountering peasants. In 'Bezhin Meadow', the narrator encounters a group of peasant boys telling ghost stories. We experience the sketch through the hunter's first-person perspective, and our perception of the boys is filtered through his observations while eavesdropping. Turgenev's sketch dwells on imagined death as a catalyst for fear in scary stories, relying on its reader's ability to perceive an intertextual relationship between his narrative frame and earlier Western Gothic tropes. These had entered the Russian cultural landscape through translation in the late eighteenth and early nineteenth centuries, sparking a 'gothic craze', which reached its peak later than in the West and proved a source of 'remarkable influence on Russian writers' (Tosi, 2006: 327, 328). Chekhov's 'A Dead Body' has a third-person limited narrator, and the story is told from the perspective of two peasants sitting by the side of a road in a forest with a dead body; they encounter a traveling pilgrim who grows frightened at the sight of the corpse. Chekhov's story plays with reader expectations: the centrality of the dead body in the story leads the reader (and the traveller) to anticipate an outcome such as those in Sensation Fiction, a genre that emerged from the Gothic, was intensely visual, and deliberately played with sensational themes and horrific images grounded not in the brooding past, as in classic Gothic fiction, but in modern life. As Henry James explained, 'The supernatural ... requires a powerful imagination in order to be as exciting as the natural, as [Sensation novelists], without any imagination at all, know how to manage it' (1865: 593).

Contemporary readers saw *Sketches from a Hunter's Album* (1851) as part of the 'new writing' heralded by Belinskii and others who advocated for more naturalist literature based in verisimilitude. In this context, it is surprising that Turgenev uses a Gothic frame in 1851. By the 1880s, however, readers had more exposure to Sensation Fiction, and the movement was already becoming a cliché; one could read the major novels of Dostoevskii and Tolstoi as a collection of murders, suicides, passions, illicit affairs, and illegitimate children in company with philosophical discourse. In 1866, Dostoevskii's *Crime and Punishment* and Tolstoi's *War and Peace* (1865–1867) were both being serialised in *The Russian Messenger* alongside a translation of Wilkie Collins' Sensation novel *Armadale*. Dostoevskii's frenetic tale of an axe murderer's motivations and the psychology of guilt parallels Collins' stream of murders, violence, and mysterious dreams. These sensational novels resonate with the late nineteenth-century Russian interest in true crime and punishment, which coincided with the advent of the trial by jury and the rise of mass journalism (McReynolds, 2012: 113–40).

The Gothic setting tends toward the exotic, but Turgenev and Chekhov, in setting their Gothic-framed tales in rural nineteenth-century Russia, enunciate the anxiety and terror inherent in real life, what James called the 'most mysterious of mysteries … which are at our own doors' (1865: 593). Intriguingly, both Turgenev's sketch and Chekhov's story end without resolution or explanation, leaving the reader to contemplate the conflicting views of death they raise. Just as these shorter works bookend the age of the great Russian realist novel, they also frame its existential questions about life and death.

'Bezhin Meadow' begins with Turgenev's hunter walking in the forest. As the forest darkens and the hunter-narrator realises he is lost, his description of his surroundings takes on Gothic overtones: night rises around him 'like a thundercloud' (как грозовая тучка), the mist colludes with the darkness, small creatures are mindlessly consumed by terror, and the 'sullen murk' (угрюмый мрак) looms.[7] He concludes, 'the hollow itself was so still and silent, the sky above it so flat and dismal that my heart shrank within me'.[8] The narrator's feelings and moods constantly shape the landscape in the *Sketches* and Turgenev uses this device to influence the feelings of his reader here as well; as the narrator feels lost and frightened, so, too, the reader, used to picking up on Gothic cues in popular fiction, begins to feel anxious for the narrator.

Lost in this environment, the narrator stumbles across the cheerful sight of a group of peasant boys exchanging stories around a campfire.

Turgenev specifically juxtaposes the Gothic frame with the tales of the boys, contrasting the traveller-narrator's literary language with the peasants' folkloric narratives. As he tells their stories back to his reader, he reveals the complicated web of folk and Christian beliefs that informs their worldview. Kostia tells of a village carpenter who encounters a *rusalka*, a folkloric female spirit who lures men to their deaths, in the forest and saves himself from drowning by crossing himself. Fedia recounts the tale of a squire, discontented after death, who haunts a nearby village. Each of the stories have elements of fear related to the contemplation of death, but only Iliusha's stories evoke real fear in the boys. Iliusha shares his terrifying encounter with a goblin or possibly a demon, then, later, tells of a mysterious demonic lamb that appeared on a drowned man's grave. In these tales, the supernatural is mysterious and lies outside of the boys' well-ordered belief system. By contrast, in Kostia's tale, the carpenter encounters a *rusalka*, but is able to save himself through ritual. In Fedia's tale, the squire's death and ghostly afterlife seem natural, the spectral squire benign, discontented in death as he was in life. Iliusha's tales, in engaging with elements that go beyond the conventions of folk belief, show the boundaries of the peasants' belief system, and the terror that the inexplicable evokes.

For the boys, the spirit world has its rules and explanations, just like the material world. Iliusha frames the story of his grandmother's death omen with the explanation that 'you can see dead people at any time [...] but on Parents' Sunday you can also see the people who're going to die that year'.[9] Within this frame, his tale of real deaths foretold is accepted by the boys; his grandmother's encounter with her own foretold death merely elicits the remark that her death has not yet come to pass. Similarly, when Pavlusha reports that he has just heard a drowned boy calling his name from a nearby river, the boys take it as an omen. Rather than reacting with fear, Pavlusha 'declare[s] resolutely' (произнес решительно) that 'your own fate you can't escape'.[10] In this belief system, death is a transitional process that separates life and afterlife.

A later exchange similarly and more explicitly exposes the fluid boundaries between the spirit world and the boys' world, and also brings the tension between the sketch's Gothic frame and folkloric core to the forefront. The boys hear a sudden noise, which is described as 'strange, sharp, sickening' (странный, резкий, болезненный) (107; 114). Kostia fears the unknown sound while Pavlusha calmly identifies it as a heron's cry. This prompts Kostia to tell a story:

> What was it, Pavlusha, I heard yesterday evening? ... So, mates, I walked past this
> tarn an' suddenly someone starts makin' a groanin' sound from right inside it, so
> piteous, piteous, like: Oooh – oooh ... oooh – oooh! I was terrified, mates. It was
> late an' that voice sounded like somebody really sick. It was like I was goin' to
> start cryin' myself ... What would that have been, eh?[11]

Introduced with the narrator's Gothic voice, Kostia's colloquial
description of his terror at encountering an unfamiliar and uniden-
tifiable sound recalls the narrator's Gothic descriptions of the forest
at night that introduce the boys' stories. There, however, the literary
Gothic descriptions play to the readers' expectations, evoking fear and
dread, whereas here Kostia's story relates a Gothic trope in colloquial,
somewhat jovial speech. Both Gothic and colloquial descriptions
emphasise aspects of the psychology of fear, but the reader, attuned to
Gothic convention, is able to experience that fear from the narrator's
description. Kostia's account discloses his fear, but, in mimicking the
heron's cry, becomes almost comical. The scene continues:

> 'The summer before last, thieves drowned Akim the forester in that tarn,'
> Pavlusha remarked. 'So it may have been his soul complaining.'
> 'Well, it might be that, mates,' rejoined [Kostia], widening his already enormous
> eyes. 'I didn't know that Akim had been drowned in that tarn. If I'd known, I
> wouldn't have got so terrified.'[12]

The subsequent discussion, in which the boys suggest both natural
(frogs) and supernatural (wood-demon) causes for the sound, shows
that, in their world, the supernatural is natural. Pavlusha's calm identification of the unfortunate Akim's soul complaining and Kostia's reply,
'If I'd known, I wouldn't have got so terrified', underscores this belief
structure. While, within the bounds of the Gothic, a tarn haunted by a
drowned man would be a catalyst for dread, for the boys it is a natural
explanation for a frightening sound, like frogs or wood-demons.

Mark Simpson argues that Pavlusha acts as a Gothic hero in
Turgenev's sketch, 'a kind of Melmoth, a sign of the dangers inherent in skepticism ... Only the Gothic hero aims to explain the many
unknowns and the many fears which confront us' (Simpson, 1986:
87). Pavlusha's explanations are not drawn from some Melmoth-like
wisdom, however, but from the peasants' own belief system. If any
character in the sketch embodies the role of Gothic hero, surely it is
the narrator. His tendency to delve into a Gothic mode of description
frames the boys' stories, and ultimately gives a fatalistic, frightening
context to Pavlusha's foretold death when he leaves the boys at the
story's conclusion and adds the note, 'I have, unfortunately, to add that

in the same year Pavlusha died',[13] with prosaic details about his demise. Pavlusha's reaction to hearing his name called by a drowned boy seems nearly ambivalent, accepting of his fate; this type of omen is an aspect of peasant belief, at least in Turgenev's depiction.

The narrator's addendum to the sketch adds a prosaic observation, an element from everyday life that disrupts the Gothic and folkloric modes of narration. The Gothic frame, however, leaves the reader feeling uneasy. Within a realist framework, the boundaries between life and death are clearly delineated, but the Gothic frame emphasises dread and mystery, and hints at the possibility that Pavlusha's death omen may have a basis in reality. The Gothic framing device brings the peasants' belief system into the bounds of a realist structure. In this way, Turgenev legitimises a belief system that offers a more comforting view of death than his own positivist and materialist views allowed. For the peasants, death is merely another facet of life, entrance into a world that exists parallel to ours, at times overlapping, whereas Turgenev viewed death as a definitive end, a state of non-existence.

Published some thirty years later, Chekhov's 'A Dead Body' similarly explores fear in the face of death. While the Gothic frame in Turgenev's sketch is in keeping with his generic experimentation in other works, the Gothic frame in Chekhov's story is unusual within his *oeuvre*. Nearly all scholarship surrounding Chekhov and Gothic has focused on the story 'The Black Monk' (1894), which deals with the notion of apparitions as a symptom of mental illness.[14] 'The Black Monk' has the most overt instances of the supernatural in Chekhov's corpus, but other stories also entertain Gothic themes or tropes. In 'A Dead Body', a traveling pilgrim encounters two peasants keeping overnight vigil with a corpse. Suddenly they hear 'a long drawn-out, moaning sound in the forest':

> Something rustles in the leaves as though torn from the very top of the tree and falls to the ground. All this is faintly repeated by the echo. The young man shudders and looks enquiringly at his companion. 'It's an owl at the little birds,' says [Sema], gloomily.[15]

The younger peasant defers to the older peasant's wisdom, and finds reassurance in his explanation. Similarly, although the peasants talk about their fears, staying overnight with the corpse is a necessary part of the peasants' funeral ritual, and this sense of duty normalises the task for them. When the pilgrim comes across them, however, he becomes afraid to venture further through the woods alone, ostensibly because of the corpse. He experiences what Julia Kristeva (1982) terms abject horror, a reaction caused by a confrontation with the threatened break-down of the boundaries between self and other. According to Kristeva, the corpse is a source of horror because it traumatically reminds man of his own demise, forcing him to face 'the border of [his] condition as a living being' (3). In Chekhov's story, the pilgrim expresses his fear of death through Gothic cliché, complaining, 'The dead man will haunt me all the way in the darkness'.[16] Intriguingly, Chekhov's pilgrim demonstrates consciousness of his fear's irrationality, continuing, 'I am not afraid of wolves, of thieves, or of darkness, but I am afraid of the dead. I am afraid of them, and that is all about it!'[17]

The pilgrim's declaration stems from an expectation of potential outcomes for a tale of a lonely and lost traveller encountering a dead body at night: perhaps it is an unlucky omen or will be reanimated, and stands in opposition to the folkloric ritualised worldview of the peasants. Chekhov subverts the Gothic by introducing a new narrative strand, one based in economics. While the pilgrim's initial reaction is to flee, he encounters difficulty in convincing the peasants to leave the dead body and show him the way, as, for them, breaking the vigil is unlucky. Finally, he convinces the younger peasant to accompany him onwards by offering five kopecks. For this sum, the younger peasant is willing to chance bad luck. This exchange introduces the notion of an economy related to death, which Chekhov builds up to humorous effect. The pilgrim offers to leave a kopeck for the burial, but upon learning that the man is possibly a suicide, he rescinds the offer, saying that he would not stay by the body for a thousand kopecks. The prosaic moment of barter undermines the pilgrim's earlier, fearful exclamation and distances the characters from the reality of the corpse.

As in Turgenev's sketch, Chekhov's reader is struck by the story's Gothic frame, which evokes the sensational in this everyday setting. From the story's beginning, a Gothic landscape is in evidence:

> A still August night. A mist is rising slowly from the fields and casting an opaque veil over everything within eyesight. Lighted up by the moon, the mist gives the impression at one moment of a calm, boundless sea, at the next of an immense white wall. The air is damp and chilly.[18]

The 'opaque veil' of mist rising up from the fields at times resembles a calm but endless sea or a gigantic white wall; it recalls Turgenev's sketch. In 'Bezhin Meadow', the familiar landscape becomes a Gothic one, with a steep menacing wall, and white mist shrouding the clammy damp grass. This opaque veil shrouds the world, rendering it unfamiliar and impenetrable. In 'A Dead Body', the crackling of the peasants' cheerful fire quickly dispels this initial atmospheric description and brings the reader back to the present. However, the story ends on a Gothic note:

> A minute later the sound of their steps and their talk dies away. [Sema] shuts his eyes and gently dozes. The fire begins to grow dim, and a big black shadow falls on the dead body … [19]

The last sentence provides Gothic atmosphere, but following the humorous exchange with the pilgrim and Sema's quiet dozing, seems disjunctive. As in 'Bezhin Meadow', the Gothic frame, provided by the realist narrator, seems at odds with the blurred boundary between this life and an afterlife, our world and the spirit world in the folk beliefs expressed colloquially by the peasants.

Three unmistakable Gothic moments appear in the text: the 'opaque veil' of mist and initial landscape description; the sudden unknown cry that startles the younger peasant; and, finally, the shadow that falls over the corpse and closes the tale. These moments are what savvy readers familiar with Gothic conventions expect from a story called 'A Dead Body'. Each could be understood humorously as melodramatic elements that contrast with Sema's rational worldview. The older peasant's cheerful fire chases away the initial gloom and cold mist. He recognises the unknown sound as an owl, providing it with context and so dispelling the younger peasant's fears. Sema's quiet dozing sharply contrasts with the black shadow falling over the dead body. However, the final ellipsis forces us to question this reading. Even if the pilgrim's fears are gently mocked and exposed as irrational, they are nonetheless real fears.

The Gothic elements in 'A Dead Body' play on the reader's irrational fears. Inserting them in the story adds to the overall feeling that something unnatural *could* happen, such as the corpse's sudden reanimation or a ghostly apparition. Chekhov's late-nineteenth-century reader understands that the text suggests fear because of these atmospheric set pieces. The final shadow on the corpse and ellipsis adds subtly but significantly to the story's effect, building on the previous Gothic moments and leaving the reader with a vague sense of disquiet.

In another story from approximately the same period, the potential for Gothic atmosphere exists but is dispelled through humorous narration. 'In the Graveyard' (1884) features a party of friends visiting a graveyard at night. While the setting could be rendered frightening as in 'A Dead Body', it is not, as we understand from the opening lines:

'The wind has got up, friends, and it is beginning to get dark. Hadn't we better take ourselves off before it gets worse?' The wind was frolicking among the yellow leaves of the old birch trees, and a shower of thick drops fell upon us from the leaves. One of our party slipped on the clayey soil, and clutched at a big grey cross to save himself from falling.[20]

The first two sentences conjure a classic Gothic scene – the dark and stormy night. The description that follows is far from Gothic, however. The 'frolicking' wind, yellow-coloured leaves, and fat raindrops, not to mention the man slipping and grabbing a cross to keep from falling, dispel any notion of the Gothic. As the story continues, the narrator introduces multiple Gothic or sensational conventions in addition to the 'dark and stormy' setting. For example, a mysterious stranger appears from behind shadowed gravestones.

'And here, under this tombstone, lies a man who from his cradle detested verses and epigrams … As though to mock him his whole tombstone is adorned with verses … There is someone coming!' A man in a shabby overcoat, with a shaven, bluish-crimson [physiognomy],[21] overtook us. He had a bottle under his arm and a parcel of sausage was sticking out of his pocket.[22]

The appearance of a ragged stranger with a discoloured face following a meditation on tombstones has Gothic or sensational potential. However, the mode breaks with the word 'physiognomy'. This ironic reference combines with 'bluish-crimson' to reinforce the humorous observation on a tombstone covered in epigrams. The second sentence, with its protruding bottle and sausage packet, banishes the Gothic potential entirely as we realise the mysterious stranger is a drunken vagrant.

Another example of Gothic convention later dispelled in 'In the Graveyard' is the presence of multiple coffins containing fresh corpses. In the short story, the party encounters one dead body after another until, finally, someone remarks, 'We've only been walking here for a couple of hours and that is the third brought in already … Shall we go home, friends?'[23] In a Gothic tale, each encounter with a dead body would usually lead to a suspenseful narrative build-up and the protagonist's growing anxiety. In Sensation Fiction, the corpses would mount, culminating in some fresh, delectable horror. In Chekhov's story, the dark night, wind, storm, and even the appearance of multiple coffins containing fresh corpses and a stranger who appears from behind the shadowed gravestones, seem like classic Gothic markers. But they are not coloured with Gothic exaggeration, cause no alarm, and their inherent sensationalism is destabilised by humour.

The clichéd setting of 'In the Graveyard' allows for a humorous yet realistic encounter with prosaic death. While not so funny, the Gothic frame in 'A Dead Body' fulfils a similar role: it informs an encounter with the materiality of death. Chekhov frames the episode with Gothic convention, subverts this atmosphere with prosaic elements, then reintroduces the Gothic, and in so doing, creates a mode in which the readers suspend their disbelief and has the potential for experiencing their own fear. The Gothic frame in 'Bezhin Meadow' evoked the recent Romantic literature that still lingered vividly in the Russian reader's imagination; Aleksandr Pushkin's celebrated 'The Queen of Spades' (1834) was not yet twenty, and Dostoevskii's *The Double* (1846), with its account of a mysterious *doppelgänger* that may or may not be a hallucination, had appeared less than five years earlier. Chekhov's Gothic, however, engages with a different readership, one for whom the age of the realist novel has ended and Sensation Fiction grounded in reality is passé. For Chekhov's readers, the frisson of doubt at the end of 'A Dead Body' is a delicious hint that, within the bounds of literature, the possibility of corpses reanimating or a ghostly apparition exists. Neither Turgenev nor Chekhov can be called Gothic writers, but in their works the Gothic adds an extra-textual layer, a mode to direct a reader's reaction, to play with reader expectations, and to access the reader's own capacity for fear. Reading the Gothic moments in these texts becomes an exercise in experiencing terror.

In Chekhov's 1892 story 'Terror', two characters ruminate on the relationship between fear and the unknown. Dmitrii Petrovich asks the narrator, 'Why is it that when we want to tell some terrible, mysterious, and fantastic story, we draw our material, not from life, but invariably from the world of ghosts and of the shadows beyond the grave?' The narrator responds: 'We are frightened of what we don't understand.' Dmitrii Petrovich continues:

> Our life and the life beyond the grave are equally incomprehensible and horrible. If any one is afraid of ghosts he ought to be afraid, too, of me, and of those lights and of the sky, seeing that, if you come to reflect, all that is no less fantastic and beyond our grasp than apparitions from the other world. … What I mean is, apparitions are terrible, but life is terrible, too. I don't understand life and I am afraid of it, my dear boy.[24]

The notion that 'our life and the life beyond the grave are equally incomprehensible and horrible' hearkens back to the 'medieval' peasant truths about collective death that Tolstoi explores, and which Turgenev and Chekhov touch upon. With advances in science and medicine, death may be deferred, but ultimately remains a constant terminus for each life. While this nineteenth-century clash between 'old' and 'new' worlds evokes the Gothic in and of itself, in the end both 'old' and 'new' succumb to terror. As illustrated in 'Bezhin Meadow' and 'A Dead Body', the unknown is frightening but, as Chekhov's provocative story makes clear, there is terror in living and in dying. Just as Turgenev's peasant boys try to negotiate the boundary between their world and the spirit world, so too does Chekhov's pilgrim come face to face with his own existential fear when confronted with a corpse.

Dmitrii Petrovich initially sets the Gothic and realism in direct opposition; 'terrible, mysterious, and fantastic' stories draw their material not from life as they do in realism, but from 'the world of ghosts and of the shadows beyond the grave', the unknown. His conclusion that life is incomprehensible gets at the heart of realism and simultaneously exposes the Gothic's potential as a literary mode that depicts the incomprehensible and folk belief's ability to categorise, ritualise, and explain the unknown. The realist Gothic frames and their folkloric interiors in 'Bezhin Meadow' and 'A Dead Body' help mediate the tension between the irrational and the prosaic, the abject and the mysterious. However, as in folklore and the Gothic, both works ultimately leave their ruminations on death open to the reader's interpretation.

Notes

1 'Наша жизнь и загробный мир одинаково непонятны и страшны … страшны видения, но страшна и жизнь.' Chekhov, A. P. (1974–1983: 130–1). Translated by C. Garnett (2006: 69–70). All quotations from Chekhov are this edition followed by this translation.

2 'Жизнь и действительность в их истине.' Translation my own.

3 Vinitsky (2009) presents Mikhail Saltykov-Shchedrin's *The Golovlev Family* (1875–1880) as an example of a text that resonates with both spiritualism and Gothic, pp. 113–15.

4 'Без естественных наук нет спасения современному человеку, без этой здоровой пищи, без этого строгого воспитания мысли фактами, без этой близости к окружающей нас жизни … где-нибудь в душе остается монашеская келья и в ней мистическое зерно, которое может разлиться темной водой по всему разумению.' A. I. Herzen (1919–1925: XII. 106). Translated by C. Garnett (1982: 88).

5 'В бесконечном времени, в бесконечности материи, в бесконечном пространстве выделяется пузырек-организм, и пузырек этот подержится и лопнет, и пузырек этот – я.' L. N. Tolstoi (1935: XIX. 369). Translated by C. Garnett (2000: 891).

6 Scholars have studied these authors' fascination with illness and their own mortality. On Turgenev's preoccupation with death, see Utevskii (1923), especially p. 7; for a broader discussion of death's thematic importance for Turgenev, see Vinitsky (2015). On Chekhov's relationship with his illness, see Finke (2005), pp. 99–138 and Finke (2007).

7 Turgenev, I. S. (1960–68: 94). Translated by Richard Freeborn (1967: 101). All quotes from Turgenev derive from these editions.

8 'В ней было немо и глухо, так плоско, так уныло висело над нею небо, что сердце у меня сжалось.' p. 94; p. 101.

9 'Покойников во всяк час видеть можно … Но а в родительскую субботу ты можешь и живого увидать, за кем, то есть, в том году очередь помирать.' p. 104; p. 111.

10 'Своей судьбы не минуешь.' p. 111; p. 118.

11 'А вот что я слышал. … вот пошел я мимо этого бучила, братцы мои, и вдруг из того-то бучила как застонет кто-то, да так жалостливо, жалостливо: у-у…у-у… у-у! Страх такой меня взял, братцы мои: время-то позднее, да и голос такой болезный. Так вот, кажется, сам бы и заплакал … Что бы это такое было? ась?' p. 111; p. 118.

12 'В этом бучиле в запрошлом лете Акима-лесника утопили воры,' заметил Павлуша, 'так, может быть, его душа жалобится.' 'А ведь и то, братцы мои,' возразил Костя, расширив свои и без того огромные глаза… 'Я и не знал, что Акима в том бучиле утопили: я бы еще не так напугался.' pp. 107–8; pp. 114–15.

13 'Я, к сожалению, должен прибавить, что в том же году Павла не стало.' p. 113; p. 120.

14 On the Gothic's function in this story, see Komaromi (1999). For a reading of the story as an example of the Gothic-fantastic, see Whitehead (2007). For a comprehensive overview of additional scholarship on the subject, see Poliakova and Tamarchenko (2008), pp. 239–49.

15 'Вдруг в лесу раздается протяжный, стонущий звук. Что-то, как будто сорвавшись с самой верхушки дерева, шелестит листвой и падает на землю. Всему этому глухо вторит эхо. Молодой вздрагивает и вопросительно глядит на своего товарища. "Это сова пташек забижает," говорит угрюмо Сема.' IV, p. 127; X, p. 133.

16 'Всю дорогу в потемках покойник будет мерещиться…' IV, p. 129; X, p. 136.

17 'Не боюсь ни волков, ни татей, ни тьмы, а покойников боюсь. Боюсь, да и шабаш!' IV, p. 129; X, p. 137.

18 'Тихая августовская ночь. С поля медленно поднимается туман и матовой пеленой застилает всё, доступное для глаза. Освещенный луною, этот туман дает впечатление то спокойного, беспредельного моря, то громадной белой стены. В воздухе сыро и холодно. Утро еще далеко.' IV, p. 126; X, p. 131.

19 'Парень поднимается и идет с ряской. Через минуту их шаги и говор смолкают. Сема закрывает глаза и тихо дремлет. Костер начинает тухнуть, и на мертвое тело ложится большая черная тень.' IV, p. 130; X, p. 137.

20 '"Господа, ветер поднялся, и уже начинает темнеть. Не убраться ли нам подобру-поздорову?" Ветер прогулялся по желтой листве старых берез, и с листьев посыпался на нас град крупных капель. Один из наших поскользнулся на глинистой почве и, чтобы не упасть, ухватился за большой серый крест.' III, p. 75; XI, p. 275.

21 Physiognomy is my amendment of Garnett's translation; she uses the more romantic word 'countenance' for the Russian 'fizionomiia'.

22 '"А вот под этим памятником лежит человек, с пеленок ненавидевший стихи, эпиграммы... Словно в насмешку, весь его памятник испещрен стихами... Кто-то идет!" С нами поравнялся человек в поношенном пальто и с бритой, синевато-багровой физиономией. Под мышкой у него был полуштоф, из кармана торчал сверток с колбасой.' III, p. 75; XI, p. 275.

23 'Гуляем мы здесь только два часа, а при нас уже третьего несут... По домам, господа?' III, p. 77; XI, p. 80.

24 'Почему это, когда мы хотим рассказать что-нибудь страшное, таинственное и фантастическое, то черпаем материал не из жизни, а непременно из мира привидений и загробных теней?' 'Страшно то, что непонятно.' 'Наша жизнь и загробный мир одинаково непонятны и страшны. Кто боится привидений, тот должен бояться и меня, и этих огней, и неба, так как всё это, если вдуматься хорошенько, непостижимо и фантастично не менее, чем выходцы с того света. ... Что и говорить, страшны видения, но страшна и жизнь. Я, голубчик, не понимаю и боюсь жизни.' VIII, pp. 130–1; IV, pp. 69–70.

References

Ariès, P. (1981) *The Hour of Our Death*, trans. H. Weaver (New York: Vintage Books).

Ariès, P. (1974) *Western Attitudes Toward Death: From the Middle Ages to the Present*, trans. P. Ranum (Baltimore, MD: Johns Hopkins University Press).

Belinskii, V. G. (1956) *Polnoe sobranie sochinenii* (Moscow: Izdatel'stvo Akademii nauk SSSR).

Berthin, C. (2010) *Gothic Hauntings: Melancholy Crypts and Textual Ghosts* (Basingstoke: Palgrave Macmillan).

Bewell, A. (1989) *Wordsworth and Enlightenment: Nature, Man, and Society in the Experimental Poetry* (New Haven, CT: Yale University Press).

Bowers, K. (2013) 'The city through a glass, darkly: Use of the Gothic in early Russian realism', *The Modern Language Review*, 108.4: 1199–215.

Chekhov, A. P. (2006) *Tales of Chekhov*, trans. C. Garnett (New York: Ecco).

Chekhov, A. P. (1974–83) *Polnoe sobranie sochinenii i pisem v tridtsati tomakh* (Moscow: Nauka).

Fedotov, G. P. (1960) *The Russian Religious Mind*, Vol. 1, *Kievan Christianity: The Tenth to the Thirteenth Centuries* (New York: Harper Brothers).

Finke, M. C. (2007) 'Heal thyself, hide thyself: Why did Chekhov ignore his TB?', in

M. C. Finke and J. de Sherbinin (eds), *Chekhov the Immigrant: Translating a Cultural Icon* (Bloomington, IN: Slavica), pp. 285–97.

Finke, M. C. (2005) *Seeing Chekhov: Life and Art* (Ithaca, NY: Cornell University Press).

Gertsen, A. I. (1919–25) *Polnoe sobranie sochinenii i pisem v 22 tomakh* (Petrograd: Lit. izd. otd. Narkomata po prosveshcheniiu).

Herzen, A. I. (1982) *The Memoirs of Alexander Herzen: My Past and Thoughts*, trans. C. Garnett (Berkeley and Los Angeles: University of California Press).

Howells, C. A. (1982) 'The Gothic way of death in English fiction, 1790–1820', *British Journal for Eighteenth-Century Studies*, 5: 207–15.

Jakobson, R. (2001) 'On realism and art', in L. Matejka and K. Pomorska (eds), *Readings in Russian Poetics: Formalist and Structuralist Views* (Chicago: Dalkey Archive Press), pp. 38–46.

James, H. (9 Nov. 1865) 'Miss Braddon', *The Nation*.

Komaromi, A. (1999) 'Unknown force: Gothic realism in Chekhov's *The Black Monk*', in N. Cornwell (ed.), *The Gothic-Fantastic in Nineteenth-Century Russian Literature* (Amsterdam: Rodopi), pp. 257–75.

Kristeva, J. (1982) *Powers of Horror: An Essay on Abjection* (New York: Columbia University Press).

McReynolds, L. (2012) *Murder Most Russian: True Crime and Punishment in Late Imperial Russia* (Ithaca, NY: Cornell University Press).

Masing-Delic, I. (1992) *Abolishing Death: A Salvation Myth of Russian Twentieth-Century Literature* (Stanford, CA: Stanford University Press).

Poliakova, A. A. and N. D. Tamarchenko (2008) '"Chernyi monakh" A. P. Chekhova i sud'by goticheskoi traditsii', in A. A. Poliakova and N. D. Tamarchenko (eds), *Goticheskaia traditsiia v russkoi literature* (Moscow: Rossiiskii gosudarstvennyi gumanitarnyi universitet), pp. 239–49.

Simpson, M. S. (1986) *The Russian Gothic Novel and its British Antecedents* (Bloomington, IN: Slavica).

Tolstoi, L. N. (1935) *Polnoe sobranie sochinenii v 90 tomakh* (Moscow: Gosudarstvennoe izdatel'stvo 'Khudozhestvennaia literatura').

Tolstoy, L. N. (2000) *Anna Karenina* [1877], trans. C. Garnett (New York: Modern Library).

Tosi, A. (2006) *Waiting for Pushkin: Russian Fiction in the Reign of Alexander I (1801–1825)* (Amsterdam: Rodopi).

Turgenev, I. S. (1967), *Sketches from a Hunter's Album*, trans. R. Freeborn (London and New York: Penguin Classics).

Turgenev, I. S. (1960–68) *Polnoe sobranie sochinenii i pisem v piatnadtsati tomakh* (Moscow: Izdatel'stvo Akademii nauk SSSR).

Utevskii, L. S. (1923) *Smert' Turgeneva 1883–1923* (St. Petersburg: Atenei).

Vinitsky, I. (2015) 'The thinking oyster: Turgenev's "Drama of Dying" as the decay of Russian realism', in K. Bowers and A. Kokobobo (eds), *Russian Writers and the Fin de Siècle: The Twilight of Realism* (Cambridge: Cambridge University Press), pp. 249–67.

Vinitsky, I. (2009) *Ghostly Paradoxes: Modern Spiritualism and Russian Culture in the Age of Realism* (Toronto: University of Toronto Press).

Watt, I. (2001) *The Rise of the Novel: Studies in Defoe, Richardson, and Fielding* [1957] (Berkeley and Los Angeles: University of California Press).

Webster Goodwin, S. and E. Bronfen (eds) (1993) *Death and Representation* (Baltimore, MD: Johns Hopkins University Press).

Whitehead, C. (2007) 'Anton Chekhov's "The Black Monk": An example of the fantastic?' *The Slavonic and East European Review*, 85.4: 600–29.

12

Vijay Mishra

Afterdeath and the Bollywood Gothic noir

In monotheistic eschatology, death is life-affirming because it is a temporary state that will be transformed into blissful eternity on the Day of Judgment or, as it is called in Islam, at the moment of *Qayamat*. This positive narrative of death and afterlife, hope and affirmation, is for the believer or, failing that, for people who have led peaceful, God-fearing lives untainted by doubt, or those who have otherwise made peace with God before their time of death. For those who fail to live up to religious dictates, culture developed the idea of unhealthy souls forever roaming this world or some other underworld until such time when they might find redemption. The Second Coming is, in this context, the ultimate sign of hope. This is more or less the easy, comfortable narrative of death and afterlife, and it is comfortable because reason has created it as largely non-threatening.

The Gothic – here read as the underside of reason – intervenes in the logic of this consoling narrative of death and redemption through a transgressive act grounded in an alternative logic designed to explore not afterlife but 'afterdeath'. This alternative logic – or anti-logic – is not an attack on belief, but a question of the encounter with our own selves, our own mortality, not as metaphysics but as 'corporeality', as body qua body. What is the evocative power of the dead body, its stench, its skeletal remains, its final extinction and absolute transformation into dust? What is the nature of the affects of the 'dead' body, a concrete 'thing', different from death as a metaphysical 'idea'? Death and the 'dead' now begin to occupy different spaces; they generate different meanings. The dead is an uncanny presence for which a new, 'nauseous' discourse becomes essential. This discourse is the discourse of the Gothic with its dark, anti-Romantic semantics and its narrative of the 'return' and the 'double', because the dead is our Other. It is not so much a discourse of terror and fear as a statement about our own complicity in the desire for death. This desire, this compulsion to repeat the pleasure principle, an urge towards the oceanic sublime, transforms the reassuring idea of death found in saviour religions into an atavistic, primal longing for dissolution in the dead body itself.

In this discourse, it is space – of the mansion, the castle – that is often the key signifier that triggers in the mind (the signified) the repressed narrative of desire. As a nightmare house, the mansion/castle is also the space of the dead, which will confine the subject whose fascination with this space marks the beginnings of the subject's complicity in the unspeakable narrative that the castle contains or to which it gives impetus. In the canonical literary Gothic by such authors as Walpole, Reeve, Radcliffe, Lewis, and Maturin, the castle draws into its space the reader who is a second-hand participant in the transgressions that may take place in it. But in spite of the threats that it poses to the subject, and to the reader, it has this enormous power of attraction as it draws them both into its mysteries, and provides them with residual unconscious material that would threaten sanity through the return of the repressed. This space is no more than a mental precipice that challenges us to jump into the abyss without the law of reason deterring us. In the classic Gothic formulation, this is where '*I and the Abyss*' (after Ralph Waldo Emerson) become one (Mishra, 1994: 250).

We see this compulsion and, indeed, the alternative narrative of death graphically in a foundational text of the Gothic discourse of afterdeath, Charles Maturin's *Melmoth the Wanderer* (1820). In the classic corpus of the literary Gothic, no character is faced with the eternal recurrence of death to the same degree as Melmoth, the eponymous anti-hero of the novel, who is damned to be forever 'there': 'Yes! – THERE I must be, and for ever! And *will* you, and *dare* you, be with me?' (Maturin, 1972: 323). 'There', capitalised in the text because it is the space of Death occupied by Melmoth, makes him, in terms of the logic of Gothic power, compulsively attractive to whomever he meets. The pure demonic in him, as in Faust, is the new *mysterium tremendum*, the tremendous mystery that theology associates with the figure of God who, to make life livable, has to be allegorised and transformed into a moral principle. Charles Maturin's work defers death through writing (manuscripts are systemically redacted in the tale-within-a-tale structure) as the search proceeds for someone willing to take on Melmoth's agonisingly endless presence through an act of will. His destiny, though, is so frightening that no one could possibly participate in it. 'None can participate in my destiny', he says, 'but with his own consent – *none have consented* – none can be involved in its tremendous penalties, but by participation' (author's emphasis) (537). Yet his attractiveness is so strong that he becomes, in the words of one of the characters in the novel, Stanton, 'the necessary condition of one's existence' (59). The condition is disturbing but it attests to the uncanny logic that informs an alternative, non-religious theorising of death.

Melmoth is a restless, damned spirit; his Faustian pact is such that he needs someone to take his place. But Maturin keeps writing Melmoth's story, embedding each tale into another as if the act of writing itself is a deferral of death because the latter is 'unpresentable' to consciousness. The Gothic, as a discourse, responds to a need, the need to blast open representation itself, to question its assumptions through rebellious, alternative reasons. But the advent of the Gothic in the mid eighteenth century (Horace Walpole's *The Castle of Otranto* appeared in 1764) also coincides with the high point of European imperialism. It became one of the more readily available and heavily consumed literary discourses under colonialism even in America. It follows that the Gothic quickly became part of a world-literary system along the lines theorised by Franco Moretti (2011) and as such, elsewhere, outside of Europe, it entered into a compromise with local literary conventions and forms of representation. One such compromise was the Indian compromise. The question arises: What happens to the Gothic when the genre enters a different definition of afterdeath where the latter is defined not as an instance of the demonic in us (the figure of the impure, the unsanctified, the satanic 'undead') but as a principle of rebirth and reincarnation that informs the Hindu way of life? When, in India's greatest epic, the *Mahābhārata* (VI.xv. verse 15 and V.lx. verse 193), the heroic family patriarch Bhīṣma refuses to fight Śikhaṇḍin because, in his previous life, Śikhaṇḍin was a woman, his action changes the course of the epic. Bhīṣma's principled stand invokes a code of honour that applies to people both in and out of lived historical time, in other words, to the living as well as the dead. This new idea of death, which has karmic consequences in an afterlife, is built into language, here Sanskrit, which has, alongside the common word for death – *mṛtyu* – other words such as *antakāla* (the end of time), *vināśa* (destruction), and *pralaya* (apocalypse), among many more. The Bhīṣma–Śikhaṇḍin encounter, within a comparative context, challenges us to reframe Melmoth's 'unspeakable', 'unutterable', 'indescribable' destiny in an Indian narrative of reincarnation.

In a world-literary system, the Gothic circulated as a discourse with its idioms, narrative conventions, and atmospherics. These idioms (or matters of style) prioritised dark, brooding melancholy, the language of sentimentality, the troublesome logic of the uncanny and an obsessive but uneasy familiarity with death. But Gothic death was still very much linked to a Christian understanding of death and a dualistic conception of man's relationship with God. The Indian compromise had to transpose both the discourse (its formal elements) and the epistemology (its knowledge base) onto a monistic conception of self and God and the principle of an eternal recurrence that is rebirth or reincarnation. This reformulation of the Gothic began initially as a literary compromise but found its most powerful articulation not in Indian literature but in the Bollywood film.

It is important to note that this filmic articulation was never unmediated, never a case of a straightforward appropriation of the Gothic under the sign of Hindu demonic sacralisation or monistic polytheism. It was, instead, yet another compromise, a compromise between the local and the Hollywood global, for the fact remains that the Bollywood Gothic film mode – the Bollywood Gothic noir – is directly indebted to the Hollywood Gothic noir, a cinematic form distinguished by a visual style borrowed from film noir. The exemplary text of the latter form is *The Postman Always Rings Twice* (1946) whose cinematic style and narrative technique – voice-over, flashback (both from a privileged male point of view), *mise en scène*, and use of space – made it a definitive text of the genre. Before it became indistinguishable from the horror film, or merged into it, the Gothic noir films extended the sub-genre of the film noir mystery thriller by exploring the darker side of killers. Its narratives too became a lot more menacing, ambiguous, and irresolvable. Over a very short and concentrated period, in films such as *The Lodger* (1944), *The Body Snatchers* (1945), *Bedlam* (1946), *Ivy* (1947), *Moss Rose* (1947), *So Evil My Love* (1948), and *Reign of Terror* (1949), the Gothic noir found its own style: deep, ominous shadows that exposed a character's inner turmoil and sense of alienation from the world, expressionistic chiaroscuro contrastive lighting and, generally, an intrusive visual style about which the spectator was always conscious (Svetov, 2009). At all levels – visual representation, sonality, narrative, characterisation of the femme fatale and the alienated and doomed anti-hero, and invocation of an earlier, darker, age – the Gothic noir (and its film noir antecedent) has what may be called a schizophrenic register, and a particular 'look and feel' throughout.

An informed analytic of the Bollywood Gothic noir shows that, whilst the principles of representation in it can be readily explained with reference to its Hollywood counterpart – two defining Bollywood Gothic noirs are contemporaneous with the Hollywood 'moment' of the genre – its narrative intentionality, its semantic content, its mood, and indeed, its overall ideology, are much more problematic and require theorisation of a different order. Before its genre collapsed into the Gothic horror (or horror generally), Gothic noir had nothing to do with 'afterdeath' (as theory and practice) as its interest was in exploring the darker, repressed side of the human mind. In this context its interest was more with the tormented, selfish, sexually disturbing aspects of the human condition than with the supernatural or the paranormal. If the latter existed at all, it was present in the film's visual form, and primarily captured in the film's *mise en scènes*. The shift to the Bollywood Gothic noir necessitates a more capacious reading of the Gothic noir in that the supernatural has to be factored in. Hindu reincarnation implied that a key feature of the Gothic – the idea of the uncanny – was a pre-given available to consciousness because its prior occurrence in an earlier life could be recalled. Past lives shadow present existence; like numbers in Indic culture, they 'read' us. This was something that the American transcendentalist Ralph Waldo Emerson was certainly aware of as he read Charles Wilkins' translation of the *Bhagavadgītā* (Mishra, 1994: 249).

The filmic form of the Gothic noir was given a local semantic content as the Gothic entered a world-literary system. Melmoth's endless agony is within time; in the Bollywood Gothic noir, the encounter with Death is not something that the subject has experienced in history but outside of history or in a trans-history. As a minor reincarnation sub-genre within a capacious Bollywood genre of melodrama, the Bollywood Gothic noir reworks an empowering but 'virtual' Hindu reincarnation teleology (noted in the Bhīṣma–Śikhaṇḍin episode) and instantiates it as a lived experience in the here and now. The Gothic noir in its Bollywood avatar erupts to challenge a karmic narrative, which stipulates that since our lives have already been written in terms of our previous lives, selves as agents are less important than selves as carriers of one's past lives. To the grand narrative of reincarnation, the Bollywood Gothic noir – given its colonial antecedents in Gothic sentimentality and the powerful presence of film noir – brings the culture's everyday demotic (its language of ghosts, spirits, and the *āsurīm*, the demonic principle) into play and disturbs its seamless metaphysical understanding of a recurring afterlife in search of the nirvanic/oceanic sublime (Mishra, 1998: 76–7). Selves become agents of change as, in the reincarnated life, the errors of the previous life are corrected, or the narrative of one's previous life is replicated with a sense of redemption. In this respect, the Bollywood Gothic noir theoretically parted company with the Hollywood Gothic noir that, drawing on film noir, gradually turned into a brooding, dark form that, with the advent of colour, used a dark palette as its visual medium (Mishra, 2012).

To the general analytic of the coupling of the Gothic and Death – the repressed underside of discourses of Death in the Enlightenment, the idea of the 'undead' as a satanic instance of Christian retributive justice, and generally its uncanny presence in culture (features that made their way into the German Expressionist Friedrich Murnau's silent horror film from 1922, *Nosferatu*) – the Bollywood Gothic noir brings the idea of an afterlife as an epistemology of reflection and self-correction of one's own erstwhile fragility. But since the genre as received – that is, the genre of the Gothic – is one of excess, dread, horror, and the unpresentable, carrying as it does the ghost of Melmoth, it disturbs one's conventional understanding of reincarnation narratives grounded in a positive and energising theory of one's larger ethical responsibilities in the dual context of this life and an 'other' life. In this respect, the Bollywood Gothic noir exposes, perhaps unconsciously, the darker underside of karmic retribution: 'I am become death, the destroyer of the worlds', says the Dark Lord in the *Bhagavadgītā* (ch. XI, verse 32). And in its use of film noir modes of visual representation, the Bollywood Gothic brings about, at least in its black-and-white films, a disturbance in the spectator's culturally conditioned reading of death and rebirth. The conditioning is linked to the comforting Hindu-Buddhist principle of reincarnation that incorporates an ethics of living: our present karma influences our future reincarnated lives. In this reading, the Dead is not a spectral, haunting presence that disturbs the mind and the laws of reason, nor, moreover, is it a presence that questions the construction of meaning through our senses alone. The Dead is our own past, the recall of which, in the Bollywood Gothic noir, is presented as an incomplete narrative that requires completing in the here and now. This is the invariable logic of this filmic form, which is also its contribution to the larger discourse of the Gothic within a world-literary and filmic system.

I turn now to two films – Kishore Sahu's *Nadiya Ke Paar* (*Across the River*) (1948) and Kamal Amrohi's *Mahal* (*The Mansion*) (1949) – made at the high point of the Hollywood Gothic noir, through which to commence consideration of reincarnation narratives as a variation on the Gothic spectres of Death.

What are the establishing shots in *Nadiya Ke Paar*? A doctor gets off a train and finds that no one is waiting to take him to his landlord patient in a village some distance away. He gets on a horse and makes his way, only to find that he has to spend the night in a *bastī* (a small settlement) as the night is stormy and no one is willing to take him across the river. The film establishes some of the classic features of the Gothic noir, including thunder, lightning, rain, the chiaroscuro effects of light and dark, strange sounds, a madwoman's laughter, howling winds, and screams. The villagers refuse to take him across even when he is willing to pay good money. He is told that no one has crossed the river at night and returned, for it holds the spirits of lovers who died five years earlier. The doctor replies in English, 'What nonsense!' but is persuaded to spend the night in a small hut that has remained closed over that time. As he tries to sleep, the window latch keeps opening, not unlike Lockwood's experience on his first night at Wuthering Heights in Emily Brontë's haunting novel. The door also opens and closes; he tries to pull a sheet that keeps being dragged back. He hears voices, a cry, and then someone slaps him, and he falls. He calls the villagers and says they told him the truth about the spirits.

The retrospective story, the flashback recounting how the class-crossed lovers could not be together and drowned during a fracas between the rival parties, begins in the typical Gothic noir style. The villagers speak of voices that are still heard, and the interdiction on crossing the river in the night remains. The expression used – *janam janam tak saṅgh rahemge*, 'in each life they will be together' – becomes a refrain in all Bollywood Gothic noir as corporeal return in reincarnated bodies is a foregone conclusion. *Nadiya Ke Paar* remains spectral because whatever happened to the doctor in the hut is known only to him (and the spectator). The film establishes many of the elements of visual style that get picked up in later films. This visual style is limited, however, to the first moment of encounter when the outsider enters the spectral space. What is recalled, by the newcomer or by the people affected by the supernatural, is given as a more or less realist melodramatic narrative. It is as if the uncanny space alone holds ghostly secrets and the experience within that space constitutes the defining moment of the Bollywood Gothic noir. In *Nadiya Ke Paar*, it is the space of the hut; soon after, this space is transformed into a mansion, the *mahal*, the *havelī*, the Indian version of the Gothic castle.

Unsurprisingly, the next Gothic noir is in fact called *Mahal*, which is unarguably the first significant Bollywood Gothic noir. In spite of its many subsequent imitators, *Mahal* remains unsurpassed in the genre. Cinematographed by the German-Indian Josef Wirsching, it foregrounds the space of a mansion/castle in its title, a space that is often the nodal point for Gothic texts. In *Mahal*, mystery surrounds the mansion; neglected for years, it is the home of a gardener and an elusive veiled woman whose voice is heard first as she sings the haunting *āyegā āyegā … āgeyā āne vālā* ('He'll come, he'll come, my lover is destined to come'). Other establishing features of the Bollywood Gothic noir follow: a portrait that is an uncanny duplicate of the new owner of the mansion, a clock that chimes at two o'clock every morning, the sense of synchronicity, swinging chandeliers, and strange statements about the arrival of a newcomer who will complete an unfinished tale of tragic love as a kind of compulsive return through rebirth. The engine of the narrative is an enigma built around a young woman awaiting the return of her lover who, it seems, in his previous life, looked exactly like the new owner of the mansion (see Figure 12.1).

But the fulfilment of desire in this narrative of eternal recurrence is possible only in death: to die is to be reunited. At one point, the girl in the mansion who says she has been waiting for his return all these years, asks the new owner, 'You desire me? Do you know the consequences of desire?' 'Yes', he replies, 'My death'. But desire must remain unfulfilled and the film ends without an adequate closure. Shankar, the new owner of the mansion, dies looking exactly like his duplicate in the portrait. Kamini the veiled woman, the object of desire, the uncanny woman who is here and in the past, will remain waiting until, in another life, another stranger will enter the mansion. *Mahal* is the great precursor text of the Bollywood Gothic noir. It remains the defining achievement precisely because of these ambiguous moments. What is noteworthy here is the way in which the Bollywood Gothic noir has internalised a colonial discourse onto which are strategically grafted elements from the vast tradition of Indian thought. The use of the Hindu theory of reincarnation, in fact, expands the capacities of the Gothic form and ultimately connects it with an underlying impulse toward the sublime that characterises Hindu aesthetic theories generally.

Although *Udan Khatola* (*The Flying Machine*) (1955), is a romantic

12.1 *Mahal* (*The Mansion*), Kamal Amrohi (1949) – The uncanny resemblance to past life.

fantasy about waiting for the return of a lover, now dead, and the wish to unite with her on the part of the man left behind, it is *Madhumati* (1958) that provides us with the consummate text of the Bollywood Gothic noir. Although crafted in the genre of melodrama to a degree greater than the other films previously discussed, the film destabilises the received reincarnation ideology with features both cinematic and thematic. The cinematographic techniques are more clear-cut, as is the threat of sexual violation within the confines of the Gothic mansion or *haveli* (Mishra, 2002: 55–9). Two people, an engineer (Devendra, played by Dilip Kumar) and his doctor friend (played by Tarun Bose), enter a decaying mansion on a stormy night. They are welcomed by an old inhabitant who flashes a hurricane lamp on the strangers before they enter the mansion (see Figure 12.2).

The doctor remains nonchalant, seeking a fire to warm himself. The engineer Devendra is disturbed as he has an uncanny sense of 'having been here before'. His agitation is rendered through the use of light and dark, shadows on the wall, curtains moving in the wind, and sounds that he alone hears, sounds of someone scratching, sobbing, and calling from afar while a clock chimes eight o'clock in the evening. A painting

12.2 *Madhumati,* Bimal Roy (1958) – Entry into the mansion.

hanging on the wall falls and Devendra exclaims, 'These are my own brush strokes, this is my painting' (see Figure 12.3).

The disturbed Devendra begins to remember his past life when, as Anand, he came as a colonial government forest overseer to these parts. He meets a girl, Madhumati, and falls in love, all standard Bollywood sentimentality, with intertextual connections made via song syntagms: the central song of *Mahal* (*āyegā, āyegā*) is replaced in the later film by *ājā re pardesī* ('O come to me stranger'), and punctuates the film at crucial moments. Against the pastoral serenity of the country, the space of the one standout house, the impressive mansion of the landlord, is the stronghold of evil. Herein resides Ugra Narayan, rapist of women as well as of the environment, and it is in his mansion that one of the great repressed themes of the Gothic is played out: the mansion as the space of violation and murder. Bollywood reincarnation narrative meets its absolute Other here in the tale of unspeakable horror as Madhumati is raped and killed. This is the tale that Devendra recalls in the mansion and it is a tale in which the ghost of Madhumati, after it had played a role in establishing Ugra Narayan's guilt in her own ghostly afterdeath, invites Anand to his own death as he follows the spectre to the edge of the mansion's flat roof. Although the recalled narrative carries the

12.3 *Madhumati,* Bimal Roy (1958) – 'These are my own brush strokes'.

obvious elements of the Bollywood melodrama by way of those spectres of sentimentality that define the form, it is the horror of violation
and the death of the lovers that remain at the narrative's centre.

In as much as its recalled narrative of a past merges with the present,
Madhumati is the definitive text of Bollywood Gothic noir. It could
have ended with the recalled narrative that explained Devendra's feelings of the uncanny in the space of the decaying Gothic mansion. It
does not, however, as, in afterdeath, the incomplete narrative of love-
in-union (*sambhoga* in Sanskrit terminology) of the inset incarnation
story concludes in redemption. The storm at an end, Devendra goes to
the station to collect his wife and child. There had been a train accident
but his family is unharmed. The wife is a spitting image of Madhumati.
This feature of a reincarnated life as a corrective to a prior life functions
as the larger frame narrative of the Bollywood Gothic noir but even as
it functions as such, the discourses of film noir infiltrate the representation, inserting in the recollected past narrative uncertainty and perhaps even doubts about reincarnation's truth-value, its non-negotiable
validity in culture. The visual elements of the received form thus dis-
turb a metaphysics of the reincarnated life as a corrective to the real or
palpable errors of one's past life. Given that the 'feeling tones' come

from elsewhere – in the case of the Bollywood Gothic noir from the English texts of the coloniser and from Hollywood Gothic noir films – reincarnation narratives are now 'wounded' by imported generic conventions. The uncanny and, with it, death, enter the Bollywood Gothic film noir: in *Mahal*, Shankar's earlier 'reincarnation' is drowned; in *Madhumati*, the spirit of the dead girl lures Anand to his death. (See Figure 12.4). It is the mansion, the space of transgression, where the rape of the innocent occurs, which begins to define the Indian Gothic noir. This *mahal*, the *haveli*, the Indian version of the Gothic castle, will also contain sounds, a painting of someone at the crux of the narrative, dark corridors and staircases, chandeliers, an ancient servant, and eerie noises that recall something that reason cannot immediately grasp. Upon entering this space, a space that also encapsulates British imperial architecture as a colonial space, memory is triggered and the stranger, stranded on a stormy night, recalls his past. What *Madhumati* avoids is heavy metaphysical coding as there is simply a secular acceptance of eternal recurrence, rebirth as a karmic event without religious connotations. In this sense, the Indian Gothic noir tames the unpresentable by transforming it into a life-event, albeit one that occurred in one's previous life.

12.4 *Madhumati*, Bimal Roy (1958) – The double and colonial architecture.

The Bollywood Gothic noir effectively ends with *Madhumati*. When reincarnation themes, albeit within a thematic register that includes the mandatory entry into the space of the mansion noted above, appear again in *Milan* (*The* Union) (1967), *Mehbooba* (Beloved) (1976), *Karz* (Debt) (1980), *Kudrat* (Divine Power) (1981), *Janam Janam* (Forever Together) (1988), *Banjaran* (The Gypsy) (1991), *Karan Arjun* (1995), *Om Shanti Om* (2007), *Karzzz* (Debt) (2008), *Phhir* (Once Again*)* (2011), and *Dangerous Ishq* (Dangerous Liaisons) (2012), the films are made in colour, thus sacrificing the formal cinematic elements of visual representation that defined the Gothic noir. Without noir's visual register – the 'atmosphere of fear and paranoia' and 'moral ambivalence' (Conrad, 2006: 1) that governs film noir generally – these reincarnation films are invested with heavy metaphysical baggage where the narrative of Bhīṣma (that, with its gods, ascetics, and revenge motifs, was always ambivalent) is replaced by the directive of Krishna to Arjuna in the *Bhagavadgītā* (ch. II, verse 13): *tathā dehāntaraprāptir* ('And likewise it attains another body'). The Bollywood Gothic noir becomes a lot more schematic with retributive justice (in the specifically karmic sense) at its core, as the goddess Kali in both her dark and destructive, as well as her benign, supportive, and caring *Durga* form, enters the text. One senses that the Bollywood Gothic noir, which always carried a sense of the uncanny, is now replaced by memorial recall as a mode that re-enacts a past act and life or fulfils the uncompleted narrative of one's past life. Since reincarnation as a religious principle is offered as absolute truth, the recall itself cannot be contested.

The one 'colour Gothic noir' that captures something of the earlier black-and-white Gothic is *Talaash* (2012), which carries the English subtitle 'The Answer Lies Within'. In this whodunnit thriller, a police inspector, Surjan (Aamir Khan), suffers from bouts of hallucination after the drowning of his son for which he feels he was responsible. In trying to unravel the inexplicable cause of the death of film star Armaan Kapoor, he comes across the call-girl Rosie who gives him important clues about the crime. It transpires that Rosie is revealed to be non-existent, a figment of his imagination. However, when he returns to the desolated foreshore where Rosie used to take him to discuss her life, he digs up a small patch of earth and discovers the remains of a dead body. On the skeleton's finger is a large purple ring that he had seen on Rosie. Although shot in colour, *Talaash* rediscovers the genre. It bypasses the parallel reincarnation narratives of the later years beginning with *Milan* (1967), and reconnects with *Nadiya Ke Paar*, *Mahal* and *Madhumati*, the classic black-and-white Bollywood Gothic noirs. In all of them, spectres of the past inform peoples' lives as there was always an eerie sense of the presence of the other-worldly incorporated as a disturbing and dangerous supplement. *Talaash* introduces this dangerous supplement as the narrative is not a reincarnation narrative of recall: the spectre is both real and unreal.

The *mysterium tremendum* that informs reincarnation narratives and the idea of Hindu Godhead generally insinuates a different order of the compulsion to repeat/return. The uncanny is not part of affect. Neither is it pathological or a function of the return of the repressed, but a narrative capable of memorial recall. The pure demonic in Melmoth, for whom salvation requires that someone else takes up his burden of eternal recurrence, is replaced by a recurrence that can be both mysterious and redemptive. Herein lies the dilemma, as the classic Bollywood Gothic noir is faced with a complex problematic, one that conjoins an alien literary and cinematic form, with its ambiguous, contradictory, and psychological themes, to a local grand and religiously sanctioned narrative of reincarnation. It is this fusion that disrupts the redemptive and often retributive nature of reincarnation stories and takes the spectator to the latent, under-theorised law of the uncanny in Indian culture. Through this fusion, the Bollywood Gothic noir insinuates a disturbance in the received grand narrative of Hindu reincarnation by suggesting that our past lives haunt us like spectres: they were not redemptive then, and are not now. The message of the traditional British Gothic attains another register and theme when transposed, in world-literary terms, onto a belief system featuring reincarnation.

References

Allen, L. (1948) (dir.) *So Evil My Love* [Film] (USA: Paramount Pictures).

Amrohi, K. (dir.) (1949) *Mahal* (The Mansion) [Film] (India: Ashok Kumar Production).

Anand, C. (dir.) (1981) *Kudrat* (Divine Power) [Film] (India: B. S. Khanna Production).

Bhatt, V. (dir.) (2012) *Dangerous Ishq* (Dangerous Liaisons) [Film] (India: ASA Production).

Brahm, J. (dir.) (1944) *The Lodger* [Film] (USA: Twentieth Century Fox).

Conrad, M. T. (ed.) (2006) *The Philosophy of Film Noir* (Lexington, KY: University of Kentucky Press).

Dhamija, G. (dir.) (2011) *Phhir* (Once Again) [Film] (India: ASA Production).

Garnett, T. (dir.) (1946) *The Postman Always Rings Twice* [Film] (USA: Metro-Goldwyn-Mayer).

Ghai, S. (dir.) (1980) *Karz* (Debt) [Film] (India: Akhtar Farooq & Jagjit Khuram Production).

Kagti, R. (dir.) (2012) *Talaash* (The Search) [Film] (India: Amir Khan Production).

Kaushik, S. (dir.) (2008) *Karzzz* (Debt) [Film] (India: Gulshan Kumar Production).

Khan, F. (dir.) (2007) *Om Shanti Om* [Film] (India: Shah Rukh Khan and Gauri Khan Production).

Malhotra, H. (dir.) (1991) *Banjaran* (The Gypsy) [Film] (India: Om Prakash Mittal & Ram Singh Production).

Mann, A. (dir.) (1949) *Reign of Terror* [Film] (USA: Eagle-Lion Films).

Maturin, C. (1972) *Melmoth the Wanderer* [1820], ed. B. Vickers (Oxford: Oxford University Press).

Mishra, V. (1994) *The Gothic Sublime* (Albany, NY: State University of New York Press).

Mishra, V. (1998) *Devotional Poetics and the Indian Sublime* (Albany, NY: State University of New York Press).

Mishra, V. (2012) 'The Gothic Sublime', in D. Punter (ed.), *A New Companion to the Gothic* (Oxford: Wiley-Blackwell), pp. 288–306.

Mishra, V. (2002) *Bollywood Cinema: Temples of Desire* (New York: Routledge).

Moretti, F. (2011) 'Conjectures on World Literature', in L. Connell and N. Marsh (eds), *Literature and Globalisation* (London: Routledge), pp. 99–103.

Murnau, F. W. (dir.) (1922) *Nosferatu* [Film] (Germany: Film Arts Guild).

Rao, A. S. (dir.) (1967) *Milan* (The Union) [Film] (India: L. V. Prasad Production).

Ratoff, G. (dir.) (1947) *Moss Rose* [Film] (USA: Twentieth Century Fox).

Robson, M. (dir.) (1946) *Bedlam* [Film] (USA: RKO Radio Pictures).

Roshan, R. (dir.) (1995) *Karan Arjun* [Film] (India: Rakesh Roshan Production).

Roy, B. (dir.) (1958) *Madhumati* [Film] (India: Bimal Roy Production).

Sadanah, V. (dir.) (1988) *Janam Janam* (Forever Together) [Film] (India: Goel Cine Production).

Sahu, K. (dir.) (1948) *Nadiya Ke Paar* (Across the River) [Film] (India: Kishore Sahu Production).

Samanta, S. (dir.) (1976) *Mehbooba* (Beloved) [Film] (India: Munshir Ria Production).

Sunny, S. U. (dir.) (1955) *Udan Khatola* (The Flying Machine) [Film] (India: Sunny Art Production).

Svetov, M. (2009) 'Noir and the gothic' [Part 1], *Noir City Sentinel* [Online] (Oct./Nov. 2008) and 'Gothic noir' [Part 2], *Noir City Sentinel* [Online] (July/Aug. 2009). Available at: www.transatlantichabit.com/noir/Noir-and-Gothic-pt1–2.pdf. Accessed 12 May 2015.

The Bhagavadgītā in the Mahābhārata (1981) ed. and trans. J. A. B. van Buitenen (Chicago: University of Chicago Press).

The Māhabhārata (1944–59) (Poona: Bhandarkar Institute).

Walpole, R. (1982) *The Castle of Otranto* [1764], ed. W. S. Lewis (Oxford: Oxford University Press).

Wise, R. (dir.) (1945) *The Body Snatchers* [Film] (USA: RKO Radio Pictures).

Wood, S. (dir.) (1947) *Ivy* [Film] (USA: Universal Pictures).

Part V

Twenty-first-century Gothic and death

13

Michelle J. Smith

Dead and ghostly children in contemporary literature for young people

The Gothic has become a popular genre in children's and young adult literature published in the past decade. Stephenie Meyer's 'Twilight' series (2005–08) is the most visible and bestselling example of fiction for young people concerned with the boundaries between the living and the dead. However, there is a large and growing body of contemporary popular fiction for young readers that focuses on interactions with vampires, werewolves, zombies, and ghosts. Many of these novels, as in the paranormal romance genre, depict human teen protagonists who must grapple with the challenges of falling in love with, or being threatened by, the dead.[1] Less common, however, are novels for young readers in which the child protagonists themselves are dead or ghostly. The death of children is particularly problematic in literature intended for young people given perceptions of childhood innocence and the contemporary Western practice of shielding children from the disturbing truth of mortality.

While the combination of childhood and death, as Kathryn James points out, is 'unsettling', examining how death is depicted in children's texts 'can provide an unusually clear opportunity to understand some of the ways in which meaning is created and shared within a society' (2009: 2). Gothic children's literature displaces the anxieties that ordinarily accompany the representation of child death in realist fiction. The fiction examined in this chapter, including Sonya Hartnett's *The Ghost's Child* (2007), Chris Priestley's *Uncle Montague's Tales of Terror* (2007), Neil Gaiman's *The Graveyard Book* (2008), and Ransom Riggs' *Miss Peregrine's Home for Peculiar Children* (2011), represents spectral children who, in diverse ways, interact with history by rewriting past wrongs committed, or experienced by, adults. The intended readership of these texts ranges from pre-teens for Priestley's collection of short stories to young adults in the instance of Hartnett's novel, yet they all operate in ways distinct from that of contemporary Gothic fictions for adults. Steven Bruhm argues that Gothic literature for adults typically emphasises the role of '*children* as the bearers of death' (emphasis added) (2006: 98). In contrast, this chapter demonstrates how recent Gothic fictions for young people mobilise ghostly children to critique or remedy adult actions, often expressing distrust in adults as authority figures. The dead or ghostly children in these works do not unsettle other characters or the reader as they do in many ghost stories, but instead expose the serious harms posed to children by selfish or evil adults.[2]

Theorising and historicising the ghostly child

Ghosts occupy a liminal space between the living and the dead, not yet having 'passed over' to an imagined afterlife and, instead, haunting the living with their spectral presence. Similarly, children occupy a transitional state between infancy and adulthood. The genre of ghost stories, Julia Briggs notes, constantly challenges 'the rational order and the observed laws of nature … reintroducing what is perceived as fearful, alien, excluded or dangerously marginal' (2012: 176). Ghostly children combine two threateningly marginal categories. Yet in recent Gothic children's literature, they are not constructed as engendering fear, as in the traditional ghost story for adult readers. As Dale Townshend explains, ghost stories were historically excluded from literature intended for young people; from the origins of children's literature as a distinct form in the eighteenth century, 'culturally approved forms of children's literature become everything that the Gothic is not' (2007: 21). With shifting perceptions of childhood and the purpose of children's reading, recent children's literature has embraced the Gothic tropes of ghostly and dead children.

While the genre largely avoided Gothic conventions in order to conform to adult expectations of didacticism and moral improvement, nineteenth-century children's literature, in particular, commonly represented dead and dying children. Indeed, Judith Plotz explains that 'the high tide of cultural concern with death is contemporary with the emergence of children's literature' (1995: 3) and argues that literary

representations of childhood death were 'part of the enabling conditions for creating and recognizing children's literature' (1995: 4). In
the kinds of fiction to which Plotz makes reference, death acts as a
'stranger preserver' (1995: 3), producing 'immortal children, freed by
one tactic or another from the dilapidations of time and history' (1995:
17). Kimberley Reynolds shows that nineteenth-century fiction used
child death to provide religious warnings, social critique, and dispose
of troublesome girl protagonists (2000: 169–70). Yet she also builds
on Plotz's contention by arguing that in fantasy literature of the period,
the death of child protagonists is celebrated and depicted as desirable, stemming from the idea of innocent childhood as 'the closest
humans get to perfection' (2000: 171–2). In these books, including
Charles Kingsley's *The Water-Babies* (1863) and George MacDonald's
At the Back of the North Wind (1868–69), death is the beginning of
an adventurous and 'important phase of life' (Reynolds, 2000: 173).
Both Reynolds and Plotz highlight the process by which child death
in nineteenth-century children's literature elevated the status of
childhood – making it 'more real' (Plotz, 1995: 17) than adulthood –
and resisted the sense that a dead child was a loss to be mourned.

Indeed, in reality, the need to mourn lost children was common. Pat
Jalland records a death rate in England and Wales varying between 148
and 154 per 1,000 live births for children under the age of one across the
period 1840 to 1900 (1996: 3). In response to the frequency of child
death owing to diseases such as scarlet fever, surviving siblings and parents commonly understood child death as a 'fact of life' (Jalland, 1996:
133). Given this high rate of infant mortality in the Victorian period,
the existence of comforting and reassuring stories about child death,
influenced by Christian beliefs about heaven, are unsurprising.

Dramatic decreases in the likelihood of infant death did not occur
until the twentieth century, during which the rate fell from 100 in 1916
to less than 16 in 1983 (Jalland, 1996: 120). This improvement in
child mortality rates, and substantial decrease in the lived experience
of child death, corresponds with the decline of death as an appropriate
subject matter for inclusion in children's literature. Emer O'Sullivan
proposes that death was 'ousted' from realistic children's fiction from
the late nineteenth century, remaining absent until the 1960s and
1970s when European children's literature adopted a 'matter-of-fact
and educational', rather than religiously oriented, approach (2005:
26). In English children's literature, Lynne Vallone suggests that
child death re-emerges in novels from the 1950s in which post-war

feelings of childhood alienation are 'resolved by Uncanny-Children' (2007: 33).

In recent Gothic children's literature, child death or ghostliness is not entwined with idolisation of the state of childhood, nor is death depicted as the gateway to a unique period of adventure. Instead, as will be illustrated in the following section, ghostly children serve as reminders of the passage of time, and of the adult failings that have produced historical wrongs. Ghostly children in contemporary Gothic fiction do not function as pathways for human child protagonists to find a place to belong, as in post-war fiction, but as a corrective for adult misdeeds or missed opportunities. Death is not depicted as the path to immortality or an endless, idealised childhood. Instead, child death is presented as an unnatural event that is to be regretted, with childhood understood as only a temporary phase in the necessary path to maturation into adulthood.

Contemporary Gothic children's literature

In Neil Gaiman's *The Graveyard Book*, the protagonist Nobody Owens ('Bod') is perched precariously between life and death throughout his childhood. The illustrated novel begins with the Man Jack, a member of the Jacks of All Trades secret society, attempting to murder baby Bod after already having slain the rest of his family. Bod escapes and is raised by ghosts within a nearby graveyard who protect him from the society. He is given the Freedom of the Graveyard, which enables him to see 'as the dead see' (Gaiman, 2008: 78), and is taught the supernatural abilities of Haunting, Fading, Slipping, and Dream Walking. His appointed guardian, Silas, who has the ability to visit the human world to procure food for Bod, is most likely a vampire. Unlike traditional representations of ghosts as discontented or needing to right wrongs connected with their death, *The Graveyard Book* depicts a seemingly infinite period of ghostly existence for every human who dies. The graveyard is home to ghosts who lived as people during all periods of British history, dating back to the Roman occupation. Ghosts, therefore, are afforded a natural, rather than threatening or troubling, status and it is humans who are constructed as evil and dangerous.[3] For instance, it is a pawnshop owner, Abanazer Bolger, and his associate, who imprison Bod, attempt to steal a priceless brooch he recovered from a grave, and plan to surrender him to Jack for a monetary reward.

The Othering of the ghost in *The Graveyard Book* is also diminished in the dance of the 'Macabray' (Danse Macabre), in which the grave-yard residents may leave the graveyard and interact with the living in the town for one night. Death is personified in the form of the Lady in Grey who rides on horseback, and with whom Bod shares the final dance of the evening. The dance that 'had been ancient a thousand years before' (159) comes intuitively and unconsciously to both the living and the dead, emphasising the universality and inevitability of death. The thin line between the living and the dead is traversed in both directions through the conditions of the graveyard. Bod's ghost parents, for example, are able to make the physical contact with him required to care for an infant. In contrast, Bod utilises the 'the way of the dead' (105) to pass unnoticed ('almost ghostly' [183]) once he leaves the safety of the graveyard to attend school.

The jovial graveyard community supports Bod's development in a way that mirrors an ideal human community. In this respect, *The Graveyard Book* shares a link with late Victorian children's fiction that provided comforting and fantastic depictions of otherworlds inhabited by dead children. The novel is indeed distinct among the contemporary examples I shall discuss in this chapter for its overwhelmingly posi-tive portrayal of death, in which the comic possibilities of the Gothic, rather than its potential to evoke fear or terror, are exploited. However, Gaiman's demystification of death for the child reader through a reas-suring portrait of a ghostly society stops short of valorising child death or presenting it as a gateway to adventure as in earlier children's fiction. Instead, the dead continually remind Bod that he will not be one of them 'for a lifetime' (163). As Silas explains to Bod who is naively untroubled by the notion of death because of his life among friendly ghosts:

> they are, for the most part, done with the world. You are not. You're *alive*, Bod. That means you have infinite potential. You can do anything, make anything, dream anything. If you change the world, the world will change. Potential. Once you're dead, it's gone. Over. You've made what you've made, dreamed your dream, written your name. (179)

Throughout the novel, Bod straddles 'the borderland between the living and the dead' (270), but the forces of good continually work to ensure that he is able to mature into adulthood, something that will spell the end of the Jack of All Trades order according to an ancient prophecy. Vampire Silas and werewolf Miss Lupescu are members of the Honour Guard who are described as guarding 'the borderlands' and protecting 'the borders of things' (303). In defending Bod's life, the Honour Guard ensure the rightful place of the child among the living, and valorise childhood's transitory state. *The Graveyard Book* presents death as something less than fearful through the comical interactions between the graveyard inhabitants who enjoy relatively peaceful after-lives. Instead, it pinpoints evil adults who bring about premature death to children as constituting a greater threat than the eventual, natural end of life. Unlike the graveyard's 'family of Victorian children who had all died before their tenth birthdays' (65), Bod's rightful place is in the world outside, among the living in the present. The potential of the child's future 'Life' (307) – a crucial element in the story as Gaiman's capitalisation of the word suggests – is far more significant than fixing children in an innocent state through death, although Gaiman does not shy away from reminding the child reader that Bod will eventually 'return to the graveyard or ride with the Lady on the broad back of her great grey stallion' (307).

In contrast with the supernatural protection afforded to Bod, which enables him to reach his teenage years and embark upon an independent life among the living, almost all of the children in *Uncle Montague's Tales of Terror* cannot be saved. The protagonists of each of the short stories become ghosts or 'shadow children' because they are not sufficiently protected by adults, or because they exhibit traits that defy notions of childhood innocence. While a *Guardian* review of the collection, the first in a series of three books, describes it as 'convincingly Victorian in tone', its representation of childhood death is diametrically opposed to the treatment of the subject in Victorian children's literature (Mangan and Williams, 2010). The protagonist, Edgar, listens as his uncle recounts a series of tales about children who have come to horrifying ends. In this respect, Priestley's collection appears influenced by author and illustrator Edward Gorey, whose abecedarian book *The Gashlycrumb Tinies* (1963) macabrely describes the various demises of twenty-six children in rhyme with a glee that challenged conventional maudlin representations of child death. However, *The Gashlycrumb Tinies*, like Gorey's *oeuvre* more generally, confronts 'the brutal truths' (Shortsleeve, 2002: 31) of childhood and other children with dry humour, rather than the serious danger or horror enacted by adults upon children, as does Priestley.

Priestley's first tale, 'Climb Not', tells of Joseph who is raised with great physical and emotional distance from his parents, as his father spends each week in London working, while Joseph attends school as a boarder. With little parental attention and supervision at home, Joseph is drawn to a mysterious elm tree with the words 'climb not' etched into its bark. At the top of the tree, he finds dozens of valuable metal objects hammered into the wood. When Joseph attempts to retrieve a gold brooch, a shadowy creature with claws closes in on him; he is later found dead at the bottom of the tree, with the expensive pocket watch, gifted to him by his father, missing. The watch, a symbolic substitute for fatherly instruction and presence, is implicated in Joseph's demise, as is his unchecked defiance of adult authority in his refusal to listen to the warnings of the gardener. Other stories Uncle Montague tells also highlight the potential for children to be deceptive, greedy, or evil, contrary to parental perception, thus dismantling Romantic notions of childhood innocence. Robert, a clergyman's son, in 'Offerings' is encouraged by his 'special friend', a mangy cat who appears to be a channel for evil spirits, to kill animals by nailing them live to a plank of wood (Priestley, 2007: 100). While in 'Winter Pruning', blind Old Mother Tallow 'tames' ill-intentioned children by transforming them – and the protagonist Simon, who sneaks into her home to rob her – into apple trees (109).

Nevertheless, at the core of this series of tales are the failings of an adult who was entrusted to educate children and assist in their growth into adulthood. In the final story, it is revealed that Uncle Montague is haunted by the children whose stories he tells, and that these are the strange, silent children Edgar has seen on his walks through the woods to his uncle's home. As a school teacher, Uncle Montague became addicted to gambling and began to steal from his pupils. He blames one child, William, for the thefts and, as a result, William is badly beaten and subsequently commits suicide. Uncle Montague continues to gamble and enjoys a prodigious winning streak, but the ghostly children who are drawn to him become his 'punishment' (217):

> They come to me and tell me their tales. They bring me some token of their story and these accursed objects now litter my house… It is a magnet for creatures of a twilightworld, Edgar, a world you cannot imagine. (218)

Unlike the Victorian fiction that represents the dead child as free from the constraints of time, the children who haunt Uncle Montague are shown as trapped or 'lost' (220). Indeed, they are acutely conscious of the deprivations of death, exhibiting a dislike and sense of disturbance when they are described as 'dead' (220). While the shadow children are unsettling, the implied reader is encouraged to pity them for never having had the chance to live into adulthood. As Uncle Montague tells Edgar when one of the children attempts to touch him with hands that have the power to chill: 'Forgive them, Edgar. They are drawn to your beating heart, to your body's warmth. They have a terrible hunger for life' (221). Though it mobilises horror in comparison with Gaiman's strategy of humour, Priestley's collection similarly understands child death as unnatural and tragic, with an eternal childhood in death represented as painful and lacking, rather than a triumph over ageing or pathway to adventure.

Miss Peregrine's Home for Peculiar Children engages with 'dead' children on two complex levels. First, because the novel is illustrated with vintage vernacular photographs assembled by Riggs and other collectors, most of which are of children who would likely be dead, or at best, very elderly, in the present.[4] Second, because of the narrative in which the sixteen-year-old American protagonist from the present, Jacob Portman, travels through time to 1940 to continue his grandfather's work of helping to save the lives of 'peculiar' children who possess supernatural powers. In the present time on the isolated Welsh island of Cairnholm, the residents understand that the old orphanage where the children resided was bombed by Germany during World War II, killing all of the children who lived there. However, the children, guided by Miss Peregrine, an 'ymbryne' who can manipulate time and is charged with the responsibility of protecting the peculiar children, safely inhabit a time loop in which they repeat the same day (3 September 1940, just prior to the bomb's fall), *ad infinitum*. As a result, the children do not physically age in their 'perpetual deathless summer', but the stasis of their lives is understood as 'sealing them in their youth like Peter Pan and his Lost Boys' (Riggs, 2011: 166). Lynne Vallone suggests that J. M. Barrie's immortal Peter Pan is 'the most ghost-like, haunting, character of all' (2007: 26), yet Riggs' peculiar children are always precariously perched on the brink of death. Not only are the peculiars emotionally arrested, they are trapped in the past; if they return to the present that Jacob inhabits and linger even momentarily, the years of ageing they have evaded will come upon them in an instant.

Two kinds of past wrongs haunt the present Jacob inhabits: the historical reality of World War II and another, imagined evil quest for unnatural power. Jacob's Jewish great-grandparents were starved in a Nazi death camp and their bodies incinerated, with the trauma revisited on each generation of descendants as a 'poisonous heirloom' (104). Moreover, the peculiar children, in the actual passage of time, 'had been burned up and blown apart because a pilot who didn't care pushed a button' (104). Riggs uses the story of the 'hollowgast' to create a fantasised mirror of the Holocaust. The hollowgast are shadowy creatures described as 'a kind of living damnation' (225). They were created at the beginning of the twentieth century by disaffected peculiars who sought to use time loops to become eternally young by 'mastering time without being mastered by death' (255). In 1908, the renegade faction of peculiars, including Miss Peregrine's two brothers, conducted an experiment in Siberia with this unnatural aim. The gigantic explosion that results, which recalls the spectre of a nuclear bomb, transforms those who sought immortality into monstrous hollowgasts, who were 'all dead, beyond killing or punishing or any kind of reckoning' (104).

The hollowgasts are driven to murder peculiar children in order to feed upon their souls, stealing life from those who ordinarily symbolise potential, though the peculiar children remain trapped in time loops in which they cannot mature in order to hide from these monsters. If the hollowgasts consume enough children's souls, they evolve into a 'wight', a being that resembles a human, with the exception of its blank, white eyes. Yet their ultimate aim is to kidnap the ymbrynes, harnessing their ability to manipulate time, in order to successfully repeat the experiment and become 'deathless demigods' (322). In this schema, Jacob's grandfather is described as confronting a 'double genocide, of Jews by the Nazis and of peculiars by the hollowgast' (248) and these historical hauntings continue to be visited on his grandson, Jacob. The connection between Jewish persecution, the diasporic movement of Jewish people around the world, and the peculiar children is furthered when one of the children explains their own struggle to find a place of peace and acceptance: 'the larger world turned against us long ago. The Muslims drove us out. The Christians burned us as witches. Even the pagans of Wales and Ireland eventually decided that we were all malevolent faeries and shape-shifting ghosts' (130).

The connection between the liminal period of youth and the liminal space of the ghostly is emphasised in *Miss Peregrine's Home for Peculiar Children*. Nevertheless, as in *The Graveyard Book* and *Uncle Montague's Tales of Terror*, the preservation of childhood in death is represented as sad and grotesque rather than as a path to freedom, adventure, and magic. In order to travel to the island of Cairnholm, Jacob must first cross a 'nautical graveyard' (67) created during World War II. Soon after his arrival, Jacob visits the small Cairnholm Museum, in which there is an exhibit of the fossilised remains of a sixteen-year-old boy who perished 2,700 years prior, known as 'the old Man'. The curator explains to Jacob that the boy had been strangled, drowned, disembowelled, and suffered a blow to the head, but that he had likely gone to his death 'willingly': 'Eagerly, even. His people believed that bogs – and our bog in particular – were entrances to the world of the gods, and so the perfect place to offer up their most precious gift: themselves' (90). The bog, as an 'in-between place' that is neither water nor land, is understood to be a path to heaven for the young person who straddles the border between childhood and adulthood (101). The Old Man is symbolic of lost potential, of life sacrificed in the pursuit of existence on a higher plane, akin to the peculiars who sought immortality and eternal youth. It is the boy's tomb, or 'cairn', that serves as the portal in time that allows travel between the present and the time loop in 1940 that the peculiar children inhabit, and it is also a symbolic reminder of the futility and waste associated with child death.

Hartnett's *The Ghost's Child* eschews the most recognisable Gothic conventions with respect to ghosts and death, such as graveyards, tombs, murder, and evil, as found in the other three texts discussed in this chapter. However, the reader learns at Hartnett's novel's conclusion that it is framed by a conversation between the recently deceased elderly protagonist, Matilda, and the ghost of her unnamed miscarried son, who appears to be approximately eleven or twelve, the age at which she had usually visualised him. It is premised on a highly unusual acknowledgement of children who die before they can be born. Indeed, the disconcerting nature of this subject, as Jacqueline Rose notes, can have 'no place' in a children's play like *Peter Pan* (1984: 38). In the second draft of the 1908 ending, Barrie wrote an annotation that describes Peter as 'a sort of dead baby – he is the baby of all the people who never had one' – but this material was excised from subsequent versions (quoted in Rose, 1984: 38). While Matilda mourns the loss of a potential child life, Harnett does not privilege the state of childhood, instead focusing on the way in which Matilda builds a fulfilling life despite several tragic disappointments and losses. As Matilda tells the tales of her past to the boy who has arrived unannounced in her home, she describes her love and loss of a wild-spirited man named Feather with whom she conceived a child that 'would have been the most beloved thing in the world' (Hartnett, 2008: 108). When Matilda loses the baby, she attempts to drown herself in a pond, deciding that '[s]he could follow the fay [her name for the child *in utero*] easily if she merely waited and was brave'. Instead, she is rescued by Feather (110).

While Matilda becomes a successful eye doctor in later life, she never marries or has children. She remains, nevertheless, pragmatic about the decisions she has made, describing paths not taken as 'ghost roads, ghost journeys, ghost lives, … always hidden by cloud' (22).

As the logical extension of contemporary Gothic children's literature that problematises and refuses the notion of endless childhood, *The Ghost's Child* celebrates the process of ageing and the experiences of a lengthy life. When the boy asks Matilda if she is angry that she is old, she recalls her own childhood experience of being frightened of an old woman:

> I knew she had once been a small girl too, but I couldn't believe it. She was old-ness and nothing else. She was like an abandoned nest you find in a bough, tatty and disintegrating to dust. Even now, the memory of her makes me shiver. It is strange, that oldness is so hard to love or forgive. (18)

The simile of the discarded nest is particularly significant given that Matilda did not fulfil the social expectation for women to bear children. However, she counters any negative perception of ageing as a process of decline, instead reconfiguring old age as arriving at the summit of a mountain: 'I have climbed a long, long way' (19). The boy, the ghost's child, helps Matilda to recall her journey to the top and to be content with its outcome. The concluding image of Matilda, now relieved of the pains of her worn-out body, willingly setting out in a wooden boat with the boy and her dog Peake, shows a freedom that comes with death after a life fully experienced. Unlike the premature, unnatural deaths of ghostly children in other Gothic fictions that emphasise the stasis and imprisonment of death for the young, Hartnett emphasises the beauty and rightfulness of a life that ceases at its rightful time, when all its potential has been exhausted.

Changing the death script in Gothic children's literature

In the first book-length study devoted to Gothic children's literature, Anna Jackson, Karen Coats, and Roderick McGillis suggest that 'children's Gothic just might be a site for recalculation, reassessment of how things are, and hence even the disestablishment, dismantling, or at least a questioning of the status quo' (2007: 8). Certainly, in a number of Gothic texts for young people, the dead or ghostly child is produced by adult sins or failings in the past. Adult characters are often critiqued for corrupting imagined childhood innocence and the rightful process of maturation into adulthood by attempting to harm children and trapping them, through death, in the state of childhood. Nevertheless, as children's literature is a socialising agent, which both moulds and is shaped by cultural norms, these texts mirror contemporary understandings of death. In comparison with many children's fictions of the Victorian and Edwardian era, in which child death was common, these recent works are unable to represent child death in a comfortingly favourable light. Instead, at a time in which the loss of children is rare and parental investment in the lives of typically fewer children is all-consuming, the very possibility of child death must be rejected and rendered abnormal and grotesque. The child reader is positioned to understand his or her worth and importance as a future adult. Hartnett's novel, however, is an exception, and a rare acknowledgement of the commonality of miscarriage, a form of child loss that has often been minimised as not constituting a 'real' death to be mourned. *The Ghost's Child*, however, like all of the Gothic children's literature considered in this chapter, thoroughly affirms the potential of life and the priceless experience of ageing into adulthood and beyond.

Notes

1 Clare Bradford argues that within the paranormal romance genre, 'relatively tame vampire figures … play out cultural anxieties about the sexuality of young women' (2013: 124).
2 This unravelling of faith in adults as reliable authority figures might be understood in light of revelations about the historic, systemic abuse of children within a range of institutions including orphanages, schools, and churches from the late twentieth century onwards, as well as prevailing concerns about paedophilia.
3 Though Bod is placed in danger by ghouls who wish to transform him into one of their own kind.
4 Some of the children in the novel give their ages as follows: Horace (83), Olive (75), Enoch (117 or 118), and Millard (86).

References

Avery, G. and K. Reynolds (2000) *Representations of Childhood Death* (Basingstoke: Macmillan).

Bradford, C. (2013) 'Monsters: Monstrous identities in young adult romance', in Y. Wu, K. Mallan and R. McGillis (eds), *(Re)Imagining the World: Children's Literature's Response to Changing Times* (New York: Springer), pp. 115–25.

Briggs, J. (2012) 'The ghost story', in D. Punter (ed.), *A New Companion to the Gothic* (Malden, MA: Wiley-Blackwell), pp. 176–85.

Bruhm, S. (2006) 'Nightmare on Sesame Street: Or, the self-possessed child', *Gothic Studies*, 8.2: 98–210.

Gaiman, N. (2008) *The Graveyard Book* (New York: Harper Collins).

Hartnett, S. (2008) *The Ghost's Child* (London: Walker Books).

Jackson, A., K. Coats, and R. McGillis (eds) (2007), *The Gothic in Children's Literature: Haunting the Borders* (New York: Routledge).

Jalland, P. (1996) *Death in the Victorian Family* (Oxford: Oxford University Press).

James, K. (2009) *Death, Gender and Sexuality in Contemporary Adolescent Literature* (New York: Routledge).

Mangan, L. and I. Russell Williams (2010) 'The best children's books: 8–12-year-olds', *The Guardian*, 12 May. Available at: http://www.theguardian.com/books/2010/may/12/best-childrens-books-eight-twelve-years. Accessed 2 March 2015.

O'Sullivan, E. (2005) *Comparative Children's Literature* (London: Routledge).

Plotz, J. (1995) 'Literary ways of killing a child: the 19th-century practice', in M. Nikolajeva (ed.), *Aspects and Issues in the History of Children's Literature* (Westport, CT: Greenwood Press), pp. 1–24.

Priestley, C. (2007) *Uncle Montague's Tales of Terror* (London: Bloomsbury).

Reynolds, K. (2000) 'Fatal fantasies: the death of children in Victorian and Edwardian fantasy writing', in G. Avery and K. Reynolds (eds), *Representations of Childhood Death* (Basingstoke: Macmillan), pp. 169–88.

Riggs, R. (2011) *Miss Peregrine's Home for Peculiar Children* (Philadelphia, PA: Quirk Books).

Rose, J. (1984) *The Case of Peter Pan, or the Impossibility of Children's Fiction* (London: Macmillan).

Shortsleeve, K. (2002) 'Edward Gorey, children's literature, and nonsense verse', *Children's Literature Association Quarterly*, 27.1: 27–39.

Townshend, D. (2007) 'The haunted nursery, 1764–1830', in A. Jackson et al. (eds), *The Gothic in Children's Literature: Haunting the Borders* (New York: Routledge), pp. 15–38.

Vallone, L. (2007) 'The child ghost in "Haunted" children's literature', *GRAAT*, 36: 21–34.

14

Carol Margaret Davison

Modernity's fatal addictions: technological necromancy and E. Elias Merhige's *Shadow of the Vampire*

In an interview conducted over a century ago on his eightieth birthday in 1908, Leo Tolstoy offered up his views on the new visual technology known as the motion picture. 'You will see', he said, 'that this little clicking contraption with the revolving handle will make a revolution in our life – in the life of writers. It is a direct attack on the old methods of literary art. We shall have to adapt ourselves to the shadowy screen and to the cold machine.' Tolstoy further characterised cinema as a unique and uncanny medium that was, in his words, 'closer to life' than literature, yet eerily capable of rendering its living subjects 'undead' (Starr, 1972: 32). Thus was this realistic medium, this 'cold machine' born of such scientific technologies as the camera, the projector, and sound recording (Neale, 1985: 1) – technologies largely developed in the nineteenth century – regarded as possessing a deadly yet death-defying occult power. The mixed characterisation of cinema as both supernatural and scientific positions it at the threshold of modernity, at the Enlightenment crossroads of Old and New Worlds – an era that likewise witnessed the inception of Gothic literature, a new cultural form fittingly fascinated by boundaries and their transgression. Cinema's liminal status has been most astutely characterised by Stacey Abbott in her accomplished study *Celluloid Vampires: Life After Death in the Modern World* (2007), as 'technological necromancy' (44), a description that, given the objectives of necromancy to predict the future by way of communication with the dead, resonates remarkably with Tolstoy's own predictions about Europe's cultural future. Implicit within both Tolstoy's statements and Abbott's definition is the idea that cinema is an ambivalent technology that transgresses, in concerning ways, the boundary between the living and the dead. As such, cinema's uncanny and literally spectacular powers rendered its uncanny, spectacular, death-wielding yet death-defying monsters perfect subjects, a role they had served from the time of that technology's inception.

Although we cannot be certain, Tolstoy's observations probably came in response to the work of the French cinematic pioneer and illusionist Georges Méliès, and thus pre-dated the Edison Studios' production of *Frankenstein*, which saw a train of silent monster movies in its wake, including Louis Feuillade's *Les Vampires* (1915–16). Tolstoy's perceptive and prescient comments gesture nevertheless towards the insights of various contemporary critics that 'film bears striking parallels with vampirism' and the revenant (Abbott, 2007: 43). According to Steve Neale, 'A photograph embalms the ghosts of the past; film brings them back to life' (1985: 8), a sentiment echoed by Abbott in her description of film as '[m]ade up of still images, ghostly shadows of the dead that are reanimated through technological means' (2007: 43). Notably, this nascent link between the visual technology of the cinema and the revenant did not go untapped. An early cinematic pioneer, Friedrich Murnau, masterfully exploited it in his technically accomplished classic, *Nosferatu: A Symphony of Horror* (1922). That production, as Abbott observes, 'imbues its vampire with the filmic and photographic qualities of the cinema as a means of exploring the inherent vampirism of this new technology' (2007: 62). That Murnau does this in a film based on Bram Stoker's *Dracula* (1897) is especially fitting given that novel's preoccupation with modern technologies, ranging from the typewriter and the telegraph to the phonograph, the Kodak camera, and the Winchester rifle.[1]

As Jennifer Wicke has observed in her seminal article examining the role of modern technologies in *Dracula*, the vampire's relationship to those technologies is nothing if not ambivalent – while he is, on one hand, their victim, he also harnesses their power in the sense that 'the social force most analogous to Count Dracula's … is none other than mass culture, the developing technologies of the media in its many forms, as mass transport, tourism, photography and lithography in image production, and mass-produced narrative' (1992: 174). A similar situation obtains in *Nosferatu* where Murnau marshals the power of visual technology to manufacture Count Orlok's terror. Neither of that film's key attack sequences – the first on Hutter in Orlok's castle and the second on Ellen in Wisborg in the film's compelling closing sequence – involves Orlok directly. Instead, they feature the projection of his disembodied shadow onto objects, making him, as Abbott nicely observes, 'an embodiment of technology, his vampirism emerging through the filmic process itself' (2007: 45).

Fast-forwarding almost a century from the production of *Nosferatu*, it remains the case that the vampire, on both the big and the small screen, emblematises 'technological necromancy', retaining the role as the monster of choice for mediating our ambivalent responses – both our anxieties *and* desires – to modernity and its proliferating technologies. In the wise words of Jeffrey Weinstock, 'vampires are always cyborgs, always produced and defined by the technologies that are needed to detect, identify and destroy them ... To view the vampire cinema then is to engage with desires and anxieties concerning the human relationship with technology' (2012: 92). Extrapolating from Weinstock's insights, I would suggest that the significance of vampire cinema extends beyond the mediation of our ambivalent attitude towards technology to include our attitude towards death, which assumed a heightened level of ambivalence in the wake of the secularising Enlightenment whose driving ideal – rational empiricism – undermined long-established Christian certainties about the existence and nature of a soul and an afterlife. The mixed sentiments of denial, dread, and desire that thereafter took social and cultural root were especially projected onto the figure of the corpse, a socio-cultural body that paradoxically serves, as Alan Bewell has rightly noted, 'as the nexus of all spiritual imagery ... [as] all narratives about life after death can be reduced to and derive their formal organization from a primary confrontation, which every culture and every individual repeats, with the bodies of the dead' (1989: 190). More specifically, such repressed anxieties were projected onto the abjected female corpse that represents our actual, inevitable mortality (Bronfen, 1992: 86). This projection phenomenon was registered in the proliferation of the supernaturally grounded and uncanny undead featured in the Gothic, a new literary form concurrently in development. It is also evidenced in the vampire film that, along with so much of our other cultural productions, registers the curious contemporary paradox in our socio-cultural attitude towards death – namely, that death is 'rejected as a presence in everyday life [while being] excessively staged' publicly (Goodwin and Bronfen, 1993: 16).

Body politics are at the core of such mediation in the form of our corporeal, mortal bodies, bodies that are always gendered in vampire cinema, just as they are in representations of death (Goodwin and Bronfen, 1993: 20), and onto which are projected – like a film screen – very specific fears and desires. While the vampire may be said to *bite both ways*, thus serving as a conduit for the expression of technophilia *and* technophobia, a tendency exists, as feminist film scholar Mary Ann Doane has perceptively noted, to displace the terror of technology 'onto the figure of the woman or the idea of the feminine', especially 'in the genre which most apparently privileges technophilia, science fiction' (1990: 163). This projection is in keeping with the identification of film as 'an erotic medium which splits the audience in terms of gender: while the women are "carried away", men are positioned voyeuristically' (Gelder, 1994: 89).

Commenting on the connection between technology and the body, Tim Armstrong has persuasively argued that modernity 'brings both a fragmentation and augmentation of the body in relation to technology; it offers the body as lack, at the same time as it offers technological compensation' (1998: 3). Two very gendered bodies seem to be implied in Armstrong's statement, with the vampire, notably, serving as the emblem for each case. On one hand, the vampire exhibits bodily limitations and lack; it possesses a corpse-like body that has already died despite its now being undead. As such, it may be said to represent anti-technology as it is enslaved by drives, instincts, and appetites as illustrated in the vampire's need for the blood with which his or her body is associated. On the other hand, the vampire exists in alignment with technological compensation as this creature defies and surpasses bodily limitations by denying death. Thus is the vampire on celluloid positioned at the crossroads between death and undeath. While the former is associated with women who are made to inhere more closely in Western cinema and culture to the body (Doane, 1990: 2) and, as Julia Kristeva cogently argues, to the abjected corpse more specifically (1982: 109), the latter is associated in feminist film theories of cinematic spectatorship with the male gaze and a modern apparatus often theorised 'as a prosthetic device, as a technological extension of the human body' (Doane, 1990: 166), that is assaultive and sadistic (Clover, 1995: 187–8) as it dominates, fetishises, and violates the vulnerable, mortal, female or feminised, body. This psychosexual theory of cinematic spectatorship is exemplified in Michael Powell's *Peeping Tom*, a cult classic from 1960 that recounts the story of an amateur photographer turned serial killer who murders women with a spike that phallically protrudes from his portable movie camera while he records their dying expressions of terror.

If a film has been produced in recent years that comments, incisively and provocatively, on the figure of the vampire in relation to the ambivalent nature of cinematic technology and the Death Question, that film is E. Elias Merhige's *Shadow of the Vampire* (2000). Set in 1921 and chronicling the production of F. W. Murnau's masterful *Nosferatu*, *Shadow* is a cinematic *mise-en-abîme* masterpiece that, sometimes *because* of its deliciously dark humour, serves as both a brilliant homage to, and a self-referential twenty-first-century commentary on, Murnau's *Nosferatu*. The purview of Merhige's film, however, is far more extensive, meditating on the 1979 remake of *Nosferatu* by Werner Herzog, the cinematic vampire more generally, the nature of cinematic subjects and spectatorship, our vexed cultural relationship both to modernity as emblematised by visual technologies and, by extension, to death, given cinema's fixation with unreal, voyeuristic death and our investment in technology as a means of defying mortality. Perhaps most brilliantly in *Shadow*, the vampire motif is brought to bear on both sides of the camera by way of a conceptual triad involving media technology–addiction–death/undeath that is also foregrounded in various recent American televisual productions featuring vampires such as Alan Ball's edgy HBO *True Blood* series (2008–14). Indeed, in its explicitly self-conscious reflections on the nature of cinema as a novel technology through which artists may create an enhanced, more realistic art form that possesses 'a context as certain as the grave',[2] and that 'will neither blur nor fade', thus ensuring the artist's immortality, Merhige's film seems to speak back to and counter Tolstoy's anxious statements about cinema's cultural revolution and its 'attack' on what the latter suggests are the truer, more realistic 'methods of literary art'. Indeed, Murnau's articulated philosophy in *Shadow* about cinema's role as a 'weapon' in the 'battle … to create art' also resonates with contentious contemporary debates amongst film theorists about cinema's subtle yet dreadful intoxicating effects in relation to gendered spectatorship and the representation of violence, particularly when employed for the purposes of propaganda.

In terms of its generic make-up, *Shadow of the Vampire* is, fittingly, a Gothic tale involving a megalomaniacal Dr Frankenstein-style director who conceives of himself as a bestower of eternal life by way of a technology associated, interchangeably, like Victor's creation of his monster, with science and art. Murnau (John Malkovich) strikes his most important Faustian bargain with a real-life vampire named Max Schreck (Willem Dafoe) who is introduced to the film crew as a Stanislavsky-schooled character-actor, but whose crucial, more symbolic role is that of a doppelgänger artist who mirrors the fanatical Murnau. (As Schreck informs Murnau in a beautifully shot face-to-face confrontation at the height of their power struggle, 'You and I are not so different'.) Murnau's bargain with Schreck involves a real-life, fatal attack on the femme fatale actress Greta Schröder (Catherine McCormack) who assumes the role of a sacrificial object exchanged, unbeknownst to her, for Schreck's participation in the film. This offer is made in conjunction, ironically, with Murnau's offer to Schreck – who is nostalgically ensnared by an unrealisable longing for his former, mortal self – of attaining a new and worthier undeath on celluloid. Given Schreck's status as a Romantic, film-going, mournful figure both on- and offscreen, he readily signs on. Greta's victimisation also carries with it the suggestion of displaced revenge given that an unidentified woman with whom Schreck only spent a single night was the source of his downfall into vampirism, a history supported by his privately repeated recitation of Tennyson's 'Tithonus' (1859). This powerful, poetic monologue recounts how the once-upon-a-time young lover of Aurora, the Greek goddess of the dawn, was granted eternal life without eternal youth, so he could remain with his divine lover beyond his natural lifespan. Schreck is, therefore, as Murnau suggests, 'chasing an altogether different ghost' than either Murnau or the script-writer, Schreck's final destruction signalling, as it does in Stoker's *Dracula*, albeit for quite different, Christian reasons, a long-awaited and desired salvation from a devastatingly loveless, solitary life of earthly suffering. Thus, rather notably, are Murnau and Schreck unlikely partners, as Murnau seeks immortality through film while Schreck, in keeping with the tradition of Gothic mortal immortals whose existence is portrayed in Christian works as accursed, chases the ghost of his mortal, emotionally connected past. True to his Gothic hero-villain status, Schreck is a melancholic, haunted man.

While some sympathy is generated for the betrayed solitary vampire in the film's lengthy and disturbing final scene during which Ellen suffers a slow and agonising death-by-blood-draining, after which Schreck breaks the cameraman's neck and then strangles the producer, the doppelgänger motif is fully realised between the blood-obsessed vampire and the fame-obsessed director. Murnau's artistic fanaticism is in evidence early on, but escalates throughout the shoot, crossing over into a madness that assumes Nazi reverberations at the film's climax with his florid anti-Semitic hate-speech. Borrowing a scene out of such Nazi propaganda films as Veit Harlan's *Jud Süss* (1940) and Fritz Hippler's *The Eternal Jew* (1940), Murnau violently directs Schreck to 'die alone in anguish, … you fucking rat bastard vampire … *Schwinehund* pig [while] the weight of the centuries venge you'. This mad, dictatorial director continues to crank the camera during a series of homicides he has engineered while proclaiming, in keeping with the film's self-conscious undermining of the line between reality and the imaginary and Merhige's commentary on the distorting, immortalising power our culture grants to cinema, 'If it's not in frame, it doesn't exist'. In this instance, Murnau merges the roles of cinema fetishist, defined by Christian Metz as a person 'enchanted at what the machine is capable of, of the theatre of shadows as such' (1975: 72), and insane cinema fanatic/junkie. That Murnau films these events – recording them on celluloid – takes the idea of cinematic reality, for which the real Friedrich Murnau was renowned, to dramatic and disturbing new heights, enhancing, by turns, what critics have failed to recognise is Merhige's crowning achievement in this revisionary film.

Film critic Michael Atkinson's condemnation of Merhige's Murnau as a 'bloody disgrace' due to the historically inaccurate portrait of a director Atkinson describes as 'a delicate artist' and 'spatial poet' who 'was the least "vampiric" of any major director this side of Renoir' (2000: 29), may possess some merit if we examine this film exclusively through the lens of historical and biographical realism. Merhige's film, however, moves beyond the biographical into the allegorical to advance a sedimented, twenty-first-century commentary on the gender and racial politics of cinematic spectatorship, and our cultural addiction to visual technologies. To this end, Merhige crafts a compelling and complex triangulated relationship between Murnau, Schreck, and Greta grounded in an addiction thematic that subsumes another central doppelgänger connection – one traditional to much vampire cinema – between Schreck and Greta. As in Stoker's *Dracula* and Werner Herzog's feminist remake of *Nosferatu* dating from the 1970s where the woman and the vampire are figured as linked in their physical abjection, animalistic sexual desire, and heightened psychic awareness, Schreck and Greta in Merhige's film – *the vamp and the vampire* – are spectacular femme fatale–homme fatal doubles whose connection possesses a historic, racialised aspect. Both were 'object[s] of the voyeuristic or fetishistic gaze in the [early] cinema', traditionally a female position according to Mary Ann Doane (1991, 20). Both were also, significantly, associated with stereotypical Jewishness in the form of economic parasitism (see Davison, 2004), the vamp being a money-seeking femme fatale possessing supernatural attributes. (Notably, the most famous cinematic vamp of the silent film era, the spectacularly provocative Theda Bara, was a Jewess who began life as Theodosia Goodman in Cincinnati, Ohio.) As such, this femme fatale and homme fatal emblematise the seductive nature of cinema and, as they become betrayed victims sacrificed to Murnau's art, a warning about its deadly costs.

Murnau's agenda to attain greater technical realism is not shown to extend, in keeping with the cinema of his day, to character make-up, especially for women. In stark contrast to the Chekhovian and Shavian theatre of the era that lent expression to female subjectivity in its complexity, cinema is gothicised by Merhige as a static technology that may be destructive, both literally and figuratively, to women. Greta speaks directly to this situation at the opening of the film when, after expressing a desire to return to the theatres of Berlin, she points to the camera, saying, 'A theatrical audience gives me life. This thing merely takes it from me.' The double sacrifice of Greta Schröder – *involuntarily and homicidal* in her real life, and *voluntarily suicidal* in her role as Ellen in the film's perverse, closing sequence that Murnau declares, just prior to her decease, 'will make [her] great as an actress' – assumes various levels of meaning. As such, this scene is as complex as that involving Ellen's self-sacrifice in Murnau's *Nosferatu* where, as Ken Gelder notes, the idea of seduction taints the idea of Ellen's purity (1994: 97), a national allegory whereby Ellen 'come[s] to represent the "German soul" … at the mercy of the property-acquiring Jew vampire' (96). In his disjunctive representation of Greta as an outspoken woman offscreen who enjoys the physical pleasures of morphine, cabarets, and sex, and her onscreen role as Hutter's morally pure and loving wife who begins the film, as Merhige's Murnau explicitly states, with 'no notion … of death', and then willingly sacrifices herself to save her plagued city, Merhige critiques the lack/absence of female subjectivity in women's film roles. This silencing is pointedly underscored by the fact of the original *Nosferatu*'s status as silent film. In this portrayal of an assertive Greta, Merhige follows Herzog's powerfully philosophical remake from 1979 that explored the emotional sublimity of death alongside our cultural death drive as exemplified by women's ultimately fatal psychosexual identification with the animalistic, sexually desiring, psychically attuned vampire. Merhige's indictment, however, is broad-ranging and deep-seated given the film's various socio-historic frames and its manipulation of different cinematic genres. Indeed, *Shadow* serves as a meditation on the horror film, particularly as that cinematic form exists in alignment with the silent film and the snuff porn film that dictate that a (usually beautiful) woman's function onscreen is to be killed into 'art', often with spectacular gusto, as constrained and silenced object of desire. Such an act underscores what Goodwin and Bronfen identify as the gendering of death – the victim is either female or feminised and always Othered (1993: 20) – while upholding Edgar Allan Poe's perverse but culturally telling declaration in 'The Philosophy of Composition' (1846) that, 'The death of a beautiful woman is, unquestionably, the most poetical topic in the world' (Poe, [1846] 1880: para. 20). Thus does *Shadow* serve, in an intensely powerful way, as an anti-horror horror film. Not only does the Frankensteinian misogynist Murnau achieve what Andreas Huyssen calls 'the ultimate technological fantasy' of 'creation without the mother' (1986: 70), a 'birth' that Murnau hopes will ensure his immortality, he readily and with sadistic intensity engenders his creation and fame out of death in the form of femicidal snuff porn. Murnau's dream is thus triumphantly realised through, and erected over, Greta's dead body.

This erection is shamelessly and spectacularly on exhibit in the drawn-out, horrifying death orgy that concludes the film. Although little flesh is revealed, the scene is essentially an extended snuff porn sequence where an actress, drugged by Murnau's assistants and rendered incapable of physical resistance, is *actually* murdered. As Gregory A. Waller has claimed, this murder doubles as a rape given Schreck's penetrating attack on his vulnerable victim (1986: 193). *Shadow* advances a fascinating but horrifically unsettling commentary about our sometimes deadly cultural *addiction* to visual technologies, a commentary that manipulates the motif of the vampire in a unique and powerful way. The addiction thematic in *Shadow of the Vampire* yokes together the film's three key players – Greta (the morphine addict), Murnau (the laudanum addict obsessed with his art and the eternal fame it may grant him), and Schreck (the blood addict). In Merhige's craftily constructed parable about cinematic technology, these different 'fixes' sometimes coalesce, such as in the snuff porn film sequence when Greta, terrified, frantic, and resistant after realising that Schreck is unnatural as he casts no reflection, is given a morphine injection against her will by Murnau so that he can finish shooting the scene. This sequence craftily advances

Merhige's brilliant suggestion that Murnau, a man Greta pointedly addresses as 'Herr Doktor' at the film's opening, assumes the role of a drug-pushing cinematographer who offers up the cinema as narcotic. After several very tense scenes chronicling their power struggle where Schreck threatens to revolt against Murnau, Schreck then resists Murnau's injunctions to wait until after his death scene to *actually* feed on Greta, attacking her in a powerfully loaded sequence that combines drug addiction and vampirism, and renders evident vampirism's function as a displacement of the traditional 'missionary position' sex act. Schreck's reaction to feeding on the morphine-suffused Greta – a 'wry twist on the notion of the satiated vampire' according to film reviewer David Sterritt (2000: 24) – also renders Schreck easier to kill in the final death-by-sunlight sequence, another key moment that is in clear violation of his 'bargain' with Murnau.

While Sterritt's is an interesting observation, it fails to take note of a new, unique, and significant craving that Schreck develops while on set. In the film's most compelling sequence, Schreck, alone on the set after a night's production (they can only film at night), explores and experiments with the movie camera. After projecting scenes from Murnau's film onto a curtain in front of him and witnessing his own elongated, shadowy fingers onscreen, Schreck kneels directly in front of the camera and projects the film's 'iris' into his own eyes/irises. In this quintessentially post-modern, meta-cinematic sequence, cinema is thus presented as Schreck's new fix, one that, notably, allows him a controlled dose of light, an element that in a greater concentration would result in his destruction, a destruction that is ultimately played out in both Murnau's and Merhige's films. Schreck is also, in this scene, positioned on *both* sides of the camera, serving as the mesmerising and transfixing subject of Murnau's film who is also himself mesmerised by this transfixing and vampiric medium. Thus is the vampire, a Gothic icon, brought to bear on a cinematic meditation about spectatorship, violence, gender politics, and our addiction to visual technologies in a scene that exemplifies the self-reflexivity found in the best examples of the horror medium (Clover, 1995: 185).

What Tolstoy called the 'cold machine' of the movie camera, is, as Merhige's film suggests, a product of what Mark Seltzer has described as the 'machine culture' of modernity and late capitalism that transforms individuals into machine-like, consumption-impelled addicts depleted of both agency and identity. Positioned before a film screen, these 'consumption-impelled addicts', fed on a steady of diet of

violence in the 'pathological public sphere' (Seltzer, 1998: 8) may be
said to become figurative vampires. They assume an ambivalent position, however, as they become vampires vampirised. On one hand,
the spectator vampirically consumes the content, thereby assuming
a morally compromised position in regard to what is being screened.
On the other, the spectator is drained of willpower, entering into a
state – to borrow a wonderfully relevant, paradoxical description from
Robert Louis Stevenson's *The Strange Case of Dr Jekyll and Mr Hyde* –
of 'voluntary bondage' (1987: 38). Merhige cunningly brings this point
home during his film's penultimate snuff porn sequence when Schreck,
impatient to suck Greta's blood, violates his contract and violently
attacks her. Rather than stop him and save Greta's life, the mesmerised
director, cameraman, and producer, who jointly represent the voyeuristic, assaultive, and sadistic male gaze, aid and abet the vampire by
frantically filming the sequence.

The subsequent scene displays Schreck asleep and snoring on Greta's
chest post-attack while the three men are seated close-up and gazing,
inert and narcotised, at the spectacle before them. Their post-coital
stance is underscored by the fact that one of them is leisurely smoking.
Given that Greta's homicide is long and pornographically drawn-out
in comparison to that involving the cameraman and producer, which
occur suddenly and swiftly, this episode plays out the gender dynamics
of Stoker's *Dracula* (1897) where the vampiric Lucy is graphically killed
and decapitated on Hampstead Heath by Van Helsing and his 'Crew of
Light'. Both episodes seem punitive, coming in direct response to their
victims' roles as sexually desiring female subjects – Greta's punishment
being undertaken by Murnau, a former lover who is portrayed as a
misogynist, megalomaniacal homosexual. Murnau's care towards his
living diva actress extends only insofar as she enables the production
of his film, her sacrifice serving to remind the spectator of Greta's
lowly objectified status in comparison with the divine, film-director
creator. Echoing the critical reading of *Dracula* as advanced by Elaine
Showalter, both episodes also involve 'gang rapes' using 'impressive
phallic instrument[s]' (1990: 181–2). In Greta's case, the 'impressive
phallic instrument' is found in both the terrifying fangs of Schreck
and the violently assaultive, sadistic camera associated with patriarchal
power and its victimising gaze.

The same camera in horror cinema that, as Carol J. Clover argues,
'plays repeatedly and overtly on the equation between the plight of the
victim and the plight of the viewing audience' (1995: 201), also fosters

collusion between the filmmaker and his or her vampire subject on one hand, and the addicted, voyeuristic spectator on the other. The *mortal* audience identifies both with the brutalised, murdered, onscreen victim – the female/feminised body of lack – and, in our ability, voyeuristically, to survive the attack, experiences a death-denying sense of immortality granted by our figuratively male compensatory body that gothically transcends mortal human limitations. Experiencing pleasurable terror over her dead body onto which are projected the repressed terrors relating to our own mortality, the viewer sits at a protected, illusory remove, embracing Edward Young's famous insight in his popular work of consolation literature, *Night Thoughts* (1762–65), that 'All men think all men mortal but themselves' (1989: 47, line 43). This death denial continues to be notably aided and abetted by way of more recent, proliferating technologies that, as in the case of the motion picture, preserve and secure our individuality by way of our doubling or, as Mark S. Roberts argues, our being grafted 'onto completely external, impersonal systems' (2003: 347).

Ultimately, the figure of the living-dead, soulless vampire in Merhige's self-reflexive vampire film is turned on the spectator, becoming our mirror, our double. Schreck is not only a fitting double for Murnau who may be described as the film's truest, greatest vampire given the blood sacrifices he makes of his onscreen heroine and film crew – sacrifices undertaken by his unwitting henchman Schreck prior to his own betrayal and physical sacrifice by his god-like director – the vampire also offers back to his viewing audience, their own reflection. It is not that we – both men and women – as transfixed addicts, *cannot* resist the spectacular, intoxicating screen but that we are, over time, from childhood onwards, seduced to become voyeurs, increasingly depleted of our moral – and our *mortal* – sensibilities so that, desensitised and duped by our deadening, deceptively empowering visual technologies, we *choose not to resist* the spectacle, experiencing countless scenes of death by proxy. Sitting enraptured in our screen-filled houses of voluntary bondage, witnessing increasingly gory and spectacular scenes of bloody violence at a remove, we are transformed into living-dead, technology wielding, consumptive vampires. Death-denying and intoxicated by such voyeuristic violence, the vampires are us.

Notes

1 Ken Gelder notes how cinema is 'one of the few popular modern technologies which is *not* mentioned in Stoker's *Dracula*' and that, in the case of Francis Ford Coppola's *Bram Stoker's Dracula*, 'there is a certain amount of ingenuity (and self-monumentalisation) involved in placing it at the centre of a cinematic "remake" of the novel' (1994: 89).

2 In the words of *Shadow*'s Murnau, cinematography will create 'paintings [that] will grow and recede; … [whose] poetry will be shadows that lengthen and conceal; … [whose] light will play across living faces that laugh and agonise. And … [whose] music will linger and finally overwhelm because it will have a context as certain as the grave.'

References

Abbott, S. (2007) *Celluloid Vampires: Life After Death in the Modern World* (Austin, TX: University of Texas Press).

Armstrong, T. (1998) *Modernism, Technology and the Body: A Cultural Study* (Cambridge: Cambridge University Press).

Atkinson, M. (2000) 'Vampire Variations', *Film Comment* 36.6: 27–9.

Bewell, A. (1989) *Wordsworth and the Enlightenment* (New Haven, CT: Yale University Press).

Bronfen, E. (1992) *Over Her Dead Body: Death, Femininity and the Aesthetic* (Manchester: Manchester University Press).

Clover, C. J. (1995) 'The Eye of Horror', in L. Williams (ed.), *Viewing Positions: Ways of Seeing Film* (New Brunswick, NJ: Rutgers University Press), pp. 184–230.

Davison, C. M. (2004) *Anti-Semitism and British Gothic Literature* (Basingstoke: Palgrave Macmillan).

Doane, M. A. (1991) *Femmes Fatales: Feminism, Film Theory, Psychoanalysis* (New York: Routledge).

Doane, M. A. (1990) 'Technophilia: Technology, Representation and the Feminine', in M. Jacobus, E. Fox Keller and S. Shuttleworth (eds), *Body/Politics: Women and the Discourses of Science* (New York: Routledge), pp. 163–76.

Feuillade, L. (1915–16) *Les Vampires* (Neuilly-sur-Seine: Gaumont).

Gelder, K. (1994) *Reading the Vampire* (London and New York: Routledge).

Herzog, W. (dir.) (1979) *Nosferatu the Vampyre* [Film] (Los Angeles: Twentieth Century Fox).

Huyssen, A. (1986) *After the Great Divide: Modernism, Mass Culture, Postmodernism* (Bloomington, IN: Indiana University Press).

Kendrick, J. (2014) 'Slasher Films and Gore in the 1980s', in H. M. Benshoff (ed.), *A Companion to the Horror Film* (Malden, MA, Oxford, and Chichester: Wiley Blackwell), pp. 310–28.

Kristeva, J. (1982) *Powers of Horror: An Essay on Abjection*, trans. L. S. Roudiez (Ithaca, NY: Columbia University Press).

Metz, C. (1975) 'The imaginary signifier', *Screen* 16.2: 46–76.

Murnau, F. (dir.) (1922) *Nosferatu: A Symphony of Horror* [Film] (London: Eureka Entertainment).

Neale, S. (1985) *Cinema and Technology: Image, Sound and Colour* (London: Macmillan Education).

Poe, E. A. (1880) 'The Philosophy of Composition' [1846], in J. H. Ingram (ed.), *The Complete Poetical Works of Edgar Allan Poe Including Essays on Poetry* (New York: A. L. Burt Company).

Powell, M. (1960) *Peeping Tom* (United Kingdom: Anglo-Amalgamated Film).

Roberts, M. S. (2003) 'Addicts Without Drugs: The Media Addiction', in A. Alexander and M. S. Roberts (eds), *High Culture: Reflections on Addiction and Modernity* (Albany, NY: State University of New York Press), pp. 339–54.

Seltzer, M. (1998) *Serial Killers: Death and Life in America's Wound Culture* (New York and London: Routledge).

Showalter, E. (1990) *Sexual Anarchy: Gender and Culture at the Fin de Siecle* (New York: Penguin).

Starr, C. (1972) *Discovering the Movies* (New York: Van Nostrand Reinhold).

Sterritt, D. (2000) 'Shadow of the Vampire (Motion Picture Review)', *Cinéaste*, 25.4: 34–5.

Stevenson, R. L. (1987) *The Strange Case of Dr Jekyll and Mr Hyde* [1886] (Oxford: Oxford University Press).

Viano, M. (2002) 'An intoxicated screen: reflections on film and drugs', in J. Farrell Brodie and M. Redfield (eds), *High Anxieties: Cultural Studies in Addiction* (Berkeley, Los Angeles, and London: University of California Press), pp. 134–58.

Waller, G. A. (1986) *The Living and the Undead: Slaying Vampires, Exterminating Zombies* (Champaign, IL: University of Illinois Press).

Webster Goodwin, S. and E. Bronfen (1993) 'Introduction', in S. Webster Goodwin and E. Bronfen (eds), *Death and Representation* (Baltimore, MD, and London: Johns Hopkins University Press), pp. 3–25.

Weinstock, J. (2012) *The Vampire Film: Undead Cinema* (London and New York: Wallflower).

Wicke, J. (1992) 'Vampiric typewriting: *Dracula* and its media', *English Language History*, 59.2: 467–93.

Young, E. (1989) *Night Thoughts, 1742–5* (Cambridge: Cambridge University Press).

15

Neal Kirk

'I'm not in that thing you know … I'm remote. I'm in the cloud': networked spectrality in Charlie Brooker's 'Be Right Back'

Welcome: _<user>

The 'Be Right Back' episode of Charlie Brooker's International Emmy-winning *Black Mirror* (Channel 4, 2011–present) fictionalises questions facing contemporary society as users of new media technologies encounter death. It depicts the reconstruction of a lost love into an interactive database comprised of photos, video, and posts to online social media sites, which later becomes housed in a biotechnical body. What begins as a means of offsetting grief and announcing Martha's (Hayley Atwell) pregnancy to her deceased boyfriend, Ash (Domhnall Gleeson), becomes a persistent, uncanny reminder of her loss. Martha ultimately accuses the embodied 'performance' of her dead beloved as 'not enough': just painful, haunting, 'ripples' (Harris, 2013).

Resurrection and immortality through technology are established conventions of science fiction. This chapter, however, focuses on the portrayal of grief and haunting in an intimate domestic setting to identify 'Be Right Back' as an expression of the overlap between technology and death in contemporary Gothic fiction. The episode forges an association with Gothic tropes by pairing the mysteries of death with similar uncertainties surrounding cultural attitudes about technological advancement. To further anchor my analysis in terms of the contemporary Gothic, I examine the episode as a ghost story rather than a robot story.

Brooker's 'Be Right Back' episode benefits from an assessment through the lens of what I call 'networked spectrality'. This concept theorises representations of ghosts in transition from the singular, linear, personal, and analogue, to the digital, multiple, participatory, systemic, and enduring. Networked spectrality is an effort to retrieve the ghost from what Roger Luckhurst calls criticism's 'spectral turn' (2002). Rather than a project of linguistic abstraction, Luckhurst calls for attention to be paid to the 'specific symptomatology' (542) of the ghost, issuing a rallying call for scholars to crack open the present absences of the ghost to situate it in its specific context. To that end, networked spectrality considers the relevant developmental, technical, social, and political dynamics of digital networks as they relate to conceptions of haunting. Thus, networked spectrality reads contemporary ghosts as intimately related to new media technologies and, as such, as a means of considering the relationship between emergent technologies and the experiences of death, grief, and remembrance.

Accordingly, this chapter uses 'Be Right Back' to exemplify and add specificity to the affordances of the Internet that danah boyd (2010) identifies as persistence, replicabilty, scalability, and searchability. It depicts the ramifications of new media on the process of grief and remembrance; the contexts of how the living remember the dead collapse when the dead have limited continued agency though mediated technical persistence. Grief and remembrance are important thematic accompaniments to the subject of death in lived social experience and fiction, especially in Gothic fictions. The episode richly demonstrates networked spectrality because it problematises grief by gothically blurring aspects of remembrance, haunting, and new media technologies.

Ash's virtual and eventually embodied return indicates a concern with present absences and the material informational dichotomies (van Elferen, 2009) associated with a ghost story. These elements of spectrality intersect with new and social media technologies complicating traditional models of haunting. I read network and spectral mechanics together as networked spectrality to help critically underpin the pairing of Ash's ghostly online presence and his embodied avatar, which is banished to the attic in conventional Gothic fashion, where he/it manifests as a multiplicity of uncanny hauntings that disrupt the lives of Martha and their daughter.

Updating: the traditional ghost story

Throughout this chapter, 'Be Right Back' is addressed in terms of the complexities of mediated persistence, context collapse, and the systemic scope of haunting, all of which help figure the embodied biotech composite of Ash as a multiply spectral present absence. These aspects of networked spectrality are informed by the structural components of networked publics, and how networked technologies serve as an interface between people and information. boyd observes four code-pendent structural affordances of networked publics:

> Persistence: online expressions are automatically recorded and archived.
> Replicability: content made out of bits can be duplicated.
> Scalability: the potential visibility of content in networked publics is great.
> Searchability: content in networked publics can be accessed through search. (2010: 46)

Networked spectrality considers these network mechanics in terms of death and haunting to account for ghosts depicted as multiple, sys-temic, and digitally omnipresent. While boyd notes that the persis-tence of information in networked publics 'is ideal for asynchronous conversations', she finds 'it also raises new concerns when it can be consumed outside of its original context' (2010: 47). In fact, the 'new concerns' accompanying networked publics, and the lack of socially defined responses to the newfound overlap between new media tech-nologies and death, are fictionalised in contemporary Gothic narratives like 'Be Right Back' as social anxieties.

There is a long cultural history of media being figured as haunted, in part because of the unseen technical animating effects of electric-ity, that Jeffrey Sconce (2000) calls 'electronic presence'. It does not take much to conceptualise boyd's affordances of networked publics as spectral contributing factors in the figuration of new media as the latest site of haunting, since much of what she is addressing are unseen technical processes that have gradually affected behaviour and use. boyd observes the following central dynamics in networked publics:

> Invisible audiences: not all audiences are visible when a person is contributing online, nor are they necessarily co-present.
> Collapsed contexts: the lack of spatial, social, and temporal bounda-ries makes it difficult to maintain distinct social contexts.
> The blurring of public and private: without control over context, public and private become meaningless binaries, are scaled in new ways, and are difficult to maintain as distinct. (2010: 49)

boyd's phrasing lends itself to the terms of networked spectrality: a lack of spatial, social, and temporal boundaries invite the possibility of systemic context collapse where binaries are meaningless and unbound. The persistence and replicability of digital information relates to multiplicity. In networked spectrality there are many ghosts and/or multiple layers of haunting. Scalability and searchability are concerned with scope: networked publics are extensive but prone to context collapse. In networked spectrality, the ghost is untethered from the personal trappings of tradition to haunt the far-reaching nodes of the network.

In her seminal work on the ghost story, Julia Briggs (1977) identifies an 'illogical logic' (16) that governs the conditions of the ghost. The illogical logic indicates an 'alternative structure of cause and effect' in which 'the supernatural is not explained away but offers its own pseudo-explanation according to some kind of spiritual law of action and reaction' (Briggs, 1999: 123). Thus, traditional spectral mechanics have set conditions and personal parameters according to which ghosts haunt specific people, places, or things. The resolution of the haunting tends to be related to the specifics that govern the ghost. The nuances of networked spectrality are extrapolated from these traditional spectral mechanics.

In an update to her findings, Briggs (1999) acknowledges Jacques Derrida's focus in *Spectres of Marx* (1994) on the processes of production and reproduction in literature as a potential post-Freudian account of ghostly returns, explaining that

> many of the most characteristic motifs of the ghost story, even the very ghosts themselves, are reproductions or simulacra of human beings, and [...] the concept of uncanniness itself is closely connected to disturbing interpretations and the discovery of resisted meanings. (124–5)

Derrida's conception of *hauntology* and its critical vogue in the early 2000s set about (de)constructing the ghost as a complex temporal and material present-absence.

Presence and absence are key elements of networked spectrality because they introduce some of the basic network mechanics surrounding digital avatar-based communication. Avatar-based communication depends on a digital representation being afforded the same social place as the actual user. Because avatar-based communication adds a layer of mediated representation to co-present and asynchronous communications, it requires a degree of trust. Since the identity of a user is not always easily confirmable as genuine, it opens a cultural space for uncertainty and moral panic often expressed as anxiety about anonymity online, cyber-bullying or stalking, or fostering other criminal or dubious behaviour. This aspect of mediated communication takes on additional complexities when death is added to the equation.

Related to the conception of the ghost as present-absence is its complex negotiation of what Isabella van Elferen calls the 'dualism of information and materiality' (2009: 99). Using a Gothic approach to cyberspace, van Elferen argues that such a dichotomy has wrought an 'age of technocultural crisis in which the presence of non-human agents has rendered our familiar world uncanny by shaking our notions of reality and humanity' (2009: 100). The structural present-absences of the ghost in terms of a material and informational dichotomy is also an important component in the development of networked spectrality. Due to the predominance of emergent technologies in lived social experiences and fictions, combined with an increasing visibility of death online and the complex effects on contemporary grieving and remembrance, networked spectrality helps contextualise the uncertainty that comes with the cultural evolution of relationships with the material and emotional remains of the digital dead. The uncertain cultural negotiations of those relationships are key elements of contemporary fictions and part of what networked spectrality illuminates about depictions and conceptions of death. In 'Be Right Back', Ash exemplifies traditional spectral mechanics – such as the continued agency of the dead, complex temporalities, the material compared to the intangible and informational, and grief – as they encounter digital technologies.

Specify user: _<Ash>

'Be Right Back' chronicles Martha's trajectory of grief after the death of her long-time boyfriend Ash. The thirty-something couple is relocating to Ash's family's country home when Ash suddenly dies. Upon learning that she is pregnant with Ash's child, Martha hesitantly communicates the news to a database collection of Ash's posts online. The relief provided by talking to the database becomes addictive. Despite constant indications of the 'creepy' implications, Martha chooses to house the database in a biotechnical body, creating an uncanny stand-in of her former beloved. The episode concludes as the schism between the biotechnical Ash and her memories of the real Ash become increasingly clear, resulting in biotech Ash's exile to the attic in the same fashion as the other material mementos of his family. As this brief summary indicates, there is a linguistic challenge in how to discuss the multiple iterations of Ash that are intentionally blurry but necessarily distinct.

The blurry distinctions between the multiple Ashes are enabled by Gleeson's portrayal of each. For the purposes of clarity, Living Ash designates Ash depicted as living, and indicates Martha and Ash's past experiences together. Database Ash is used to discuss the interactive software that is collected from Living Ash's online communications data. Lastly, Embodied Ash is used to indicate the composite of Ash's appearance, based on archived photos, the database of his social network utterances, and the biotechnical body that houses the software with its own evolving agency. I consider all representations of Ash after his death as ghostly figures. Embodied Ash is not a ghost of Living Ash in the traditional sense, however, because there is no returning supernatural agent. But through a consideration of networked spectrality, and his perfect likeness (in the actor's portrayal of all versions of the character) Embodied Ash is clearly a spectral stand-in for the deceased Ash.

As a ghost story, a hyperawareness and presentation of death permeate the whole episode, most directly expressed when Living Ash shares a digital picture of an old photograph of himself left in his family home, across his social networks:

> Ash: When I came down the next morning, all Jack's photos were gone from that wall. [Mum] put them in the attic. Is that how she dealt with stuff? And then when Dad died, up went his photos. And she just left this one here. (2013)

This dialogue invests the setting with an intimate inheritance of loss. Martha's inheritance of Ash's family home is a plot point full of Gothic significance, since inheritance is a fundamental Gothic concept. Ash provides Martha with an insight into the photo's context but neglects to share the intimate details online. The scene is referenced later when Embodied Ash makes light of the emotionally significant picture. For Martha, the moments of emotional significance replaced by the flippant 'performances' of Ash's online utterances express the extent to which she values her memories of Living Ash, and how she feels they are in danger of being overwritten by the networked spectrality of Embodied Ash.

Like the picture, Martha cannot bear to paint over a section of wall that tracks Ash's growth as a child. They are reminders of Living Ash, charged with Martha's memories of him and their time together, but compounded by loss and grief. The photo and the pencil-mark indicators of Living Ash's genuine history, both revisited later in the episode, depict the Gothic and spectral implications through the concepts of presence and absence and material/informational binaries. They suggest Living Ash's past physicality and the current immaterial, emotional remembrance of him. As a guiding definition, Chris Baldick (1992) identifies a problematic inheritance of time in an intimate domestic setting as a key element of the Gothic effect. Martha's inheritance of Ash's family home includes multiple histories of loss as well as material reminders of grief. These are the ideal conditions for a ghost story.

Following Dale Townshend's assertion that mourning is 'the fundamental obligation in Gothic writing' (2008: 75), like the traditional ghost story, networked spectrality is intimately related to the grieving process and Gothic inheritances. As Martha's friend, Sara, (Sinead Matthews) insensitively mentions, 'it wouldn't work' if Ash was not dead. In an important scene, Sara and Martha discuss a digital service, in beta development, that can supposedly help with her bereavement:

> Sara: You click the link and you talk to it [...] You type messages in, like an e-mail, and then it talks back to you, just like he would.
> Martha: He's dead!
> Sara: It's software. It mimics him. You give it someone's name. It goes back and reads through all the things they've ever said online, their Facebook updates, their tweets, anything public. I just gave it Ash's name, the system did the rest [...]. Just say hello to it. If you like it, you then give it access to his private e-mails. The more it has, the more it's him.
> Martha: It won't be him.
> Sara: No. It's not. But it helps. (2013)

Sara's claim that the software mimics a user based on their digital contributions online helps anchor the terms to describe the database that eventually gets embodied in the likeness of Living Ash. It also foregrounds the fact that Database Ash is not Ash, but is also not entirely not him either.

This scene should be read in terms of networked spectrality. Ash is dead and the resulting ghost depends on the logic of digital networks. With Ash's name, 'the system' does the rest. This anonymous system constructs a digital ghost from Living Ash's virtual remains. But this networked spectre is not static; it blurs public and private contexts in a terrifying sort of inverted consumption: 'the more it has, the more it's him'. The result is a collapsing of the present-absent, material informational context that is simultaneously not the material Ash, and more like the virtual, and thereby spectral, Ash. Such a ghost has profound implications for Martha's grieving process, and even before she chooses to embody the spectral Database Ash, the systemic, haunting implications in her life are evident: it won't be him, but …

The episode foregrounds the uncanny resolution that sees Database Ash as a systemic source of haunting in Martha and her daughter's life, which becomes all the more poignant precisely because of Martha's involvement and the constant reminders of how 'creepy' the process is. A sub-theme of the episode is the ease of use, comfort, and immersive qualities of digital technologies through which Martha becomes dependent, even addicted, to the 'help' Database Ash provides in her mourning process. Martha is complicit in her own haunting at every possible turn. In such a way, Martha's mourning process is irrevocably, Gothically, polluted. At the episode's climax, Martha finally understands that the comparatively static (re)construction of Embodied Ash is endangering her memories of Living Ash. At the heart of her growing discomfort with Embodied Ash has been a thematic concern of the entire episode: all social interaction and self-presentation is contextual, and constantly being negotiated, but this process is complicated by mediated persistence and death.

Network error. Welcome back:_<Ash>

In *The Presentation of Self in Everyday Life* (1959), Erving Goffman conceptualises social interaction using drama metaphors to explain the negotiation of public facing, front-stage performances, compared to backstage privacy. Goffman's concepts of face, face-work, and impression management are often linked with symbolic interactionism, the sociological perspective that situates aspects of identity and self as constructed through constant spoken social interactions. Accordingly, co-present communication depends on an active negotiation of context-dependent mutual social cues. But in mediated non-co-present communication, this framework breaks down as identifiable contexts collapse into infinite possible scenarios challenging the 'correct' navigation.

The application of context collapse to networked spectrality is a middle approach between Marwick and boyd (2011) and Michael Wesch (2009). Marwick and boyd observe,

> Twitter flattens multiple audiences into one – a phenomenon known as 'context collapse'. The requirements to present a verifiable, singular identity makes

it impossible to differ self-presentation strategies, creating tension as diverse groups of people flock to social network sites. (2011: 122)

Wesch's definition incorporates a far-reaching focus on personal experience in relation to something much wider and simultaneously ephemeral and semi-permanent:

it is everyone who has or will have access to the Internet – billions of potential viewers, and your future self among them […] The problem is not lack of context. It is context collapse: an infinite number of contexts collapsing upon one another. (2009: 22–3)

As a component of networked spectrality, Wesch's observation of the awkward encounter of a persistent, mediated version of one's past self in the present draws questions of authenticity into focus and widens the scope of context collapse systemically. In 'Be Right Back', it is Martha, not Ash, who experiences this collapsing of context. Ash is the context that collapses, in addition to the depiction of death as the ultimate context collapse for mediated remains.

Social navigation and impression management occur in co-present conversation too, although it is much more problematic online. At the beginning of the episode, Ash is happy to sing along with Martha but 'draw[s] the line at disco'. This prompts an otherwise forgettable argument in which Ash declares, much to Martha's wonder, that everyone likes the Bee Gees. The exchange highlights the divide between Ash's authentic self that loves the Bee Gees – 'I do' – and Martha's perception of Ash: 'It's just – not very you.' Specific signifiers of Living Ash get feedback through the collapse of the living/dead/mediated remains context to show the extent that Embodied Ash is 'not enough' of the authentic Ash of Martha's memories. Variations on the theme of the context collapse in mediated social exchanges are plentiful in the episode.

Inverting the episode's repeated warnings to Martha about the uncanny situation she is fostering, it is Martha's effort to negotiate the present/absence, material/informational context collapse of Embodied Ash that suggests the biotechnical entity's social progress. When Martha takes Embodied Ash to the famed lovers' leap (with its own emotional signifier in both Martha and Ash's relationship, and her emotional remembrance) and orders him to jump to his death, Martha asserts that the real Ash would not have simply jumped, but would be scared, pleading for life. Embodied Ash does just that, suggesting a breakthrough in its conscious social interaction. Martha does not expect this and as a final realisation of the scope of her actions and their profound implications, she screams in frustration.

Multiple errors: networked_spectrality

Embodied Ash is uncannily at odds with how Martha remembers (and wants to remember) Ash, but also how she constructed him in their social interactions. This contributes to a radical context collapse but also constructs Ash as an example of the transition from the singular traditional ghost to the multiple ghost(s) of networked spectrality. Martha's choice to reconstruct Ash based on his social media use results in multiple, enduring, uncanny versions of Ash.

The complexities of symbolic interactionism in mediated communication are not solely enough to exemplify the theme of multiplicity in networked spectrality. But with Ash's death, the context of the Living Ash's social utterances begins to collapse and become expressible in spectral terms. The episode takes these conceits further by playing out multiple levels of context collapse around the living/dead, present/absent, and material/informational binaries.

Martha broaches the uncanny digital threshold when she realises she is pregnant with Ash's child. She communicates to a database assemblage of the deceased father of her unborn child. Dead, Ash is a spectral presence, only immaterially present (the memory of Ash), but he is also absently present in the collected agency of his online utterances. Still more multiply spectral, he is absently present in the genetic make-up of his unborn child. The implications of multiplicity simultaneously point to a spectral presence and genuine absence in both Ash and the unborn child. These aspects of multiplicity reverberate with networked spectrality because the spectral mechanics depend on the past (Ash's death), influence the present (Martha's emotional state and pregnancy), and impact the future (Martha and her daughter, and even Embodied Ash who is allowed special visitation in his exile in the attic), but are inseparably linked with the persistent, replicable, scale of the affordances of networked new media technologies.

Another layer of multiplicity suggesting the systemic scope of Brooker's imagining of the overlap between technology and death is reinforced when Martha accidently breaks her mobile phone, which she has been using to stay in near constant contact with Database Ash. Dropping the phone causes a fresh experience of grief in Martha.

Distraught, she quickly charges a new phone, and frantically awaits Database Ash's call:

> Ash: I'm not in that thing you know, I'm remote. I'm in the cloud. You don't have to worry about breaking me…. I'm not going anywhere. (2013)

Although Martha has replaced her material mobile phone, the new phone readily provides access to the database. The fact that Ash is dead while there is a spectral, 'remote', digital database 'in the cloud' mimicking and allowing a pseudo-continuance in Martha's life, goes a long way in introducing the emphasis on multiplicity and technical persistence in networked spectrality. The scene also indicates the systemic scope of such persistence. Martha mistakenly associates Database Ash as 'fragile', but it is not the steadfast database that is damaged, or even contained in the phone. As a digital entity, Database Ash is persistent, replicable, and scalable.

Database Ash's ready availability on a new phone suggests another layer of multiplicity. If there were a problem with the Embodied Ash's biotechnical body, a fresh blank body could be activated and installed with Database Ash's subjectivity. The technological transfer of subjectivity, uploading or downloading one's consciousness into a new or enhanced body, and a general concern with the agency and personhood of clones, are all established themes in science fiction. In a networked spectrality reading, similar concerns are approached as Gothic when related to death and haunting. While the tone of the episode remains consistently and deeply personal, any blank biotechnical body could assume the qualities of Ash, therefore making multiple Embodied Ashes, and suggesting the themes of multiplicity doubly because any blank body could also become any number of other digital consciousnesses, possibly all at the same time. Although 'Be Right Back' resembles the personal haunting of a traditional ghost story, the implications of these multiple iterations of Ash, and multiple layers of haunting, serve to profoundly confound Martha's grief. The fact that Embodied Ash remains in Martha and her daughter's lives, albeit in exile in the attic, also indicates the systemic nature of networked spectrality, rather than the restorative resolution of the traditional ghost story. Database and Embodied Ash's spectral conditions are rooted in the digital and, as such, are not governed by an illogical logic that, if the specific spectral conditions were met, would see the haunting resolved. Instead, Embodied Ash remains a source of profound uncanny haunting in Martha's life, and suggests entirely new complexities in how her daughter relates to the memory of Living Ash, and the hyper-presence of Embodied Ash. Although their relationship is not depicted, it is suggested that the daughter does not have the same haunted relationship with Embodied Ash as her mother. But the claim stands that the daughter and Embodied Ash's relationship is fundamentally different because of the multiple layers that separate them both from Living Ash.

Unable to shut down, programmes still running

'Be Right Back' is a contemporary Gothic expression of the fears surrounding the unknown and unknowable experience of death, mixed with anxieties about the unknown and uncertain effects of technological advancement. Brooker depicts a future in which there is no easy or readily accessible 'off' button. As an allegory for contemporary media use, this episode invites viewers to reflect on their own contributions to social media networks, and how death might complicate them: What form will your enduring digital presence take? What will it say about how you lived, and what will it say about you when you are gone? Martha has to live with her choices in a multiple continuum of haunting. Reflected through Brooker's *Black Mirror*, 'Be Right Back' offers a dark meditation on new media technologies encountering death.

Where traditional ghost stories usually resolve according to their own specific spectral conditions, when ghosts assume the qualities of new media technologies, they are multiple, enduring, and have systemic ramifications. In its final sequence, 'Be Right Back' lingers over the systemic extent to which Martha is haunted by Embodied Ash. It charts the Gothic continuum of haunting and grief that includes the loss of Living Ash, but also Martha's complicity in the haunting whereby an uncanny version of Ash continues to exist in her and her daughter's present. As Martha unfolds the ladder to the attic in the background, the shot focuses on the unpainted-over pencil marks from Ash's youth. The focus shifts to Martha who hesitates before ascending at her daughter's urging. The camera lingers on Martha's expression, a chilling visual, before jumping to a medium, then to a long shot, and finally jumping to black. The effect of these jump cuts reinforces the scope of haunting as systemic; it permeates the whole house, the whole episode, and even opens into the viewer's watching space. Removing visual mementos of the dead to the attic has already been established as a means of dealing with grief in the episode. But for Martha, the mementos of Ash are forever coloured by her choice to embody his virtual remains. The final scene draws her memory of the authentic, Living Ash, into contrast with the embodied performance. Martha has not properly mourned Ash, and the Embodied Ash remains a continuous reminder of her loss, with each encounter opening that grief and regret afresh.

Housing a database in a biotechnical body that nearly perfectly resembles a human, is currently a fiction; however, there are already fully digitised databases that populate our social and technical experiences. Considering the fact that networked information can be accessed with increasing disregard to physical locations, pulled from the cloud, or accessed via a mobile device, it is increasingly common to continue posting to the Facebook page of a dead friend, attend a funeral in a multiplayer online game for an acquaintance you have never met face to face, or track the last days of a celebrity dying of an illness through posts on their personal blog. Networked spectrality offers a toolkit to consider the implications of mediated remains and technical persistence in a contemporary society that tends to identify and articulate such encounters as spectral. 'Be Right Back' questions the implications of the widespread afterlives and increasing visibility of the digital dead and addresses intentional and unintentional participation with virtual remains that are deeply imprinted with 'authentic' identifiable signifiers of self. New media technologies increase the points of contact with the digital dead, opening users to new experiences of grief and context collapse. The persistence and vast circulation of virtual remains are changing established patterns of grief, threatening to turn any mediated experience of grief into one of systemic and enduring haunting.

References

Baldick, C. (1992) *The Oxford Book of Gothic Tales* (Oxford: Oxford University Press).
boyd, d. (2010) 'Social network sites as networked publics: affordances, dynamics, and implications', in Z. Papacharissi (ed.), *Networked Self: Identity, Community, and Culture on Social Network Sites* (New York: Routledge), pp. 39–58.
Briggs, J. (1999) 'The ghost story', in D. Punter (ed.), *A Companion to the Gothic*, Blackwell Companions to Literature and Culture (Malden, MA: Blackwell Publishers), pp. 122–31.
Briggs, J. (1977) *Night Visitors: The Rise and Fall of the English Ghost Story* (London: Faber).
Goffman, E. (1959) *The Presentation of Self in Everyday Life* (Garden City, NY: Anchor).
Harris, O. (dir.) (2013), 'Be Right Back', *Black Mirror* [Television], written by C. Brooker (London: Endemol).

Luckhurst, R. (2002) 'The contemporary London Gothic and the limits of the "spectral turn"', *Textual Practice*, 16.3: 527–46.

Marwick, A. E. and d. boyd (2011) 'I tweet honestly, I tweet passionately: Twitter users, context collapse, and the imagined audience', *New Media Society*, 13: 114–33.

Sconce, J. (2000) *Haunted Media: Electronic Presence from Telegraphy to Television* (Durham, NC: Duke University Press).

Townshend, D. (2008) 'Gothic and the ghost of Hamlet', in J. Drakakis and D. Townshend (eds), *Gothic Shakespeares* (New York: Routledge), pp. 60–97.

Van Elferen, I. (2009) 'Dances with spectres: theorising the cybergothic', *Gothic Studies*, 11:1, 99–112.

Wesch, M. (2009) 'YouTube and you: experiences of self-awareness in the context collapse of the recording webcam', *Explorations in Media Ecology*, 8.2: 19–34.

Index

Pope, Alexander 21, 26
'pornography' of death 6
portrait, as uncanny double 181
post-Darwinism 119
post-Enlightenment 5, 7, 14, 16 n.2
Postman Always Rings Twice, The (1946)
    177
Powell, Michael: *Peeping Tom* (1960) 207
pralaya (Sanskrit: apocalypse) 176
pre-Enlightenment 4, 119, 135
preformationism 36
prescience 49
Priestley, Chris: *Uncle Montague's Tales of
    Terror* (2007) 191, 192, 196–8
primitivism 120
Protestantism 22
Purgatory 7, 22, 44
Pushkin, Aleksandr: 'The Queen of
    Spades' (1834) 168

Qayamat 174
Queen Charlotte 45
Queen Victoria 119, 120

Radcliffe, Ann: *The Mysteries of Udolpho*
    (1794) 27, 28, 29; *A Sicilian Romance*
    (1792) 93
Rank, Otto: *der Doppelgänger* (1914) 147
Reeve, Clara 175
Reign of Terror (September 1793–July
    1794) 5, 64, 77, 82, 84; *see also*
    September Massacres
Reign of Terror (1949) 177
reincarnation 12, 121, 128, 177–87
religious novel 9, 51, 53
resurrection 22, 24, 35, 39, 50, 218
retribution 28, 110, 118, 179
return of the repressed 63, 77, 78, 133, 187
revolution: age of 8; cultural 8, 204, 208;
    revalorisation of concept 63–4
Revolutionary Gothic 10, 63, 72
Reynolds, George: *Bantry Bay* (1797) 10,
    67, 70–2
Riggs, Ransom: *Miss Peregrine's Home
    for Peculiar Children* (2011) 191–2,
    198–200
Robespierre, Maximilien 70
Robinson, Henry Crabb 39
Roman Catholicism 6, 11, 30
Romero, George A.: *Dawn of the Dead*
    (1978) 136, 138; *Night of the Living
    Dead* (1968) 135, 136, 137, 140 n.5,
    140 n.12
Roy, Bimal: *Madhumati* (1958) 8, 182–7
Royle, Nicholas 2, 49, 126

Russian folk belief 157, 160
Russian naturalism 12
Russian Orthodoxy 159
Russian realism 12, 157, 159–60

Sahu, Kishore: *Nadiya Ke Paar (Across the
    River)* (1948) 180–1, 186–7
Said, Edward 119
Saltykov-Shchedrin, Mikhail: *The Golovlev
    Family* (1875–80) 169 n.3
Scapigliatura 12, 145–6
Schreck, Max 209–15
Schröder, Greta 209, 211
science fiction 106, 207, 218, 228
séances 121, 158
Second Coming 188
Sensation Fiction 160–1, 167–8
September Massacres 6, 70
Shadow of the Vampire (2000) 13,
    204–17
Shelley, Mary: *Frankenstein; or The Modern
    Prometheus* (1818) 3–6, 116, 205, 206,
    208, 212; *The Last Man* (1826) 108–11;
    'On Ghosts' (1824) 1, 4
Shiva, Vandana 138, 140 n.13
silent film 155 n.12, 179, 205, 211, 212
'sins of the father' 10, 90, 110, 112
slave plantations 132
slaves 140 n.3
Smith, Horace: *Mesmerism: A Mystery*
    (1845) 9, 48–60
snuff porn 212, 214
So Evil My Love (1948) 177
social contract: between the living and the
    dead 19
somnambulism 52
sororicide 70
soul 2, 8, 21, 22, 23, 25, 30, 31, 34–47,
    50, 52, 54, 55, 57, 59, 91, 99, 121, 127,
    139, 147, 158, 163, 174, 199, 206, 211,
    215
Spanish Inquisition 31
spectres 15, 28, 29, 94, 180, 183, 187, 199,
    224; of children 192, 196, 197, 201; of
    cultural decline 10, 11, 130–4; and the
    Enlightenment 22–3; and France 108
spiritualism 51, 120, 157–8, 169 n.3
Sterritt, David 213
Stevenson, Robert Louis: *The Strange Case
    of Dr. Jekyll and Mr. Hyde* (1886) 214
Stoker, Bram: *Dracula* (1897) 123, 147,
    209, 210, 214, 216 n.1
sublime/sublimity 1, 21, 24, 27, 28, 41,
    103, 104, 105, 109, 111, 112, 113, 150,
    153, 154, 175, 179, 181

Lightning Source UK Ltd.
Milton Keynes UK
UKHW050153251120
373930UK00010BA/1925